Witness and Vision
of the Therapists

In memory of
Josie O'Dwyer

Witness and Vision
of the Therapists

edited by
Colin Feltham

SAGE Publications
London • Thousand Oaks • New Delhi

First published 1998

SAGE Publications Ltd
6 Bonhill Street
London EC2A 4PU

SAGE Publications Inc.
2455 Teller Road
Thousand Oaks, California 91320

SAGE Publications India Pvt Ltd
32, M-Block Market
Greater Kailash – I
New Delhi 110 048

British Library Cataloguing in Publication data

A catalogue record for this book is available
from the British Library

ISBN 0 7619 5158 X
ISBN 0 7619 5159 8 (pbk)

Library of Congress catalog card number 98–060772

Typeset by Mayhew Typesetting, Rhayader, Powys
Printed in Great Britain by Biddles Ltd, Guildford, Surrey

Can I see another's woe,
And not be in sorrow too?
Can I see another's grief,
And not seek for kind relief?

William Blake, *On Another's Sorrow*

Utopian speculations . . . must come back into fashion. They are a way of affirming faith in the possibility of solving problems that seem at the moment insoluble. Today even the survival of humanity is a utopian hope.

Norman O. Brown (1968) *Life Against Death: The Psychoanalytical Meaning of History*. London: Sphere. p. 267.

Visionary experience is not always blissful. It is sometimes terrible. There is hell as well as heaven.

Like heaven, the visionary hell has its preternatural significance. But the significance is intrinsically appalling and the light is 'the smoky light' of the *Tibetan Book of the Dead*, the 'darkness visible' of Milton. In the *Journal d'une Schizophrène*, the autobiographical record of a young girl's passage through madness, the world of the schizophrenic is called le Pays d'Éclairement – 'the country of lit-upness.' It is a name which a mystic might have used to denote his heaven.

From Aldous Huxley (1994) *The Doors of Perception: Heaven and Hell*. London: Flamingo. p. 98.

Rearrange the [Hebrew] letters of tzara [Hebrew for 'suffering'] and you have the word tzohar, a window. Through pain one can see further, through grief one can gain remarkable vision. The pain of suffering can be turned into the pane of insight.

Rabbi Benjamin Blech, quoted in Schwarcz, V. (1997) 'The pane of sorrow: public uses of private grief in modern China', in A. Kleinman, V. Das and M. Lock (eds), *Social Suffering*. Berkeley, CA: University of California Press.

Contents

Notes on contributors

Jane Akister has been a Senior Lecturer in Social Work at Anglia Polytechnic University since 1991. She trained in family therapy in the USA with the McMaster Research Group at Brown University, Providence. She is a practitioner, researcher and teacher of family therapy, and published articles on family functioning in the *Journal of Family Therapy* between 1991 and 1995. She is currently writing a research review on attachment theory and its relevance to family therapy for the *Journal of Family Therapy*. She is a member of the Association of Family Therapists (AFT) and the Association of Child Psychologists and Psychiatrists (ACPP).

Adrienne Baker began professionally as a social worker, training over the years in family therapy, group work and psychodynamic counselling. Her work constantly confronted her with the realities of women's roles within the family – a subject she later researched for her PhD within the context of her own, very traditional culture. Subsequently, Macmillan commissioned a book based on this research – *The Jewish Woman in Contemporary Society* (1993). Her PhD opened unforeseen doors, not least of which was being appointed Director of the Diploma in Psychodynamic Counselling at Regent's College School of Psychotherapy and Counselling. She is also a wife, mother and grandmother. In addition to her academic and teaching work she is currently editing and contributing to a book on addictive shopping. She has her own clinical practice, with a particular interest in women's developmental issues.

David Brandon is Professor in Community Care at Anglia Polytechnic University, Cambridge. He is the author of more than 20 books, including *Zen in the Art of Helping* and *Advocacy – Power to People with Disabilities*. He has been a counsellor, therapist and Zen Buddhist monk over many years.

Todd Butler, MSc, a UKCP registered psychotherapist, is an Associate Teaching and Supervising Member of the Gestalt Psychotherapy Training Institute (UK). He also holds diplomas in Person-Centred Counselling and in Gestalt Therapy. He designed and implemented the Foundation Year in Gestalt Therapy for Metanoia Institute which he taught for three years. At present, he is a guest trainer with Metanoia and has trained students for various institutes and universities in London and internationally in Slovakia and Switzerland. In his practice, he has led groups, worked with individuals and couples and supervised many trainee therapists and counsellors. He is on the board of the Association for the Advancement of Gestalt Therapy.

Ian Craib received a PhD in sociology at the University of Manchester in 1973, and trained as a group psychotherapist at the London Centre of Psychotherapy, qualifying in 1987. He is now a full member of the London Centre for Psychotherapy, Professor of Sociology at the University of Essex and a group therapist for the NHS, and leads experiential groups on university courses. He has published books on social theory, and on social theory and psychoanalysis, the most recent being *The Importance of Disappointment* (Routledge, 1994). He is currently working on an introduction to psychoanalytic theory and practice.

Colin Feltham PhD is Senior Lecturer in Counselling at Sheffield Hallam University and a Fellow of the BAC. He runs or teaches on a variety of courses and maintains a private counselling and supervision practice. His publications include *Psychotherapy and its Discontents* (with Windy Dryden, Open University Press, 1992), *What is Counselling?: The Promise and Problem of the Talking Therapies* (Sage, 1995) and *Which Psychotherapy?: Leading Exponents Explain Their Differences* (Sage, 1997). He also edits two book series for Sage Publications – 'Professional Skills for Counsellors' and 'Perspectives on Psychotherapy'.

Paul Gilbert is Professor of Clinical Psychology at the University of Derby. He has researched and written about mood disorders for over 20 years and has specialized in the treatment of depression. He is currently exploring the relationship of shame to psychopathology and has recently edited, with B. Andrews, a book entitled *Shame: Interpersonal Behaviour, Psychopathology and Culture* (Oxford University Press).

Judith Hassan BSc (Hons) Psychology; Sociology; CQSW; Postgraduate Diploma in Applied Social Studies (London University) is currently Director of Services for Holocaust Survivors, Refugees and their Families for Jewish Care. She has been working with Holocaust Survivors for 20 years and was responsible for the establishment of the only Holocaust Survivors' Centre in the UK. She has helped to develop similar projects in Eastern European countries as well as being consultant to other projects in Europe. She supervises research on this subject. Her work is published widely, both here and abroad including the *Handbook of Psychotherapy* edited by Clarkson and Pokorny. She has organized international conferences and seminars for professionals working with survivors.

Bob Johnson specializes in the psychotherapy of severe personality disorders. After training at Cambridge, London and the New York Psychiatric Institute, he studied family structures as a general practitioner. He is known for his work at Parkhurst Prison, where for five years he was Consultant

Psychiatrist in the Special Unit for psychiatrically disturbed, ill-disciplined and violent lifers, widely reported in a series of *Guardian* articles and elsewhere. Most recently he has worked in Charing Cross Trauma Clinic, London, and now runs a Personality Disorder Clinic. He is consultant to the James Nayler Foundation, a charitable organization set up to implement training and research into personality disorders via emotional education using truth, trust and consent. He is currently working at Ashworth Hospital, Liverpool, as Head of Therapy.

Norman Leitman, MA, DIP INT Psych, a UKCP registered psychotherapist, is a tutor on the Integrative Psychotherapy training course at the Metanoia Institute and a guest trainer at other training institutes. He is a supervisor and has a private practice working mainly with gay men both individually and in groups.

William West is a Lecturer in Counselling Studies at the University of Manchester, where he teaches on the Advanced Diploma and Masters courses in counselling, and supervises PhD students. His MA and PhD were in Counselling Studies, both at Keele University. His PhD research topic was integrating counselling, psychotherapy and healing. He is at present doing post-doctoral research into therapy and spirituality, and is currently writing a book on psychotherapy and spirituality for subsequent publication by Sage. He is a member of the BAC research and evaluation sub-committee.

Acknowledgements

Thanks are due to Faber and Faber, Ltd., for kind permission to reproduce lines from T.S. Eliot's '*East Coker*' in Chapter 2 (Adrienne Baker). Also to Harcourt Brace & Company for permission to reprint the excerpt from 'East Coker' in FOUR QUARTETS, Copyright 1943 and renewed in 1971 by Esme Valerie Eliot.

Thanks are due to the National Israeli Center for Psychosocial Support of Survivors of the Holocaust and the Second Generation (AMCHA) and the Brookdale Institute of Gerontology and Human Development for permission to reproduce in adapted form Chapter 8 (Judith Hassan). This was originally: Hassan, J. (1995) 'Individual counselling techniques with Holocaust survivors', in J. Lemberger (ed.), *A Global Perspective on Working with Holocaust Survivors and the Second Generation.* pp. 185–205.

The editor wishes to thank Aimée Hilton for her help with the manuscript.

1

Introduction

Colin Feltham

Psychotherapeutic literature is expansive, much of it concentrating on theoretical speculation and clinical instruction. In recent years, a fair amount of literature criticizing and problematizing therapy has been published. Arguably, what has been missing or marginalized is a focus on the essence of therapy, on the ways in which practitioners become involved in it, what they think is achieved by it, what they observe or witness directly in the many hours spent with clients, what non-clinical learning is involved in these hours, what conclusions can be drawn about the place of therapy in society, and what may be inferred about the human condition from the time spent listening to so much suffering, confusion and aspiration.

This book uses a title resting on ocular metaphor: therapists witness their clients' stories, struggles, progress, limitations, pain and suffering. Since most therapists have probably themselves been clients in therapy too, they have also introspectively witnessed their own psychological suffering and its mirroring in the therapeutic process. They may also make inferences from what they witness; in other words, they may not necessarily regard themselves as exclusively and narrowly clinical workers but may regard themselves as researchers into the human condition, as data gatherers with precious gleanings to pass on to social policy-makers, as seers informed by a vision of how therapy can help more, be applied more widely, or ultimately be rendered redundant by working towards non-pathologizing social structures. It is this latter hypothesis that may be considered a kind of research question within this book: does the witness of therapists imply or issue in visions of optimal mental health and in visions of social or spiritual change?

Faber (1985) has warned that the long-standing preoccupation with ocular metaphors among western thinkers has led to a distorted spectator mentality, preventing us from going further than the merely 'mirror relationship' that is rooted in the infant-caregiver relationship. Levin (1989) too has warned against oculocentrism, or 'the hegemony of vision'. In therapy we have plenty of insight and also supervision, again ocular metaphors. Insights, supervision, the therapist's witness of her own and her clients' pain, and having visions of a better person and better world based on her work, these are all metaphors of seeing. Interestingly, if we turn to what is meant by an 'idea', we see that etymologically it is related to the look of something, its form, and that these are also related to the 'ideal'. Levin points to the etymologically identical origins of the terms for seeing and knowing in ancient Greece, in contrast with the Jewish identity of *feeling* (and listening) with knowing. Recently, social therapists Newman and Holzman (1997) have also critiqued the hegemony of knowledge and vision, advocating a need to go from spectator and interpreter to actor and activist.

Most of us cannot look at anything it seems without forming internalized images; and of course the capacity for (some might say entrapment by) inner vision, including dreams, nightmares and fantasies, precedes the capacity for language. Much therapy is about getting beneath the deceptions of language, but also about correcting unhelpful self-images, distorted images of others and often dangerous projections. As Friedman (1992) warns, any image we may have of the human being should not be static but continually re-examined and remade in actual dialogical encounters, in the form of inter-human revelation. There is also the danger that clinically we may tend to 'scrutinize' our clients, thus distancing and disempowering them and ourselves (Lomas, 1994).

Perhaps there is a danger in the present book of getting trapped in a deceptive hall of mirrors: even when we try to turn insight into 'outsight' and supervision into socio-spiritual vision, we may be trapping ourselves in some infinite regress. We may forget, as the philosopher/teacher Krishnamurti so often pointed out, the elusive holistic reality in human life that 'the observer is the observed' and that 'you are the world and the world is you'. In other words, clients are simply human beings with slightly different problems from our own, and they and we inflict our own problems on society: at some level, it is all one unbroken process, a long-standing epidemic of our species. This also reflects the theme of 'the personal is the political'. But beginnings, however imperfect, must be made, and potential traps must perhaps be risked.

Certainly the otherwise sceptical George Albee has commented that psychotherapy, for all its inadequacy, provides:

> a window on the damage done to children [and] . . . the damage done to everyone by a social system that encourages mindless competition and implicitly embraces the philosophy of social Darwinism. (1990: 373)

Redfearn analyses links between the feared nuclear holocaust of the 1980s and the psychic causes of apocalyptic trends, and comments:

As a psychotherapist I see every day how ordinary, sane, decent people like myself are, without being fully aware of it, actively bringing about self-destructive results as if they unconsciously intended to do so. (1992: 2)

Another clinician, Deikman, put his observations on the individual's wider uses of mysticism and psychotherapy, in cultivating a meditative self, very simply:

By means of the observing self, ongoing life experiences can be used to gain understanding of the human condition. (1982: 175)

Is it possible that therapists see, witness every day, nothing more than an endless stream of individual clients with unique problems, and that clinical experience leads to no theorizing or visions about the human condition and the potential for social change? It is just conceivable and it is the position of some therapists (Chasseguet-Smirgel and Grunberger, 1986). As Brown argues, however, psychoanalysis contains a logical aspiration to 'the vision of the possibility of human living not based on repression' (1968: 141) and Freud himself 'did not avoid sponsoring a *Weltanschauung*' (1968: 135). Probably many consciously enter this profession (or vocation) partly in order to make some difference to society – to help re-humanize it – and also inevitably draw conclusions about sources of damage and dysfunction. Freud drew his own conclusions about individual and social functioning from his own practice, and each major founder of a psychotherapy school since has drawn conclusions about what it is to be human, why we suffer and how we might individually and collectively come to live more productive lives. The 'greats' like Freud, Jung, Klein, Perls, Berne, Rogers, Ellis, and others, presumably do not witness the same phenomena in their consulting rooms, or they make different inferences about what they witness, and fashion quite different visions about therapy and society from their inferences. Perhaps all of us witness quite different stories and phenomena in our work, or fashion quite different visions from what we witness.

The Jungian, archetypal psychologist, James Hillman, places envisioning and revisioning high on the agenda of therapists and others. Hillman's work is 'soulmaking' and reflects as much on town planning, for example, as on psychotherapy, with vision being central to psychologizing:

The psyche wants to find itself by seeing through; even more, it loves to be enlightened by seeing through itself, as if the very act of seeing through clarified and made the soul transparent – as if psychologizing with ideas were itself archetypal therapy, enlightening, illuminating. The soul seems to suffer when its inward eye is occluded, a victim of overwhelming events. This suggests that all ways of enlightening soul – mystical and meditative, Socratic and dialectic, Oriental and disciplined, psychotherapeutic, and even Cartesian longing for clear and distinct ideas – arise from the psyche's need for vision. (1990: 55)

Brian Thorne, positioning himself far from the political and spiritual neutrality of some therapist writers (for example, Chasseguet-Smirgel and Grunberger, 1986), issues for following visionary call:

> I would like to see a trend towards the creation of a community of counsellors who are purposefully and overtly prophetic, political and spiritual. Those of us who are privileged day by day to accompany clients who often endure intolerable psychic pain are in possession of knowledge which could yet save the world. We know more than a little, for example, about birth and pre-birth and about the needs of the human infant. We are acutely aware of what destroys the human spirit and what heals and nourishes it. We daily practise empathy and are appalled at its rarity in our culture. The costly knowledge which we possess is often the outcome of relationships which have challenged us to extend ourselves to the limits of our own humanity. Such knowledge brings with it an increasing responsibility not unlike that borne in the past by prophets and seers. For an individual such a responsibility is well-nigh impossible to shoulder and that is why a corporate voice is required. I want to see a counselling community which is prepared to shout what it knows from the rooftops, to risk itself in the increasingly contemptible world of political discourse and to proclaim that persons are persons are persons – which means that we have bodies, minds, spirits. (1995: 38)

Erich Fromm (1963) has been one of the most prolific of therapist visionaries, making associations between therapy, therapeutic theory, politics and spirituality. Wilhelm Reich (1975) sought to wed psychoanalysis and Marxism and to challenge social structures with insights from clinical work. Indeed, in the heyday of humanistic therapy and the human potential movement, there were many texts attempting to shake the world from the writers' therapeutic positions (for example, Wyckoff, 1976). Contributions from what might be called a metaclinical position have been made by Miller (1984), Richards (1984), Rowe (1987), Redfearn (1992) and Samuels (1993), among many others. Interestingly there may have been a shift in the last few years away from the insistence that the public should listen to therapists, and towards the view that therapists must take greater account of social factors in their clinical work. But in reality these two positions cannot be disentwined (Hillman and Ventura, 1992).

In fact, I am unsure whether therapists do have privileged access to truths about the human condition. What we presumably do have is a special role of confidential witness to stories of human misfortune and struggle. The stuff of therapy sessions is largely invisible, private, concealed; indeed the thriving of therapy has been said to correlate closely with 'the fall of public man' (Sennett, 1986). Obviously nurses witness much physical suffering, misery and dignity, and police officers, for example, witness much human brutality, deceit and consequences for victims that therapists do not. Journalists witness numerous newsworthy personal stories and novelists turn their observations of everyday human behaviour into moving and edifying literature. Perhaps the fact that therapists tend more than some professionals to trade in conversation, in aspirations towards personal change, and to theorize prolifically, leads to greater apparent connections between their work and implications for social change and spiritual comment.

What characterizes the witness of therapists is that they are usually intentionally sought out, their work is conducted in conditions of privacy and their clients spend much time somewhere between suffering and confusion on the one hand, and searching for understanding and a better life on the other. Therapy, however flawed, may be regarded as a place in which people disclose their innermost thoughts, feelings, memories, observations, fears and dreams more unguardedly than elsewhere. We are discouraged from exhibiting strong feelings publicly, from staring at people, from seeing death; we tend to keep a straight face. Therapy is a situation that can be likened to a microscopic representation of what is happening covertly in society at large. It is also a micro-laboratory (some have called it a secret society) in which people test out possibilities, allowing themselves to envisage different futures for themselves and sharing these hopes, intentions and visions with therapists.

The extent to which many therapists have replaced priests, and the tendency for psychotherapeutic discourse to have displaced theological discourse, may have been greatly understated. Some evidence of this tendency is apparent in this book, and elsewhere the suggestion that much psychotherapy essentially is recycled religion or spirituality is growing (Halmos, 1965; Kirschner, 1996). Somewhere in this area belongs the question about the aims and power of therapy. Is it about understanding our place in the cosmos and adapting to eternal mysteries beyond our control? Does therapy have the means to lift us into higher states of consciousness traditionally experienced only by those touched by the grace of God? Is much therapy materialistically based in concrete, hedonistic objectives and too hooked into 'outcomes' altogether?

Hollis, for example, is critical of the modern fantasy of happiness, arguing that therapy must help us to live with wisdom in the inevitable suffering of the 'swamplands of the soul', and suggesting that 'a vision of the white city is vouchsafed only to those who have "gone through" the swampland of loss' (1996: 135). The white city is something like a truly Utopian (it does not exist in any place) society and/or nirvana that can only be known symbolically, emotionally or in fleeting moments, but is precious – indeed vital – none the less.

Ernest Becker, in his seminal work drawing on psychoanalytic insights and combining these with themes from anthropology, psychology, politics and philosophy, portrays his vision in these terms:

> The highest possible standard of health for man would be a humanistic-critical one that would help him develop as a free, self-reliant, independent being; the thing that prevents this kind of development is precisely his automatic conditioning into cultural *fictions*; and so, the standard of health must at all times be

'*What is real?*' As the noted anthropologist Meyer Fortes recently pointed out, to 'see what is real' is the great evolutionary problem that emerges from trans-cultural studies. (1972: 155)

The attempted separation of the real from the illusory that Becker goes on to investigate is precisely what most therapy consists of. Clients struggle to extricate themselves from constrictive and unnecessary personal and cultural narratives. Were we able to extricate ourselves significantly from the hamartic script of humanity, it could prove that the preparatory work conducted in therapy is one of the important glimpses into this extrication process. Indeed some writers view the necessarily slow, psychic chiselling process of therapy as an important evolutionary project likely to take quite some time-span to make discernible differences (Csikszentmihalyi, 1993; Langs, 1996).

Many therapists from Freud's time onwards have published case studies focusing on clinical observation, diagnosis and treatment. Fewer have focused on what may actually be learned from clients. Generalization from direct observations in consulting rooms to the world at large is of course a risky business, therapists tending like everyone to have predetermined belief structures of their own which colour their inferences and visions (Messer, 1992). We should also note the criticism advanced by some that therapists pronounce upon the world with no more right to be heard and with no greater accuracy or insight than anyone else. Freud in particular has been criticized for having made unwarranted analyses of history and civilization on the basis of very limited data and a very artful imagination. Foucauldian commentators such as Rose (1989) have been critical of the (objectifying) 'gaze of the psychologist', whose witness may translate all too easily, self-servingly and insidiously into a vision of an apparently benign but actually disempowering therapeutic state.

Carl Rogers permitted himself to 'portray the way in which I see the successive stages of the process by which the individual changes from fixity to flowingness' in his now well-known view of the seven stages of the process of becoming a fully functioning person (1967: 132). But he also allowed himself to pronounce on 'the good life':

> The view I have been presenting is that the basic nature of the human being, when functioning freely, is constructive and trustworthy. For me this is an inescapable conclusion from a quarter-century of experience in psychotherapy. (1967: 194)

Rogers went on to describe his view of the good life in mainly individual terms, in the context of the person who is committed to an actualizing process. But in *A Way of Being*, Rogers (1980) shares his larger vision of the 'world and the person of tomorrow'. On this new, emerging person, Rogers says 'I realize, too, that I saw something of this person in my years as a psychotherapist, when clients were choosing a freer, richer, more self-directed kind of life for themselves' (1980: 349). Rogers' optimistic views of human nature have been criticized by many as naive and as failing realistically to take account of evil, or of destructive impulses. But at least we know what Rogers' witness and vision consisted of. Psychoanalysts Sandler and Dreher (1996) show how difficult it is to define the aims and goals of psychoanalysis, and acknowledge that part of the problem lies with the naive claim often made that analysts have no aim but to analyse. As I have mentioned, Brown (1968) insists that psychoanalysis is in its own way necessarily visionary. Clinical work always shapes and is shaped by the selective perceptions (biased witness) and implicit visions of therapists, whether psychoanalytic, person-centred or of other persuasions.

In order to afford a glimpse into and reflections upon the clinical worlds of therapists working with quite different clients in a wide range of contexts, I have invited therapists to describe some of their personal experiences and motivations, to make any wider inferences from this that they feel able to, and to formulate any theory, observation, challenge or vision they believe may have some value for our society generally. I have also included my own observations as a therapist (or counsellor) and my own 'visions'.

It may be instructive to consider not only what each reports, but also the extent to which 'visions' are omitted, are played down (perhaps in favour of a more compelling call to individualized witness), or are quite different from each other. Can we read therapists' accounts of their work and their observations thereon without experiencing some sort of (probably visual) 'trial identification' for ourselves of the accuracy and applicability of what they depict? And we might argue that unless therapists at least grapple with their implicit aims, visions and personal theories, and lay these bare, they cannot make progress as an integrated profession or vocation. Just as clients falteringly disclose painful and shameful secrets and aspirations, therapists may be expected sometimes to disclose their secret fascinations and hopes, their tentative theorizing, and perhaps some of their painful experiences (Crouch, 1997; Jourard, 1971).

References

Albee, G.W. (1990) 'The futility of psychotherapy', *Journal of Mind and Behavior*, 11 (3, 4): 369–84.
Becker, E. (1972) *The Birth and Death of Meaning*, 2nd edn. Harmondsworth: Penguin.
Brown, N.O. (1968) *Life Against Death: The Psychoanalytic Meaning of History*. London: Sphere.
Chasseguet-Smirgel, J. and Grunberger, B. (1986) *Freud or Reich?: Psychoanalysis and Illusion*. London: Free Association Books.
Crouch, A. (1997) *Inside Counselling*. London: Sage.
Csikszentmihalyi, M. (1993) *The Evolving Self: A Psychology for the Third Millennium*. New York: HarperCollins.
Deikman, A.J. (1982) *The Observing Self: Mysticism and Psychotherapy*. Boston, MA: Beacon Press.

Faber, M.D. (1985) *Objectivity and Human Perception: Revisions and Crossroads in Psychoanalysis and Philosophy*. Edmonton, Alberta: University of Alberta Press.

Friedman, M. (1992) *Dialogue and the Human Image: Beyond Humanistic Psychology*. Thousand Oaks, CA: Sage.

Fromm, E. (1963) *The Sane Society*. London: Routledge and Kegan Paul.

Halmos, P. (1965) *The Faith of the Counsellors*. London: Constable.

Hillman, J. (1990) 'Ideas', in T. Moore (ed.), *The Essential James Hillman*. London: Routledge.

Hillman, J. and Ventura, M. (1992) *We've had a Hundred Years of Psychotherapy and the World's Getting Worse*. San Francisco, CA: HarperCollins.

Hollis, J. (1996) *Swamplands of the Soul: New Life in Dismal Places*. Toronto: Inner City Books.

Jourard, S.M. (1971) *The Transpersonal Self*, rev. edn. New York: D. Van Nostrand.

Kirschner, S.R. (1996) *The Religious and Romantic Origins of Psychoanalysis*. Cambridge: Cambridge University Press.

Langs, R. (1996) *The Evolution of the Emotion-Processing Mind*. London: Karnac.

Levin, D.M. (1989) *The Listening Self: Personal Growth, Social Change and the Closure of Metaphysics*. London: Routledge.

Lomas, P. (1994) *True and False Experience: The Human Element in Psychotherapy*, rev. edn. New Brunswick, NJ: Transaction.

Messer, S.B. (1992) 'A critical examination of belief structures in integrative and eclectic psychotherapy', in J.C. Norcross and M.R. Goldfried (eds), *Handbook of Psychotherapy Integration*. New York: Basic Books.

Miller, A. (1984) *For Your Own Good: The Roots of Violence in Childrearing*. London: Virago.

Newman, F. and Holzman, L. (1997) *The End of Knowing: A New Developmental Way of Learning*. London: Routledge.

Redfearn, J. (1992) *The Exploding Self: The Creative and Destructive Nucleus of the Personality*. Wilmette, IL: Chiron.

Reich, W. (1975) *The Mass Psychology of Fascism*. London: Pelican.

Richards, B. (ed.) (1984) *Capitalism and Infancy: Essays on Psychoanalysis and Politics*. London: Free Association Books.

Rogers, C.R. (1967) *On Becoming a Person: A Therapist's View of Psychotherapy*. London: Constable.

Rogers, C.R. (1980) *A Way of Being*. Boston, MA: Houghton-Mifflin.

Rose, N. (1989) *Governing the Soul: The Shaping of the Private Self*. London: Routledge.

Rowe, D. (1987) 'Avoiding the big issues and attending to the small', in S. Fairbairn and G. Fairbairn (eds), *Psychology, Ethics and Change*. London: Routledge and Kegan Paul.

Samuels, A. (1993) *The Political Psyche*. London: Routledge.

Sandler, J. and Dreher, A.U. (1996) *What Do Psychoanalysts Want?: The Problems of Aims in Psychoanalytic Therapy*. London: Routledge.

Sennett, R. (1986) *The Fall of Public Man*. London: Faber and Faber.

Thorne, B. (1995) 'New directions in counselling: a roundtable', in I. Horton, R. Bayne and J. Bimrose (eds), *Counselling*, 6 (1): 38.

Wyckoff, H. (ed.) (1976) *Love, Therapy and Politics*. New York: Grove Press.

2

If I am only for myself, who am I?: from trainee to counsellor

Adrienne Baker

Buber suggests a paradox:

> We are afraid of things that cannot harm us, and we know it. And we long for things which cannot help us, and we know it. But actually it is something within us that we are afraid of, and it is something within ourselves that we long for. (1970: 73)

It is evident in almost every student who comes to train. They present with all the right requirements and simultaneously convey their immense ambivalence. They carry within themselves their own (sometimes hidden) fragilities and speak of their desire somehow to make reparation in becoming a therapist. It seems to resonate with their own yearning to be healed.

Many come late to train as counsellors. Often they are women who have had an apprenticeship in caring from their own mothers. Many have nurtured their own families so that enabling other people's development, trying to make other people feel better, comes as second nature. They have done what Orbach (Eichenbaum and Orbach, 1983) describes – unknowingly sought their own fulfilment in fulfilling the needs of others. The men who train have looked at a world which seems uncaring and they want to challenge the masculine stereotype which deems competing and achieving as all-important. They see how hurt people have been in being seen as – and feeling themselves to be – unentitled, 'children of a lesser god', and as therapists they want to reverse that.

There is much in the literature (Burton, 1972; Goldberg, 1986; Miller, 1983; etc.) which suggests that the therapist has been the one in his family of origin with antennae finely tuned to the needs and sadness of others. Merodoulaki (1994: 18) further suggests 'a kind of "repetition compulsion"' – a need somehow to recreate and this time 'to understand, resolve, create meaning from' the painful areas of childhood 'in a socially acceptable way'.

What happens during training is often first a flight into the head, an intellectualizing and objectifying of pain, and a fear of trusting one's own judgement and competence. It is a time in which the feelings become increasingly raw and during which the personal development group, a source of such ambivalence, becomes the container for many negative emotions.

Gradually a process takes place in which trainees in their clinical work and through its impact on their own lives become willing to stop looking through a screen and able to 'touch' and be 'touched' by their clients' emotions. They become able to bear witness to anger and chaos and able adequately to hold and contain it. Most importantly they begin to understand the constant dynamic between a client's inner world and the external realities of clients' often very disadvantaged lives.

There follows a period of hope and despair in which the trainee, having glimpsed and been part of the other's struggle, feels almost intoxicated by the experience. But it is an excitement often soon reversed by hopelessness as the seeming stuckness of the client envelopes one, resonating with the student's own, still-fragile sense of self. The almost spiritual connection when, however rarely, we know we have touched the chords of another's soul – and they ours – can so easily be extinguished.

Tolerating the frustrations, realizing that we can contain within ourselves contradictions, uncertainties and compromise, becomes part of the counsellor's strength as we learn that they do not detract from our own or our clients' intrinsic worth. In eventually becoming and being a counsellor we learn to work within constraints, real and perceived, and to help people gain a sense of self-respect and choice in situations of seemingly little choice. Ultimately and paradoxically, the vision is in the recognition that we live in an imperfect world but that what we do in it as therapists can make the difference between a life starved of joy and a life fully lived.

What follows is a view of one psychodynamic counselling course from the perspective of a trainer. Because students have been so open about their feelings all along, we – as tutors and therapists – have been able to partake in the 'witness and vision' of the title.

Before the course starts

The *anxiety* which accompanies students throughout much of the course is with them before they begin. Maybe it is an unacknowledged aspect of the 'wounded healer', a necessary accompaniment of the desire to live life more authentically. Goldberg writes: 'In the oldest myths of healing, it is precisely because healers were vulnerable to wound and suffering that they had the power to heal' (1986: 12). And Ignatieff suggests that 'a self must be lost, before it can come to itself again' (1994: 178).

The autobiographical statements which accompany a student's application are the first hint: in some, the 'safety' of facts; in others, the rawness of re-experiencing the honesty of their own depression. But even before the application there had often been a period of ambivalence about whether or not to apply, of recognizing that such a training would cause them to question and could destabilize the tacit agreements in their present relationships.

Being oneself at interview is almost always impossible and even more so when strong transference issues influence what we explore. Then, being accepted, the time of waiting begins and as the date for starting draws near the phone calls intensify – always factual enquiries of course, about place-ments, reading lists, supervision, therapy – and behind them there seems the question which must be so familiar to us all: 'Will I be all right?'

The beginning

So many parallels exist between the first day of training and the first meeting with a client. Anxiety runs high. We try to contain it but we, too, are concerned that all should go well. As much as possible we create a safe frame, anticipating the factual questions and addressing them in the induction session and in page after page of information and guidelines – responses drawn from years of listening to students' needs and fears.

Sometimes the anxiety feels well channelled in the first day's exercise of listening and being listened to. Sometimes it needs to express itself by testing the frame, especially in relation to the personal/professional development group: 'I want to change my group; I know I can't work with that facilitator.'

Processes within the process of training

By week two, when the course starts in earnest, students begin to take on roles familiar to them. Those who find safety in the 'stuff in the head', eloquently discuss from a theoretical perspective 'the unconscious', objecti-fying pain, seeing splitting as a mechanism to which other people or clients resort. Others – with 'only' personal experience to draw on – shy away from class discussion. It is as if, despite our emphasis on self-awareness, the personal seems somehow lesser. Experiential work on defences often inten-sifies and makes overt the previously covert conflicts: 'If I'm prepared to expose myself, why the hell isn't she?' Or students who have, despite therapy, defended successfully against heart-rendering losses talk about them in a disassociated way.

But, of course, the very nature of the training and the impact of the client work bring the personal to awareness in even the most defended student. As trainers, we acknowledge the fragilities and endeavour to make the course a holding and facilitating environment. There is always a balance to be achieved, not the least of which is in allowing the expression of students' negative feelings and yet not allowing students to be overwhelmed by their own infantile omnipotence. Implicitly we offer a model of therapy which involves being able to bear confusion and pain.

The process of training seems not only to reflect aspects of the therapeutic process with all their ambivalence and fear, but equally the developmental stages with their conflicts and regression. Adolescence predominates and at times it feels that students struggle throughout the day – but in reverse order – with the progression depicted by Erikson (1968) and Marcia (1975): the identity diffused adolescent, the foreclosed adolescent, the moratorium and the identity achieved. The identity diffused stage, as expressed by Biff in Miller's *Death of a Salesman* – 'I just can't take hold . . . I can't take hold of some kind of a life' (1961: 42) – presents itself most of all in the personal/ professional development group.

Leaving the safe base of home (family, job) throws the student ill-equipped into a world where others seem to be more competent. The awareness of entering a new world, of questioning old ways of being, of acquiring knowledge – in a way a new language – brings with it great fear of envy and retribution. In excluding those they most still need from this new world, they fear being excluded from the old familiar world of home. Sometimes in the early stages of training, 'gifts' from the course are taken home where they appear to be devalued, leading the student to protect their separate life on the course and so struggling with a split self which feels as if it can never again become whole. Loss seems an underlying feeling, as if this venture into independence re-evokes earlier separations. Barwick writes:

> . . . such independence . . . seemed to echo her experience of other, earlier separations, where loss had occurred at points of heightened aggressive potency and where new independence had left her similarly 'empty': the unmodified omnipotent phantasy of the destroyed parent behind her matched by the absence of the good object . . . within. (1995: 567)

There is also the fear of being rendered invisible (which we, the tutors, can make happen) and the terror of non-recognition. Salinger's hero, Holden Caulfield, conveys the panic: 'I thought I'd just go down, down, down, and nobody'd ever see me again' (1951: 204).

Theoretical framework

Theory, the need for a framework which informs, is of course the corner-stone which, as we gain confidence, we integrate with our clinical skills and our self-awareness. For the trainee in the early stages this linking is difficult. For example, a merely intellectual understanding of transference may in the early months make the student feel immobilized – 'It seems so egocentric to talk about the relationship with me.' Only gradually, through the role plays, the placement work and the supervision does the trainee begin to feel that the theoretical concepts help us to make sense of the client's – and our own – experience. At the same time, we encourage the student to question, to understand how this or that idea might have personal meaning, that 'the safe frame', for example, takes us back to our earliest childhood memory of being safely held and that, in terms of 'human development', the turmoil of adolescence is ever-present.

Edelson suggests that a psychotherapy training should teach us how to listen to the client's story, to think about its meaning and purpose and, in trying to 'loosen the stranglehold of theory', should allow the student to draw on his own unrecognized 'deeply entrenched knowledge' (1993: 315).

Judy Tame similarly urges that we remain open to the possibility of being surprised by the client and that we avoid seeing all material as evidence of an aspect of theory. Yet, 'in defence of theory, I find it supplies a vocabulary through which we can speak about emotions and feelings which are difficult to communicate. By putting words to formless thoughts, they become symbolized and communicable. In the space between self and other we struggle to communicate our feelings by giving them meaning through words.' (Tame, 1996: 52)

One of the aspects of theory we teach is the communicative approach of Langs (1979, 1988) in which one learns to listen for the derivative communications in the client's stories that comment on the client's unconscious perception of the therapist. It is an approach which focuses on the process and interaction taking place in the room between therapist and client, and on the client's unconscious awareness of the therapist's management of the encounter or of the environment. These awarenesses are encoded in the narratives which the client tells. The communicative model attempts to redress the balance of power in the therapeutic relationship by heeding the client's innate ability to supervise the therapist in the encounter.

Beginning to recognize that the theory is not just something 'out there' is a process well expressed by this student: 'I still sometimes get involved very powerfully with a client's pathology, I become very disturbed by a client's projections. I understand the countertransference – with experience I hope to master it better – but it is inevitably anxiety-provoking.'

It is a two year training which is committed to teaching students to think and question. Its core theoretical model is psychodynamic but we avoid its becoming an orthodoxy by encouraging consideration of other approaches too. In the fourth term, by which time we believe that psychodynamic concepts are reasonably well understood, we introduce ideas and ways of working from existential thinking. Not surprisingly, it is a term when uncertainty and confusion have to be tolerated. Yet, paradoxically, the existential ideas allow students to feel freer within the very framework – the psychodynamic – which they protect so fiercely during this term in which we invite them to challenge the core model. 'I don't know why I thought that humour is divorced from a psychodynamic approach. My client made me want to laugh. Is that so bad?'

Skills training

Skills training continues throughout the course, creating new anxieties. These are mature students who mask their uncertainties well, yet old competencies, different ways of working, feel very threatening. It is as if aspects of the self are at risk – as indeed they are. The early realization that counselling skills involve the whole being fits with our urging students to hear their client's story and to listen to their own response. But it feels somehow easier to form hypotheses that to stay with uncertainty, to 'understand' in terms of theoretical formulations rather than in terms of what is provoked inside oneself.

In teaching it seems we must challenge so much – that empathy, whatever that is, may be discordant with our honest, gut-felt response; that the counsellor's questions may have no more value than being a way of assuaging her own unease; that touching breaks boundaries.

It is hard, too, for the trainee to tolerate silence and to see it as productive, particularly in the early stages when there seems to be such a need to be active. It takes time to feel at ease with the recognition that silence gives the client space to think, to feel, to be honest, and that we may understand how somebody feels – and convey that understanding – even better without words. Moja-Strasser writes:

> The therapist's silence allows the necessary space for the client to tune into themselves and get in touch with their deepest concerns . . . The corollary to the therapeutic dialogue is that by remaining silent the therapist allows the client to develop that 'inner hearing' which is . . . tuning in to oneself. In this way the therapist becomes the musical instrument with which the client's creation resonates. (1996: 100)

The learning process is a painful one; peer criticism in triad work, however constructively given, assumes personal dimensions. The role-played client material intermingles with the student's own narrative and often resonates, too, for the role-playing counsellor. The tutor's task parallels the therapeutic relationship: she must contain and hold so that it is a safe enough environment in which to learn. She must enable the student, whose first role-played sessions sometimes seem like a diagnostic interview, to develop different ways of learning to understand. She must allow the student who has mastered the art of avoiding her own feelings, once more to feel. She must encourage students to begin to make sense of what is going on.

For the trainee, as for us the trainers, the willingness to expose oneself to another person's pain risks touching our own fragile areas. Yet, of course, as it continues the skills training allows the trainee to feel easier and to develop her own style:

> One thing is beginning to happen – I'm less afraid to be myself. I don't want to become 'a skilful therapist', I want to be myself with skills.

Sometimes I recognize that I'm becoming too emotional and then I think 'do I want to become unemotional?' It is scary because then the confusion can happen: what is mine and what is theirs. The client is constantly a mirror image of our own pain and vulnerability.

Alicia Spedding, Dec. 1996

The college supervision group

The supervision group becomes the area in which sibling rivalry is re-enacted. First this revolves around securing a placement, then in having clients. Then, sometimes, a vying for time in the group is transformed into anger with the tutor or with peers. But gradually alongside this there develops something richer, an immense feeling of mutual support, so that as the course progresses the group begins to feel it is in a safe enough space to try out new understandings.

The focus of the supervision group enables a mutual learning. Week after week, shared issues arise. The presentation of clinical work reveals the tension between the student's wanting to hold the client and wanting herself to be held. Similarly, clients choosing to leave the therapy can be devastating to a student's still-fragile sense of competence.

Perhaps most of all it is around boundary issues that trainees, as they discuss their work, struggle with the disparity between what they recognize as important in order to create trust and the difficulty of maintaining the boundaries. The concept of the 'safe frame' (Gray, 1994) is central to a psychodynamic approach. It is a way of thinking about and offering containment, the analogy of the parent's 'holding' the anxious child being very relevant. It emphasizes the need for reliability in the therapeutic relationship – its place and time, its regularity and its confidentiality. It acknowledges the significance of impingements such as interruptions on an environment which the therapist should be keeping safe. It also recognizes how a client's ambivalence about therapy may be expressed by 'breaking the frame', for example by lateness or missed sessions. The request 'just this once' (and the significance of our colluding with it), hides a multitude of deviations from the frame and it is only as we listen to the client's material that we realize how unsafe it makes us feel to be boundaryless. Toni Morrison, in a different context, writes of the:

> . . . fear of being outcast, of failing, of powerlessness; their fear of boundary-lessness . . . of loneliness, of aggression both external and internal. In short, the terror of human freedom – the thing they coveted most of all. (1990: 37)

Sometimes it is the placement's different way of working which makes it difficult to hold the safe frame. Hoag (1992) discusses this within the 'deviant frame' of the general practice surgery, and suggests that '. . . the counsellor . . . may get caught up in her own ambivalence in terms of needing to be seen as acceptable and useful to the medical hierarchy in which she works'. She draws on Langs (1979) in suggesting that:

> . . . deviations in the . . . boundaries of the therapeutic setting and relationship have a wide range of deeply significant consequences . . . They include: development of a sense of mistrust, feeling of persecution, unclear interpersonal boundaries . . . and a sense of the therapist as someone suffering . . . emotional instability . . . (Hoag, 1992: 420)

As students settle in placements and clinical work, the task becomes one of how to use supervision, how to recognize what belongs in supervision and what in therapy, and how to make sense of the different approaches of college and placement supervisors:

> I had this myth that the supervisor would be the person who would sort everything out for me. They give their experience and knowledge but you still have to process it and make it your own, or not. Early on I couldn't resolve what seemed to me a conflict between what I was learning at placement and what I was learning at college. I wasn't yet at a stage of my training where I could select what I could use from each place. I was totally thrown; I was left in limbo. During this time, the client didn't come.
>
> Alicia Spedding, Dec. 1996

Commenting on the supervisory relationship, Jacobs points out that '[h]ow the supervisor and supervisee feel, relate and behave in the supervision may reflect the client. But equally so what the supervisee says about the client may reflect how the supervisee experiences the supervisor' (1996: 62).

The academic work

Writing the essays and case studies is, for many students, particularly those with little recent experience of academic work, yet another hurdle. Intense anxiety accompanies the need to submit the work on time and anticipating the results often re-evokes fears of parental admonition. Sometimes students who have had little validation of their worth as children or as adults find in the writing an opportunity to sabotage themselves. Barwick suggests that 'to complete . . . the [essay] . . . was to experience a separation and to separate in this way meant an unacceptable irretrievable loss' (1995: 569).

While for many students the fear is, of course, of failure, for others, paradoxically, it is the fear of succeeding: 'I have this real dread of completing. Then they'll say, "Well you should go on and do more – the MA, the advanced training" – and then I'm back with their voices in my head.' Yet other students seem to need to test out something old: recognizing that in the past they had 'got by', they submit something mediocre but, simultaneously, convey their desire this time round not to be allowed to do so.

Barwick's discussion of essay anxiety gives considerable insight into how it represents 'typical mechanisms of defence':

> The non-starters may attempt to avoid anxieties provoked by loss, by rejection – 'This bloody stupid essay! Who needs it?' – or dejection – . . . 'Forget the essay. Forget me.' In the first instance, denial, self-idealization, denigration of the love object, may play their part; in the second, the splitting off and projection of aggressive impulses may leave the mind empty, free from the fear of envious attack. As for the non-completers . . . Aggressive impulses are repressed so the wistful illusion that the lost object is never quite lost can be kept . . . In the case of the overly concise, controlled essay producer, the pain of working through loss is artfully side-stepped by means of intellectualization. In the case of the compliant writer, an obsessional gathering of the decimated parts of the lost object takes place, in the forlorn hope that the re-creation of the idealized object may be achieved by spewing them out onto the page. (1995: 573)

A very similar process accompanies the writing and presentation of the termly self-reflective paper. Much acting out takes place . . . 'Who'll read it?' 'What feedback will we get?' 'What's the point?' Certainly it is a fragile part of themselves which they are handing over and a part which never feels good enough.

The personal/professional development group

The personal/professional development (PPD) group – about which there is so much ambivalence – in many ways mirrors our own lifelong process, with periods of stuckness and struggle to reach a more self-accepting stage of integration – only then to be followed by more questioning. It is as Virginia Woolf writes in *The Waves*:

> Rippling and questioning begin. What do I think of you – what do you think of me? Who are you? Who am I? – that quivers again its uneasy air over us, and the pulse quickens and the eye brightens and all the insanity of personal existence without which life would fall flat and die, begins again. (1972 [1931]: 165)

The history of a PPD group is in so many ways the story of a therapy – and yet not a therapy. In the beginning anxiety is writ large and it feels that the silence has to be broken: by wit, 'I think this is a self-defence group, not a self-development group' or 'Not another group where we have to study each other's shoes!'; by leaving the room, '. . . didn't manage to go to the loo before'; or by demands for clarification about 'what we're here for exactly'. It is an early painful period which, for facilitator and student facing the unknown, recalls Bion's wisdom that the therapeutic encounter must contain 'two rather frightened people' (in this case, group members and facilitator). As Bion put it: 'In every consulting room there ought to be two rather frightened people; the patient and the psycho-analyst. If they are not, one wonders why they are bothering to find out what everyone knows' (quoted in Casement, 1985: 4).

In one way the anxiety is almost welcomed: 'I've had such fear about beginning this that I could keep other feelings at bay. Now that we've begun, now that I know what it feels like, the old agenda comes back and I've got to tackle the other things, the endings, in my real life.'

The facilitator inevitably stands in for other ambivalently felt relationships. Anger feels safer if it is expressed obliquely: 'I still feel furious at what happened in the supervision group. I wasn't listened to; I was made to feel invisible.' Drawing parallels to feelings here in this group may be denied or may provoke further anger: 'I'm sick of these analytic interpretations; I'm not talking about what I feel *here*. It seems that my anger towards . . . daren't be said; it has to be interpreted instead.'

Rivalry develops too, between group members and between participants and facilitator. It is subtle, seemingly a one-way process, and yet as facilitator I hope I adequately explore with the group what I am feeling within the group process and am able to separate off from that the still-unresolved fragilities it may stir up. Joan Hutten in fact questions the title of facilitator, pointing out that it '. . . tends to foster the illusion that the primary task of the group is to be comfortable and that learning can be made easy' (1996: 250).

Later in the history of a PPD group other issues arise. Someone speaks of loss of innocence. 'It feels as if I can no longer dream', was how it was expressed – the apprehension that to become fully adult means to give up desire, hope, fantasy. It leads to reflections on intimacy and whether the fear of intimacy is the fear of another person's needs. For another student it is the equating of intimacy with sexual intimacy which makes it difficult for her fully to enter the space in the group. Alongside that 'pairing' takes place, not the pairing which Bion (1961) suggests might save the group, but a flirtation suggesting the humdrumness of relationships outside the special reality of the group.

The change-over of tutors can provoke powerful feelings of abandonment. In one of the courses a tutor was to be away for a term to have a baby. She prepared the students in her supervision and PPD groups well in advance for her absence and for the advent of a locum, but nothing could adequately prepare her for the rage which her telling the group members provoked. Their jealousy of the baby-to-come spilled over into other parts of the course. Perhaps inevitably, this upheaval was in the context of other things going on too, particularly institutional change with its unsettling effects. The disturbance in the frame took concrete form by there being no room allocated for one of the PPD groups so that the intense anger and hostility could focus on the college's seeming abandonment of them.

The emotions were still raw when students returned after the long summer holiday. At first they threatened to overwhelm the locum tutor but she was strong enough to accept the students' anger and when her term was over their real grieving became possible, held by the return of their 'errant'

mother. That same summer we lost our Dean, suddenly and in circumstances causing us all great unease. The students feared for us and for
themselves: who would hold us? Would we be strong enough to hold them?
We were, but it was a period of profound emotions.

Inevitably, grief, loss and depression are never far away: 'They hover
waiting to catch me if for a moment I become *engaged* in something else.'
Most of all, of course, they present themselves near the end, accompanied
by intense resistance to working 'with the cliché' of endings.

The placement

'It sometimes seems that there are more trainees than clients. The frustration of not having clients is terrible.' The struggle to find a placement is
often matched by the struggle within the agency to feel adequately valued.
Many other issues arise too, not the least of which is the difficulty in
maintaining the safe frame when the agency so often operates with
inadequate resources or with different understandings of what counselling is
all about.

Linda Hoag (1992), quoted earlier in this chapter, discusses how one may
attempt to work in settings such as the psychiatric outpatients clinic or the
GP surgery where the frame is 'deviant' – where, for example, the same
counselling room is not always available or where there are interruptions or
lack of privacy. The need to maintain secure ground rules is seen as a
prerequisite to effective therapy.

The student also has to negotiate how to use supervision and the thin
divide between what is appropriate for supervision and what belongs in
therapy. The parallel processes (which Jacobs, 1996, warns against our
using as a mantra) exist throughout:

> I'm a trainee therapist but also I'm a trainee client . . . being a trainee brings
> another dimension to being in therapy and the therapy is part of my own personal
> journey . . . which includes myself in supervision.
>
> A great part of my work is with people with special needs. At one point I
> 'rescued' one of my clients because of the pain of being the therapist . . . I'm very
> aware of the power: I don't have 'special needs', therefore I'm more powerful. Yet
> with all this pain came the realization that when I am also vulnerable I'm working
> better.
>
> Irith Sassoon, Nov. 1966

Students' insecurities and growing self-awareness are at the same time an
aspect of their honesty, as this group discussion shows:

> I feel so unsure of myself when a client comes up with what is still current and
> unresolved for me. It makes me realize my own vulnerability even more.
>
> Stella Neocleous, Nov. 1996

I'm only too aware of not yet being qualified. It's all my own issue about not being good enough. Yet if you go to a professional you want to check out who on earth you're seeing. There's a disparity between how I present myself and what I know about myself. Therapy really is about two frightened people.

Jacqueline Tupholme, Nov. 1966

It's like expecting your clients to be honest and you yourself are not being honest. The invalidation process is internal and it goes on and on.

Alicia Spedding, Nov. 1966

Another student in a different intake reflected on her placement experience:

Don't ever do your counselling in a residential unit where you are also a worker. It's too painful. It really challenges all your understandings of boundaries. But the other placement, working in a psychotherapy department, was very frustrating. They were therapists, I was only a counsellor and a trainee at that . . . And yet he gave me an excellent report; I couldn't believe it was about me . . .

At first, it was difficult to contain so much pain . . . and yet also at the beginning I felt a sense of power – how easy it could be to fit into that – and at the same time so much anxiety when I make a mistake.

Martina Philips, Nov. 1966

Perhaps for us, the trainers, one of the most significant indicators of a student's beginning to feel at ease in their placement work is when we recognize their being able to work not just with the content but with the process.

I've been in therapy for so long and yet each client potentially can touch a raw spot in me. At first I felt an imbalance, that the client is further along the process than I. It made me feel extremely vulnerable sitting with someone who is prepared to dive in where I wasn't yet . . . Clients come because they want to change something in themselves – and yet the fear of change – to allow yourself to change into you don't know what – we tend to flee when we are too close to an edge. And when it becomes too unbearable, the client may not turn up and as the counsellor you lose that possibility for a while and then you go on with it . . . Whatever comes up is what happens. Resistance almost always slowly breaks itself but if you break it too quickly you lose it.

Alicia Spedding, Nov. 1996

Own therapy

Sometimes it is the seemingly composed who carry with them such sadness, never more eloquently expressed than by the student discussing his difficulty with his case study and then, after a pause, bursting out with, 'It feels as if my heart is trapped.'

As with every other aspect of training, students show their ambivalence about therapy – an ambivalence not always unjustified! Their experience of it ranges from those who have had many years of analysis or who are in therapy three or four times a week, to those who agree to go for counselling 'only because the course requires it'. Inevitably the client work, alongside relationships on and off the course, make even the most reluctant recognize their need for therapy.

Going into therapy, being able to trust one's judgement that this particular relationship is or is not right, involves all the pain of realizing that long-forgotten feelings, far from being dead and buried, live on. There is a fear too, particularly of destabilizing intimate relationships – and yet, whenever we initiate change, there is an element of our wanting to question a symbiotic relationship which has begun to feel dysfunctional.

Us, the trainers

Each group of students becomes special in its own way. Each ending is a new loss reminding us of other older losses. In many ways we mirror the processes that the students go through. Sometimes, defensively, we take on familiar roles – for me, although I challenge them throughout, they are the good mother, strongly protective, and the rescuer. Adrienne Rich suggests:

> A woman may react to her vulnerability by denying it. She may spend her life proving her strength in the 'mothering' of others . . . in the role of teacher, counsellor, therapist . . . In a sense she is giving to others what she herself has lacked; but this will always mean that she needs the neediness of others in order to go on feeling her own strength. (1977: 243)

I recognize much of that, together with the need to hold, to give a good enough feed – and the intense fear of rejection.

Tatelbaum similarly writes:

> Many people from what I earlier called the 'secret society' of mourners go on from grief to become counsellors, therapists . . . Out of loss experiences, many go on to serve, to teach, to be compassionate helpers, to enable others to enhance their lives. (1980: 141)

With insight it opens the possibility of the therapist as one who can allow the process of the client to be born in the experience of the therapist herself being adequately held.

As the course ends

> It's as if I'm making more endings happen now, too – with my job, in my relationship. And I recognize what I do: I sleep an awful lot. I really seek oblivion because I can't bear the losses.

The sense of impending loss as we go through the last term is intense, for staff and students, although of course often denied:

> I really feel quite detached from all this talk about loss. I feel angry, it's a cliché, like going on and on about breaks and endings in therapy. Yet in my guts I know it'll hit me when it's over and then I'll be alone.

Drawing a family analogy, Hutten suggests that part of the work of ending is that 'parents have to trust their children to make their own mistakes and learn from them . . . The youngsters have to manage their rebellious impulses and doubts well enough to risk trying their own wings . . . Both sides of this process can happen only when envy (of youth and of experience) is acknowledged and managed. Something of this mastery . . . is inherent in the ending of every course' (1996: 255).

Looking back as a course ends, there are powerful emotions to do with self. First, there is a real awareness of having changed and matured through all the struggles. Second, there is the feeling of not yet being quite 'good enough' – 'I'll feel more confident when I have BAC accreditation/UKCP registration.' It is not only to do with a necessary humility which enables us all to continue monitoring ourselves and learning within supervision, it is more to do with not yet believing in oneself as a counsellor.

The changes inevitably reverberated in their personal lives. One student wrote:

> I don't think I was aware how much impact my training would have on the family . . . I don't think any of us were ready for the fundamental changes in me. I had allowed my world to narrow down to the needs of my young family and my home in a small Kentish village – very safe. . . . My lectures affected me in their content – especially at the beginning when I was faced with completely new ideas; my clients affected me by bringing up stuff that I had to sort out in therapy; my therapy has affected all of us, to the extent that my husband says I am simply not the person he married . . .
>
> Carolyn Couchman, 19 Nov. 1996

This same student had earlier written:

> Another landmark . . . was the lecture on feminism. It was a very moving experience for me because I heard someone use words to describe my life in a way that I had not even dared to think of. I had barely begun to acknowledge the feelings, and yet here was someone who had already thought of the questions. As I listened to Adrienne discussing her PhD. research, I thought, 'Here is someone who knows, who understands, without my having to explain.' It was a feeling of being completely understood. It is one of those times that I can remember, frozen, like a photograph.

Interestingly, particularly considering the high level of anxiety during the course, one of the memories most often spoken of is the excitement – of new ideas, of client work, of reading and beginning to see a pattern in the way things are.

During the course, the peer group had become all-important, almost an idealized family in which it had become safe enough to be angry and vulnerable and to try out a self developing at a sometimes alarming pace. By the end, students often form themselves into smaller groups which go on meeting regularly for many years. They acknowledge one ending but keep the energy alive. As tutors, that we can express our loss becomes of immense importance too.

Some personal reflections

Some time during one of the courses I went to a performance of Tennessee Williams' *The Glass Menagerie*. It is a haunting play and this was a particularly moving performance. Its story is of a shy girl and a gentleman caller. For a while he kindles in her the spark of life, of hope, but the core of what he brings is loss. In contrast, what counselling may do is to allow the flame which is kindled to gain strength and not to be extinguished however cold the wind. Like Laura's in the play, the student's journey is one through uncertainty. For the student it leads to an awareness of quiet and ordinary truths, an awareness of the fragile, delicate ties that may break in relationships when we try to fulfil ourselves – and of the possibility that they can be rewoven in a different way and with greater strength.

It is difficult to convey the rawness of emotions and at the same time the sense of being more fully alive that a student experiences during such a training. We know, because we ourselves are not immune to the process. For a few it is too much, or the ripples in the family are too great, and they leave. Others – maybe all at some stage – go through periods of great ambivalence, but know they must stay, that the training is part of the always painful search into ourselves.

As the poet said:

> . . . In order to arrive there . . .
> In order to arrive at what you do not know
> You must go by a way which is the way of ignorance.
> >   T.S. Eliot (1959) from *East Coker*, p. 29

POSTSCRIPT

Our editor, Colin Feltham, posed several questions, my thoughts on which are listed below.

As a client in therapy there are many powerful memories. Most lasting in terms of the feelings recalled was the long, arid time of depression. Long before I recognized the process, I recognized the split between the self I was and the idealized self I thought I could never become. It was as if I had to denigrate all that I had been, to belittle the aspects of myself that had held on to traditional, nurturing roles. I reproached myself for the timidity which had left me frustrated and angry, longing for I know not what – a career that would stretch me and meet my needs, recognition, a sense of my own worth – for that was what I lacked terribly. So I had to devalue the self as wife, mother, homemaker – for in this immobilizing depression I saw myself only as defined by roles until I could acknowledge and challenge the legacy from my own mother's fragile self-esteem.

The struggle was one through therapy and through a Ph.D. to a recognition that I had choices, that I could make my world how I wanted it to be. Paradoxically then, the 'doing' things came to me and a fulfilment that I had yearned for, and it is my good fortune that through this time my family held me safe.

The other special learning was to do with the possibility of being fallible. My early experience of therapists had not been good and it was only later that I glimpsed my possible part in the scenario. Eventually, though, I came to a therapist who 'worked' for me and yet twice during my four years of therapy she made mistakes. She made them and survived and so did I. It was such an important recognition for me that one can be generous to oneself.

Yet even after nine years in psychodynamic therapy with four different therapists, it seems presumptuous to claim that these experiences of therapy have 'informed my view of human nature'. I feel confident, though, with some realizations: first, that there is a time when one is 'ready' for therapy and a time that is too early for it. Second, I am sure that what 'works' for a client is the therapeutic relationship, by which I mean the *real* relationship in the room, every bit as much as the transference relationship. And from one experience of disdainful therapy I have known what I never dared to say – that qualities of respect and honesty are more healing than 'clever' interpretations.

Along the way as client I have learned how subtle the changes can be in one's sense of self; how the slightest rebuke, a hint of ridicule in the external world, can evoke still-latent feelings of inadequacy; how one can be made and unmade daily. I believe that therapy can begin to redress this only slowly, not by reparation or reassurance but through the therapist's having the guts to stay with one through the grey winter of hopelessness to a cold sharp spring in which there is the promise of new growth, untested and fragile.

The range of client problems with which I work is small, for as a full-time trainer there is an inevitable balancing act between clinical work, teaching, administration, and an attempt to reconcile family needs with my own.

Perhaps inevitably some of the struggles which were my own, which I have lived through and written about – women within families: love, duty, ambivalence and the process of our own eventual growing-up – are the same struggles which bring clients to me. It is also, often, the stage of development which brings women to train.

One recurring theme is as Doris Lessing writes in her preface to *The Golden Notebook*: 'Once a pressure . . . has started, there is no way of avoiding it; there was no way of *not* being intensely subjective.' The theme is of ambivalence, of wanting to change and of fearing what might result.

Yet the client who has affected me most is the one whose dilemma was the opposite of these themes. She was a professional woman, in worldly terms successful but a success which had no value for her. She spoke of a sense of the meaninglessness of her life. The only relationship which had ever mattered to her had ended two years ago and the man, whom she still talked of as 'my boyfriend', was shortly to marry another woman. Her father – distinguished, remote, austere – had died four years earlier but they were a family in which feelings were taboo and she hadn't cried for him or for herself.

She recognized her idealization of the relationship with the boyfriend but he had seemed to offer her spontaneity and a sense of living life fully. She couldn't let him go because 'part of me is still in him'.

> . . . I'm guarded because I daren't risk being hurt again. And yet sometimes I lose the very thing that I most want because I don't recognize that I have it until it's too late. I was thinking about this in relation to my father; you know I could have got closer to him. With my boyfriend, it's as if I wanted something from him that he denied having. Depth. Love. So I lost him.

My sense was of a life in abeyance where there was immense safety in the bleakness of not feeling. She represented a tentativeness which echoed something only too familiar to me and I felt protective towards her, fearing for her fragility.

John Macmurray, a Scottish philosopher, wrote:

> We must choose between a life that is thin and narrow, uncreative and mechanical, with the assurance that even if it is not very exciting it will not be intolerably painful; and a life in which the increase in its fullness and creativeness brings a vast increase in delight, but also in pain and hurt. (1935: 25)

I don't know why I suddenly and vividly thought about her one summer evening at the theatre watching tango dancers. Later I could think about the issue of my boundaries but meanwhile the programme gave me an insight which seemed even more relevant:

> . . . we return to the idea of a state of mind, a state of being: the sense of solitude and of longing. Tango is the tension on the brink of the void, an energy of desperation which, instead of succumbing to it, chooses to risk its life within music.

We worked together for over a year during which her greatest achievement was that she began to feel. At first her anger particularly frightened her. It seemed that the changes she wanted to make in her internal world had to take concrete form in her external world; she chose to relinquish the safety of work and become a student again. Her metamorphosis involved her in painful confrontations with her mother. Nor had either yet grieved the loss of a husband and father. Not surprisingly, considering the powerful transference, she also expressed much ambivalence about therapy – 'I'm concerned about how addictive it could become; it can become a way of life.' But gradually she did become freer and not being in control of every aspect of her life no longer terrified her. She no longer lived in her head and when we parted she had begun to dance.

David Smail, in *The Origins of Unhappiness* (1993), urges us not to pathologize or anthropologize people's suffering but to see it as a valid response to problems within the social context of their lives.

But it is difficult to rid ourselves of value judgements. As a therapist, I learn from the mistakes I made as a mother and from the wisdom my daughters bring as mothers of their children. Sometimes this learning contradicts the ideal I subscribe to as a therapist. Painfully I recognize that the notion that it is 'a good thing' fully to fulfil one's potential can be coercive. For sometimes a child is wary of the world and to deny him the right to create his own safer world is an imposition of our own particular need.

The difficulty with any orthodoxy when we are within it is the fear of questioning it; to do so may mean expulsion. At the very least, the possibility that it can exist alongside other realities means we must tolerate uncertainty and confusion.

Perhaps the greatest gift we can give to our clients and our students is that which I think quietly can define our own lives:

> If I am not for myself who is for me? But if I am only for myself what am I?
>
> Hillel, quoted in Jacobs (1992: 10)

References

Barwick, N. (1995) 'Pandora's box: an investigation of essay anxiety in adolescents', *Psychodynamic Counselling*, 1 (4): 560–75.

Bion, W.R. (1961) *Experiences in Groups and Other Papers*. London: Tavistock. pp. 151–2.

Buber, M. (1970) *Ten Rungs: Hasidic Sayings*. New York: Schocken Books. p. 73.

Burton, A. (1972) *Twelve Therapists: How They Live and Actualize Themselves*. San Francisco: Jossey-Bass.

Casement, P. (1985) *On Learning from the Patient*. London: Routledge.

Edelson, M. (1993) 'Telling and enacting stories in psychoanalysis and psychotherapy', in *The Psychoanalytic Study of the Child*. Vol. 48. New Haven, CT: Yale University Press. pp. 293–325.

Eichenbaum, L. and Orbach, S. (1983) *Understanding Women*. Harmondsworth: Penguin.
Eliot, T.S. (1959) *East Coker*, in *The Four Quartets*. London: Faber and Faber.
Erikson, E.H. (1968) *Identity, Youth and Crisis*. New York: Norton.
Goldberg, C. (1986) *On Being a Psychotherapist: The Journey of the Healer*. London: Gardner Press.
Gray, A. (1994) *An Introduction to the Therapeutic Frame*. London: Routledge.
Hoag, L. (1992) 'Psychotherapy in the general practice surgery: considerations of the frame', *British Journal of Psychotherapy*, 8: 417–29.
Hutten, J.M. (1996) 'The use of experiential groups in the training of counsellors and psychotherapists', *Psychodynamic Counselling*, 2 (2): 247–56.
Ignatieff, M. (1994) *Scar Tissue*. London: Vintage.
Jacobs, L. (1992) *Religion and the Individual: A Jewish Perspective*. Cambridge: Cambridge University Press.
Jacobs, M. (1996) 'Parallel process – confirmation and critique', *Psychodynamic Counselling*, 2 (1): 55–66.
Langs, R. (1979) *The Therapeutic Environment*. London: Jason Aronson.
Langs, R. (1988) *A Primer of Psychotherapy*. New York: Jason Aronson.
Lessing, D. (1962) *The Golden Notebook*. London: Michael Joseph.
Macmurray, J. (1935) *Reason and Emotion*. London: Faber and Faber.
Marcia, J.E. (1975) 'Development and validation of ego-identity status', in R.W. Muuss (ed.), *Adolescent Behaviour and Society*. Random House: New York.
Merodoulaki, G.M. (1994) 'Early experiences as factors influencing occupational choice in counselling and psychotherapy', *Counselling Psychology Review*, 9 (3): 18–39.
Miller, Alice (1983) *The Drama of Being a Child*. London: Virago.
Miller, Arthur (1961) *Death of a Salesman*. Harmondsworth: Penguin.
Moja-Strasser, L. (1996) 'The phenomenology of listening and the importance of silence', *Journal of the Society for Existential Analysis*, 7 (1): 90–102.
Morrison, T. (1990) *Playing in the Dark: Whiteness and the Literary Imagination*. London: Picador.
Rich, A. (1977) *Of Woman Born: Motherhood as Experience and Institution*. London: Virago.
Salinger, J.D. (1951) *The Catcher in the Rye*. London: Hamish Hamilton.
Smail, D. (1993) *The Origins of Unhappiness*. London: HarperCollins.
Tame, J. (1996) 'The seductiveness of theory: thinking about dyads and triads in a case history', *Psychodynamic Counselling*, 2 (1): 39–54.
Tatelbaum, J. (1980) *The Courage to Grieve*. New York: Harper & Row.
Woolf, V. (1972 [1931]) *The Waves*. London: Hogarth Press.

3

Psychotherapy and community care

David Brandon and Jane Akister

This chapter will concentrate on the development of psychotherapy in three main areas in the community: *marginalized groups, family breakdown* and *carers*. There is currently developing an infinitely more self-conscious society with a proliferation of materials – especially in women's magazines and on daytime television – about 'better ways' of living. Many books on personal growth are in the bestsellers list, particularly in the United States. There is a growing familiarity with both counselling approaches and language. Such powerful trends have diverse weaknesses and strengths. As an example of the former, Rose (1986) calls the whole psychotherapeutic process: 'the professional annexation of ordinary human experiences'.

Smail (1993) describes it dismissively as a major part of 'a whole culture of disparagement'. As he puts it:

> It is extremely difficult to think of any major text in these fields which does not either belittle those who become the objects of its attention, or patronize them by holding before them an ideal of how they ought to be. At the same time, there is of course, absolutely nothing to justify such professional conceit – no evidence that the authors of such texts know better than anyone else how to live their lives, and none that the application of their methods actually leads to a significant amelioration of distress. (1993: 81–2)

These are extremely hard words.

One important drawback of the growth in counselling and psychotherapy may be to ignore the substantial socio-economic changes which drive it and so excessively individualize human difficulties. This may create a situation where Elastoplast is habitually applied in the place of a desperate need for major structural surgery. These changes include a greater movement of peoples both nationally and internationally, taking them further away from people they may love and trust; an ageing demographic profile in many parts of the world; moral structures and social rules which are increasingly changeable; the growing influences of global multi-media; and seemingly greater uncertainty in the economy, largely through increasing unemployment in most parts of Europe. All these factors and many more create an atmosphere of growing uncertainty in which counselling from perceived 'wise tribal elders' who are also paradoxically strangers, becomes ever more prevalent.

One of us has been a subject of psychotherapy and experienced directly that heady and complex mixture of healing and exploitation (Brandon, 1976). This experience involved a real sense of personal exploration as well as a shaping by powerful others in sometimes very unwelcome ways. Psychotherapy can be an illuminating conduit for liberation, as well as a considerable opportunity for the misuse of power – an outlet for a variety of egoistic forces like evangelism and sexual exploitation. Relationships established in therapy are most usually founded on an imbalance of power. Hopefully therapy can continue the further exploration of its own shadow side.

Marginalized groups

Traditionally there has been an exclusion by psychotherapy and counselling of certain groups of people existing on the social margins – especially those with chronic mental-health problems, learning difficulties, multiple disabilities, those having physical disabilities and elders. These groups are perceived as profoundly unfashionable and unattractive with very little money, power or influence and as frequently institutionalized. They are also the most socially and economically excluded and have usually been seen, especially in the case of mental handicap, as beneath the minimum threshold for psychotherapy and counselling (Brandon, 1989).

For example, the basic textbook on social work with mentally handicapped people for many years contained no references at all to direct therapeutic work with people who were 'mentally handicapped'. In its section on counselling, written by my former and much-valued psychiatric tutor at University College Hospital, London, the whole emphasis is on therapeutic work with families.

> The essence of counselling is to build up with the families of sub-normal children an on-going relationship, on the basis that all possible information has been given by the parents, in return for which the counselling service does its best to watch the child's development and to promote its welfare in every possible way. (Soddy, quoted in Adams and Lovejoy, 1972: 5)

This promotion of welfare was to be indirect, only through the parents. Thankfully that's not how he and his students practised!

Within the health and social services there has been a particularly entrenched resistance to dealing with these clients' emotional needs (Cullen,

1992). They have been seen as sub-human, animalistic and as lacking the same feelings and sensitivities as others. All over the world they have been institutionalized; shut away from the company of their fellow humans; frequently brutalized through experiences of sexual exploitation and systematic violence (Wolfensberger, 1972, Chapter 2). Oswin describes a systemic denial of pain: 'Lack of sensitivity towards bereaved people with learning difficulties living in residential care is not necessarily a flagrant unkindness but more a *denial of feeling*' (Oswin, 1991: 96, emphasis in original).

Psychotherapy, where it has been concerned at all, has been dominated by the 'personal tragedy' perspective – seeing people, particularly those acquiring a disability, as wrestling with serious emotional problems holding them back developmentally. For example, Segal comments that people with disabilities '. . . take in general two years to accept any significant loss . . . this means that people with disabilities are often mentally about two years out of date in terms of their physical situation' (Oliver, 1995: 261). This is a ridiculously negative generalization, close to stereotyping.

Developmental models of old age often ignore social contexts. 'As people grow older their behaviour changes, the activities that characterize them in middle age become curtailed, and the extent of their social interaction decreases' (Havighurst, quoted in Oliver, 1996: 135). Many therapists have been fully paid up founder members of the Pessimists' Club!

In recent years, there has been a gradual and more enlightened development of both methods and interest in these historically more marginalized areas. This reflects major processes like de-institutionalization and the struggle towards a less medically dominated and rather more social model of disability. The Community Care Act 1991 gave a great boost to individualized service systems which has nourished areas like therapy and care planning (Atherton et al., 1996). It also reflects rather more cynically the increased numbers of students training as counsellors and therapists and the consequent need to conquer new areas for gainful employment. In particular, psychoanalysis has taken a new and largely valuable interest in the area of 'mental handicap', concentrating especially on issues of sexual abuse and their consequences (Sinason, 1991).

Such interest is not without its complexities. 'Somewhat surprisingly, given the negative findings of some of the early research in this area, there is now a resurgence of interest in psychological interventions with schizophrenics' (Holloway and Carson, 1996). The authors go on: 'psychologically based treatments could play an important role', somewhat mitigating the considerable sin of cynicism (or is it simply realism?) but not, perhaps more importantly, the greater sin of depersonalization – as in 'with schizophrenics' – which accurately, if unconsciously, portrays the great ambivalence of many therapists towards this particular client group.

On one level, as Rose implies (1986, Chapter 2), this is part of the gradual colonization of various sorts of human distress. Professionals are robustly claiming expertise in ordinary living, as Smail suggested earlier, with little realistic justification. They are eager to teach grandmothers to suck eggs. Another important theme arises out of the 'care in the community' policies. In the past many people with disabilities were congregated and segregated in isolated institutions, but now they are living among us and next door to us. The damage done to them by institutions and their sometimes relatively strange behaviour can cause both us and them severe social problems.

These new potential clients present a considerable challenge to psychotherapy. They have been damaged by the so-called helping systems; have been 'taught', often through the behaviour of professionals, that others are not trustworthy; and many have little or no speech. There has been the injurious development of blanket terms like 'challenging behaviours' with their related marauding teams, representing rather institutional and often pathological ways of using community-based staff. This kind of negative terminology and the often controlling methods have tended to conceal more than reveal. They describe a client group so diverse as to render such blanket descriptions as 'challenging behaviours' almost completely erroneous.

In constructive response, there is the development of several so-called non-aversive systems, aimed at being more respectful of clients and their experiences. These attempts to replace methods which are often seen as coercive and in some cases actively punitive. In a way, they are helping to radically redefine the whole nature of counselling and psychotherapy (Brandon, 1990). They are also dedicated to spelling out some further disturbing details of the substantial iatrogenic (hindering) forces in human services (Illich, 1975, Chapter 2).

For example, Gentle Teaching is a clear and powerful reaction to what it sees as the exploitative aspects of the dominant behavioural interventions in the field of learning difficulties. Developed in Nebraska in the United States, it perceives behaviour modification and related therapies unequivocally as forces for evil – perhaps an extreme reaction to the use of the electric cattle prod and powerful drugs in some institutions in that state. It is very firmly values-based and has generated an energetic debate about whether there are any appropriate 'techniques', a debate relevant to the wider field of therapy (McGee et al., 1987).

Predominantly, this method of teaching or therapy looks in a mirror, emphasizing the often negative and disturbing reflections of the therapists and the support systems, rather than the actions of the client. Values include *mutuality* – where the process is more about changing the nature of professionals than their clients, about constantly critically evaluating the nature of their motives and interventions. The fundamental principle is that all others are our teachers. Further to this is *autonomy* – whereby people are encouraged to discover the nature of their influence and power and to develop and use it; and *solidarity* – that is, standing on the side of people who have been oppressed, excluded and devalued, who have been taught that they are worth less than others, which establishes closer links with advocacy.

Also included are *valuing* – we should value both ourselves and those we work with. There should be an atmosphere of realistic optimism. We believe that the clients can grow and learn to appreciate others more fully as well as themselves. And finally, *acceptance* and *tolerance* – that is, the practice of positive human values leading towards friendship, liking and love; strongly aiming to nourish others where the means never justify the ends. There has been a powerful tendency, especially in behaviouristic interventions, to justify methods involving present indignity in the subject in terms of some perceived gains in the future.

These overall approaches, what Gentle Teaching calls a posture, try to communicate to people the essential worthwhileness of contact with others, the inherent merits in bonding. It is about relating to people who through their long injurious experiences have often been taught the exact opposite.

Work with such clients challenges the whole nature of psychotherapy, which has often reflected the wider social attitudes about their inferior status. Such interventions can hardly be neutral in the fact of systemic and crushing oppression (Barron, 1996). The therapist often has difficult issues to confront.

Rosemary is 46 years old and lived in a long-stay mental-handicap hospital for more than 25 years. She has Downs Syndrome and a chronic heart condition. During those years there were several allegations made about physical violence and sexual abuse. Two particular male staff members were accused. The police investigated and uncovered insufficient evidence to justify taking the case to court. One staff member was retired early and the other was moved to another ward.

Rosemary received no emotional support except from an aunt, a younger sister of her mother, who had died two years earlier. The fixed staff belief was that 'Downs people are like rubber balls. So cheerful that they get over events like this easily and anyway they don't feel the distress which would knock normal others down.' The ward staff regarded her as 'hysterical'. Rosemary comments: 'Those men did things to me. I didn't agree with it but they didn't take notice. Nobody did anything about it. The police came but they didn't believe me and did nothing.'

Her regular bed-wetting was a great problem for staff and treated behaviourally, but she didn't respond to this approach. It wasn't until she left hospital to live in a local group home with three others that any connection was made between the alleged sexual abuse and the bed-wetting. She received weekly psychotherapy. Very hesitantly, she told the long and detailed story of a number of unwelcome sexual experiences, including rape by a hospital staff member.

These several incidents were very frightening to Rosemary and her bed-wetting incidents increased when she began to discuss them. She felt she had not been believed and that the two people involved had lied and got away with it. 'They should have gone to prison.' The police investigated and decided once more that there was insufficient evidence for referral to the Crown Prosecution Service. Some staff commented that she was just 'attention seeking'.

The psychotherapist provided a safe setting to talk of dangerous events and people, but first she had to gain some trust. She encouraged Rosemary to develop her communication through halting speech and drawing large pictures. The two male hospital staff were shown on a dozen sheets of paper as hugely dominating, dark shadows towering over a tiny Rosemary. Another poignant sheet shows a wretched little girl soaking wet in an immense rainstorm.

During these prolonged sessions, where Rosemary became very tearful, her bed-wetting ceased completely for a time. Crying at one end, apparently, could affect crying at the other. However, the bed-wetting began again after several months as she described fresh bullying by a male staff member in her new group home. The matter was referred to the police by the manager. The police sergeant commented wearily and unenthusiastically, 'the mentally handicapped make rotten witnesses'.

The psychotherapist was working right on the edge of an overall oppressive system with a strong tendency to abuse, from which there seemed little escape. Rosemary remains fundamentally devalued and seemingly unsafe outside the therapy room. She is often depressed and at other times absolutely furious. She feels that nobody believes her. She made several further allegations about abuse, with at least one case of actual bodily violence.

It was even hard for the professional therapist to get a hearing within the large organization running the group homes. This particular therapist was very unhappy in the role of advocate but could not remain passive in the face of such experiences. After nearly a year, another staff member was a direct witness to the abuse. She saw her colleague punch Rosemary. She told the manager who was most reluctant to move the staff member because of strong union pressure that he was being victimized without real evidence and before any investigation was complete. Eventually, after a few weeks, in which Rosemary was very frightened, he was moved to another post. How can individual psychotherapy avoid colluding with extremely powerful and negative social forces? What is the most effective interplay between advocacy and therapy? These are issues likely to become ever-more pressing in these difficult areas.

Joanna is in her forties and has recently been discharged from a large psychiatric hospital after 18 years as part of a run-down and closure programme. She had received very little treatment for her diagnosis of chronic schizophrenia: some years of powerful anti-psychotic drugs resulting in tardive dyskinesia, mixed with two dozen sessions of 'frightening shock therapy'.

I was never liked within my family. They wanted to get rid of me and so got me carried off to the lunatic asylum just because I was a loner and a bit eccentric. I wandered around the local streets in all weathers picking up bits of rubbish. After all these years I'm just as bad as ever. Being in here hasn't helped at all.

She has become heavily institutionalized, making it very difficult for her to survive as an ordinary citizen in the world outside.

Weekly psychotherapy focuses on her growing anger about the abuse and neglect she has experienced. She has also had great loss to contend with as some friends from the hospital were dispersed over a wide area as part of the overall resettlement policy. She finds it hard to write letters and cannot easily use the phone, so it is almost impossible to stay in contact.

> I didn't like it in that place but I miss my good friends, Winnie, Frieda and Mary. I've known them for years. We used to have such a good giggle. I'm more lonely nowadays because I don't have much in common with the other women here.

At the beginning of most weekly sessions, she shakes and grimaces silently for several minutes before launching into a disjointed tirade about staff, including a nurse who deliberately broke her spectacles, grinding them under his foot. Each meeting ends with some regular breathing exercises to help concentrate her energies more fully. 'I feel much better after the breathing. It's fun and helpful. I also practise in my bedroom.'

This anger has been very long repressed in a setting in which Joanna felt completely crushed. In the early therapy periods, it was difficult for her to say anything; those sessions were punctuated by the relaxing music she loves and breathing exercises.

> There was so much inside me that it went sour. I couldn't get hold of it. I felt blocked and the breathing really helped. In the hospital my feelings were never ever taken into account. There were long years of boredom, waiting many hours for the nurses and doctors. I was made to feel like nothing. No real treatment and little human contact. Nobody explained anything. Nobody ever listened to me.

She now lives in a group home with three other women ex-patients whom she doesn't like.

> I still feel very inferior to everyone. I still feel that people are all staring at me; talking about me on the streets. I know it isn't true but it feels that way especially when I'm bad. Nobody understands what it was like to be in those awful places. I often get depressed and suicidal and then that makes it worse because I get frightened they'll take me back into the institution.

Arising from psychotherapy, Joanna was put in touch with an advocacy service. She wishes to pursue complaints against particular hospital staff. The psychotherapy sessions focus on helping her to feel less devalued. The fact that she knows the psychotherapist has a long-term connection with psychiatric hospitals and was a service user himself seems to help. There is an element of peer support within the therapeutic process (Segal et al., 1996).

When she feels a bit more confident and balanced, Joanna wants eventually to move into a bedsit.

At the moment I am struggling and very angry. When I feel more settled and quieter I want to move away from these women and the group home and start my own life. I'm middle-aged now and I've hardly had any life at all. I need a bit more therapy so I can understand what is going on inside my head.

Family breakdown

The proliferation of therapies raises many questions for those seeking assistance with divorce and separation. Family breakdown is an ever-increasing phenomenon in the West. There are serious questions about how and from whom such fragmented families may seek help and what ways there are of assessing and evaluating any help they may receive.

Currently there is a developing trend for people to seek help with interpersonal difficulties not from their community of friends and relations but from professionals outside their local community. The reasons for this are not clear and frequently involve statements like 'professionals are more objective and detached'. These people are seen in some senses as 'secular priests'. Certainly there is a view that people are increasingly isolated and have no one to turn to. The perceived lack of a community is an important context.

Many people previously would not have come to the attention of the 'helping' services nor would they have been deemed 'ill'. They are mostly a new group, sometimes called the 'worried well', seeking psychotherapy and counselling in the community, not using traditional gatekeepers like social workers or medical practitioners. At the same time as there are increases in families seeking help, many with considerable difficulties are still likely to delay seeking help partly because of the perceived stigma. A community sample of intact families given the Family Assessment Device (a self-report questionnaire on family functioning) showed 16 per cent reporting clinical levels of dysfunction (Akister and Stevenson-Hinde, 1991). This indicates a reluctance to seek help as well as difficulty in identifying when things are going wrong.

Families contain and work through many difficulties, often very serious, making it hard to decide when outside help could be relevant and useful. Fear of admitting failure in marital and parental roles is still problematic. There is still scope for encouraging the process of exploring and working on relationships. Workshops like 'marital enhancement weekends' are steps in this direction.

Is psychotherapy always the answer? Are there times when self-help is better? Where should people seek help? These questions are important keys to the psychotherapeutic experience. If a family experiences difficulties they may decide that the problem lies with one individual and seek help for him or her. They may decide it is a marital problem and seek help with the marriage. They may decide on a particular solution, for example to separate and seek mediation. Even within the traditional realms of therapy, a family has to make decisions about who to approach, crucially determining their subsequent experiences.

There is the fundamental question of what families want from therapy. There have been numerous studies on the effectiveness of family therapy (Gurman et al., 1986), but the specific factors remain elusive. A process study (Frosh et al., 1996) looked at the 'attitude to change' in one recently separated family. Having made the separation the father feels that change should be left to evolve whereas the mother feels that it should be managed. As Frosh et al. put it:

> As family members move in and out of different discourses on change over the course of therapy, they seem to become more comfortable with each others' perspective and more able to acknowledge the complexity of their relationship and their emotional state. (1996: 160)

This work investigated the subtleties of the experience of therapy for the family in altering their appreciation of their own and each others' positions.

In this example, the experience would have been very different if the mother had sought help alone. There would have been no opportunity for the reappraisal of each other's position. While there is no 'correct' way to seek help, people need an awareness of the various options and implications regarding who does and does not get involved in the process.

When there is no agency advising on where to get help, where can people start? This depends on availability and what the person knows, but perhaps it is best to start with a psychotherapist skilled in relationship work. A family or marital therapist can then refer on for individual, group or even no psychotherapy as considered appropriate. If the starting point is individual therapy then opportunities to work on relationship issues with those involved in the relationships are less likely. Caution is none the less needed and David Howe's look at consumers' views of family therapy highlights the need for therapists to be clear with their clients as to what they are able to offer and whether this is either what the family wants or needs (Howe, 1989).

The experiences of some families will help to explore the complexities of who the real client is and who, if anyone, is in need of psychotherapy and in what shape or form it is needed.

Mr Adams resigned from his job, which included accommodation for the family. He was unable to obtain work with similar pay and status. The family moved to a new town and Mrs Adams had to go out to work. The family had no friends or support in the new community and she became extremely stressed and angry with their changed situation. Her husband withdrew and would not talk to her. The relationship deteriorated with Mrs Adams becoming more and more angry and hostile to both her husband and their two children (aged eight years and six years). After a bitter 18 months, they sought marital counselling with a view to separation.

Marital counselling resolved some issues for the couple and they decided to try and continue their relationship. The counselling also identified that Mrs Adams had some serious unresolved issues from her family of origin which the current difficulties had brought to the surface, and individual counselling was recommended.

Mr Adams' resignation from his job precipitated problems for his family in dealing with a major change. It might have been expected that if anyone needed individual counselling it would be Mr Adams. The move resolved some of his dilemmas but caused problems for others in the system. Marital work helped the couple with relationship difficulties and identified problems occurring for the individuals. If they had sought help alone, problems experienced in their relationship could not have been so easily tackled and they would have been left with an individualized view of their situation, possibly blaming themselves or each other rather than having the opportunity to see the interrelatedness of their concerns.

When an individual is considered to have all the problems, he or she can be burdened with this role for many years. In the Greg family the mother had for some years been identified as the problem. At the time they were describing their experiences, the Gregs had three children – two daughters aged nine years and six years and a son aged four years. Mrs Greg had experienced numerous bouts of depression following the birth of her second daughter. These episodes lasted for up to six weeks during which she would become increasingly dysfunctional, at times sitting all day in a chair ignoring the children's demands. Treatment was sought through her general practitioner who prescribed anti-depressants. The husband was not seen or involved in the treatment and no specialist psychiatric help was sought.

During an episode when the younger daughter was four, Mrs Greg became aggressive towards her husband who felt unable to cope any longer. Following this incident he sought advice through his workplace counselling facilities. Family counselling was recommended enabling the whole family to share their concerns and experiences. A process began whereby the family were able to sustain their relationships through the depression and Mrs Greg received individual psychotherapy to complement her anti-depressant medication.

The Gregs were seen together as a family over four sessions, to express their reactions to Mrs Greg's depression. This enabled them to move on from repeated episodes, which everyone had tiptoed around. As a whole family they approached some problems in therapy while Mrs Greg had individual attention. Often a combination of approaches is needed with the whole system approach enabling all family members to be engaged in and understand the processes. This also enabled Mrs Greg to receive some specialist help but not to be seen as the 'problem'. The family were able to work together to preserve their integrity and to have a shared notion of difficulties, rather than believing that everything was down to Mum's depression.

These views of one person carrying all the negative responsibilities can be held for many years and the randomness of what kind of help is received is worrying. First, the person with difficulties may be ready to take on the role of being the 'problem', and second, there is no doubt that the beliefs and values of the person first approached for help determine what is offered and received. There has to be some role for advocacy in negotiating the maze of psychotherapeutic possibilities.

Although there are times when people's experiences are essentially individual, there are repercussions for others. Often in crises everyone is relieved to deal with the immediate concerns. When Mr James was suffering from stress at work and developed an acute anxiety response, eventually attempting suicide, he was admitted to a psychiatric unit and treated through anxiety management. Everyone was relieved about the success of the treatment and he was home four weeks later. Neither Mrs James nor the three children (aged nine years, six years and four years) were involved. When he returned home his wife began to get extremely anxious about the possibility that he would get ill again and kill himself. This stressed the relationship and the couple sought marital therapy. The therapist advised a joint consultation with Mr James' psychiatrist. Importantly, the marital therapist identified that there was no need for marital therapy. It would have been easy to embark on unnecessary treatment.

This is a good example of what can happen when someone is treated and their partner is not. Whenever a person is involved in life-threatening incidents, whether a heart attack or attempted suicide, there are major concerns about recurrence and handling rehabilitation. A conjoint session enables issues to be aired and helps the family resume their lives. Failure to have such sessions increases the possibility of secondary problems occurring, for example, resulting in anxiety in other family members.

Differing approaches to problems often lead to very different outcomes. In working with relationships it is important to include all family members who are prepared to be involved so as to optimize the outcomes of any intervention. 'Evaluation for "good' practice requires that purposes are debated and acknowledged' (Everitt and Hardiker, 1996: 33). Good practice also requires an awareness of different ways of working rather than relying on standard procedures. Further to this, it involves an awareness that 'doing nothing' is sometimes appropriate. The James' were fortunate their marital therapist recognized that they did not need marital therapy. There is a considerable risk of therapists seeing all who approach them as able to benefit from their skills; it is a difficult judgement as to whether intervention is necessary.

Carers

In the care of older people, there is a great and welcome growing emphasis on choice and supporting older citizens to remain in their own homes. This is fundamentally positive and based on giving older people and their carers wider choices. As with all changes, new issues arise and psychotherapy has a role to play in facilitating such choice, in acknowledging and exploring issues like loss, and perhaps even in moderating the more fiercely dogmatic aspects of evangelism in the institution versus community debate.

One familiar difficulty is who to approach and when. Doris, in her eighties, was admitted to hospital in the terminal stages of a progressive illness. Doris had been cared for over many years by her husband Jim to whom she had been married for 55 years. The medical team felt it was unrealistic for Jim to continue to care for his wife, who needed constant nursing care, and that she should enter a residential nursing home. The social worker talked with Doris about this and also separately with Jim. Both were extremely distressed at the prospect of admission to residential care and the separation involved. To avoid further distress, no conjoint meeting was held. Arrangements were then made for Doris to move into a residential home without the couple talking it over with the social worker. As McGoldrick put it:

> All change in life requires loss. We must give up certain relationships, plans and possibilities in order to have others. And all losses require mourning, which acknowledges the giving up, transforms the experience to take into ourselves what is essential, and allows us to move on. (1995: 127)

There are still many caring situations where discussing loss in joint sessions is avoided. Sometimes the rationale is that it is too painful for people to talk together. Is the greater reality perhaps that it may be too painful for the worker? Certainly for Doris and Jim it is 'too painful', but avoidance can lead to even more pain. Sometimes there is no really relevant rationale but it is just not the way the organization is run. This is particularly true of institutions like acute general hospitals, where the main task is physical treatment rather than a focus on work with relationships. Any care package which alters people's previous arrangements for living should be discussed together with the significant persons. If this is not the case, then although one individual may exercise choices, someone else is having decisions foisted upon them in profoundly undemocratic ways.

A further personal example: marriage to Althea in 1963 brought a father-in-law – Leslie. He had retired early and developed arteriosclerosis and moved in with us. That was a very difficult experience for all of us for several years. He was extremely forgetful and untidy. Looking after Grandpa and the two young children split us in various ways. It was often like having an elderly cuckoo in the nest. Over time, he got even worse, was often doubly incontinent and required much greater attention. It was difficult to banish the smell of stale urine from the house. We rarely went out socially. We almost never invited people to our home. We became very stressed and our own relationship was extremely strained. We felt completely isolated.

Treatment for Grandpa's worsening cataracts was arranged in the nearby Preston Royal Infirmary. He was supposed to be there for only a few days but things got really bad. He became restless and confused. They transferred him to the geriatric ward and then for convalescence. Eventually he was discharged to our care and we had an immediate crisis. He couldn't manage on his own at all. He just wandered around restlessly, not knowing where or even who he was. He lived mostly in previous decades.

A social worker visited. He carried a briefcase full of forms and talked initially of assessment and of the social services department's problems at great length. Was Leslie a health or social services responsibility? There was obviously a substantial battle going on behind the scenes. We talked very practically and politically for something like 15 minutes – about commodes, wheelchairs, the lack of home-help services, possible admission to old people's homes, etc. Then I realized that the conversation had turned into therapy. This young man for whom I had very little respect had become an unwelcome and intrusive therapist.

It was based on subtle blackmail, sometimes not so subtle. In my role of caring relative, I didn't really exist in my own right. I wasn't the client. The single client was and had to be Grandpa who wasn't a person any more but a series of conditions and syndromes. Both my wife and I were simply adjuncts, a means of supporting his infirmity. She and I were unpaid members of a professional team which included him and the community psychiatric nurses. Without our agreement or any discussion, we had become 'carers'. No one at all tended to our grief and distress because we weren't the clients. We needed to break down psychiatrically and become a case in our own right to be seen and heard and to qualify for some help. There was some slight possibility of real support and help but to receive it we had to be seen as cooperative, open and compliant. We had to share fully our wounds and vulnerabilities to compete effectively with many unseen others in the lottery for help. It felt like a form of abuse (Brandon and Jack, 1997).

Leslie was admitted quite unnecessarily to psychiatric hospital, eventually going into a new elderly severely mentally ill (ESMI) unit. This inflexible service was unable to listen or to react either to his needs or to ours and so spent excessive amounts of resources on a service which nobody wanted and injured us all. We wanted some inexpensive support like 'meals on wheels' to continue caring for Grandpa in our community, not an in-patient admission to a grim institution and then further transfer to an inorganic Startrek unit.

Angela was married to Norman who had a psychiatric diagnosis of manic-depressive psychosis (now commonly called bi-polar disorder). It had been a roller-coaster of a relationship over many years. She was a practising and very competent lawyer but had to give up her job to care for him. He was admitted several times a year to mental hospital.

> He was very violent to me and then would get depressed for many months at a time, hardly moving or talking at all. There were several dozen suicide attempts over the years. Periodically he would get on a high and run up huge bills on various hi-fi equipment, cars, word processors . . . He was such a huge worry. I often felt I was his nurse not his wife.

Angela went through the usual exhausting round of psychiatric review meetings and visits from interminable professionals, drinking endless cups of tea.

> I came into psychotherapy because I was beginning to lose any sense of myself. I felt that very powerful others saw me as having no rights. I began to see myself exclusively as his wife, entirely designed to support him. That was my purpose in life, all my training at university had become meaningless. I didn't want to be a psychiatric nurse when I grew up, I wanted to become a lawyer.
>
> The various professionals never saw my needs, never even recognized my distress or the loss because he was not the man I married all those years before. He had become a sort of monster, which is a terrible thing to say. I became largely the unpaid member of the psychiatric team who did all the weekend shifts; that was what partnership meant for them. I wanted to leave him and set up a real life for myself but the pressure from the team is immense and extremely self-centred. It would put much more pressure on them if I didn't do the weekend shift! Their pressure and my guilt and feelings of marital failure are enormous.

In those various sessions Angela tried to disentangle various feelings of obligation and responsibility and search once more for her individual self. Eventually she decided to leave Norman and set up a life with someone else. Norman found out where she lived and that she was living with someone else and tried to wreck the situation. She was both furious and frightened and returned to psychotherapy to deal with the feelings.

These examples indicate a need for much more flexible responses and genuine therapeutic means. It requires that carers be seen also as individuals in their own right and not simply as vital but unpaid elements in an informal support service. It is worrying therefore that a very recent text defines the tasks of 'supporting elderly people and their caregivers at home means: helping caregivers to carry on supporting the older person . . .' (Askham, 1997). The dominant use of the term 'caregiver' accentuates the barriers that Angela faced as well as the lack of attention to the relatives. The professionals tend to identify a single client/patient, rather than working with systems, with the result that everyone else is defined as irrelevant and unpaid auxiliaries in supporting that client, and not seen as people in their own unique right. This often leads to an injurious and undemocratic process, as the examples given above illustrate.

Conclusion

With the expanding range of therapies available some mechanisms are needed to assist informed choice by users. Marital or family psychotherapy offers techniques which can be extremely useful in situations where well-established patterns of living need changing. The range of therapies based not primarily on verbal communication is increasingly yearly, allowing professionals to work increasingly with people with little or no speech. Those in the 'helping, caring and medical' professions need to constantly reappraise their knowledge of what is available and where research indicates effectiveness.

In particular, some studies show that psychotherapists may not be more effective than social workers or nurses with little therapeutic training. A series of studies showed no differences between the two compared professional groups across four of the most common categories of patient complaints. We are still seeking the Holy Grail of psychotherapeutic effectiveness (Christensen and Jacobson, 1994). We still have little idea whether that effectiveness is more to do with the personality of the therapist than his or her training and techniques. Whatever else we need, humility is vital.

Psychotherapy in the community covers a wide range of exciting possibilities. There is a place for traditional psychotherapy, working with individuals often intensively and over long periods of time, but there is also a place for brief focused interventions. These are not always based on 'problems' in the sense of experiencing failure to cope. Frequently they may involve looking at life changes, adapting to new situations or decisions to be made, and using the presence and skills of a therapist as well as the experience and frequently the wisdom of the client(s). What is needed is a wider appreciation of where the skills of the family, couples or group therapist, advocate, mediator and others can be useful.

Naturally such benefits come with side-effects. Many marginalized clients live and work within fundamentally oppressive settings where they are devalued just like Rosemary. Their pain and suffering can easily be pathologically individualized into therapy while ignoring fundamentally unjust systems. As we have seen, this institutionalized oppression poses challenges when the turbulent waters of therapy and advocacy meet (Brandon, 1995).

Even the development of self-consciousness can have a very high cost. Thomas Merton, a Trappist monk interested in Buddhism and Taoism, commented:

> The more 'the good' is objectively analyzed, the more it is treated as something to be attained by special virtuous techniques, the less real it becomes. As it becomes less real, it recedes further into the distance of abstraction, futurity, unattainability. The more, therefore, one concentrates on the means to be used to attain it. And as the end becomes more remote and more difficult, the means become more elaborate and complex, until finally, the mere study of the means becomes so demanding that all one's effort must be concentrated on this, and the end is forgotten. (1965: 23)

There is a great danger that the inherent process of objectivization of human events, especially transitions, is made even more difficult through increasing self-consciousness. Even more dangerous is therapy becoming yet another expression of that reaching for perfection which usually results in the rejection of human ordinariness.

Any attempt to introduce sound psychotherapeutic principles into intensely darkened areas, like the learning difficulties services and old people's homes, should anticipate negative reactions that are often very intense. At their best these principles and methods, if properly applied on a clear values base, can generate great light. 'The forces of light usually stimulate a reaction from the forces of darkness' (Skynner, 1989). We must continue to anticipate powerful corrosive forces both from inside these systems as well as from the outside.

However dark it may sometimes seem in the therapy field, one of us just received a Christmas card from a former schizophrenic patient who was seen in psychotherapy over three years against considerable psychiatric advice. The loudly expressed professional view was 'You are wasting your time.' He had never been employed and had spent ten years in a Victorian mental hospital, the son of two parents both diagnosed as schizophrenic. He has been working consistently over the last three years and will probably and hopefully qualify as a social worker in six months time. Not bad for someone who was written off by most professionals!

References

Adams, M. and Lovejoy, H. (eds) (1972) *The Mentally Subnormal – Social Work Approaches*. London: Heinemann.

Akister, J. and Stevenson-Hinde, J. (1991) 'Identifying families at risk: exploring the potential of the McMaster Family Assessment Device', *Journal of Family Therapy*, 13: 411–21.

Askham, J. (1997), in Ian J. Norman and Sally J. Redfern (eds), *Mental Health Care for Elderly People*. New York: Churchill Livingstone.

Atherton, K. et al. (1996) *Care Planning Handbook*. London: Positive Publications.

Barron, D. (1996) *A Price to be Born – My Childhood and Life in a Mental Institution*. Harrogate: Mencap Northern Division.

Brandon, D. (1976) *Human Being Human*. London: Quaesitor.

Brandon, D. (ed.) (1989) *Mutual Respect – Therapeutic Approaches to Working with People who have Learning Difficulties*. London: Good Impressions.

Brandon, D. (1990) *Ordinary Magic*. Preston: Tao Preston.

Brandon, D. (1995) *Advocacy – Power to People with Disabilities*. Birmingham: Venture Press.

Brandon, D. and Jack, R. (1997) 'Struggling with services', in I.J. Normal and S.J. Redfern (eds), *Mental Health Care for Elderly People*. New York: Churchill Livingstone.

Christensen, A. and Jacobson, N.S. (1994) 'Who (or what) can do psychotherapy?', *Psychological Science*, 5 (1).

Cullen, C. (1992) 'Introduction', in A. Waitman and S. Conboy-Hill (eds), *Psychotherapy and Mental Handicap*. London: Sage.

Everitt, A. and Hardiker, P. (1996) *Evaluating for 'Good Practice'*. London: Macmillan.

Frosh, S., Burck, C., Strickland-Clarke, L. and Morgan, K. (1996) 'Engaging with change: a process study of family therapy', *Journal of Family Therapy*, 18 (2): 163–83.

Gurman, A., Kniskern, D. and Pinsof, W. (1986) 'Research on marital and family therapies', in S. Garfield and A. Bergin (eds), *Handbook of Psychotherapy and Behaviour Change*. New York: Wiley.

Holloway, F. and Carson, J. (1996) 'Interventions with long-term clients', Chapter 9 in M. Watkins et al. (eds), *Collaborative Community Mental Health Care*. London: Edward Arnold.

Howe, D. (1989) *The Consumers' View of Family Therapy*. Aldershot: Gower.

Illich, I. (1975) *Medical Nemesis – The Expropriation of Health*. London: Calder/ Boyars.

McGee, J. et al. (1987) 'Gentle Teaching – A Non-aversive Approach to Helping Persons with Mental Retardation'. Nebraska: Human Sciences Press.

McGoldrick, M. (1995) *You Can Go Home Again: Reconnecting With Your Family*. London/New York: W.W. Norton.

Merton, T. (1965) *The Way of Chuang Tzu*. London: Unwin.

Oliver, J. (1995) 'Counselling disabled people: a counsellor's perspective', *Disability & Society*, 10 (3): 261–79.

Oliver, M. (1996) *Understanding Disability*. London: Macmillan.

Oswin, M. (1991) *Am I Allowed to Cry*? London: Human Horizons, Souvenir.

Rose, N. (1986) 'Psychiatry – the discipline of mental health', in P. Muller and N. Rose (eds), *The Power of Psychiatry*. London: Polity Press.

Segal, S.P. et al. (1996) 'Self-help mental health programs', *Breakthrough*, 1 (1): 23–4.

Sinason, V. (1991) *Mental Handicap – A Human Condition*. London: Free Association.

Skynner, R. (1989) *Institutes and How to Survive Them*. London: Routledge. p. 191.

Smail, D. (1993) *The Origins of Unhappiness*. London: HarperCollins. p. 193.

Wolfensberger, W. (1972) *The Principle of Normalisation*. Canada: NIMR.

4

Therapy with gay men in the era of AIDS

Todd Butler and Norman Leitman

N: Is there a significant difference between therapy with gay men and other clients?

T: No, I don't think so. Over the years I have found that I don't work differently with my gay male clients than I do with my other clients. They don't usually present gay issues, but come with depression, anxiety, work problems, relationship problems (why can't I find one?) and, almost always, low self-esteem.

N: That is pretty much my experience, but the problem of self-esteem in gay men is exacerbated by internalized homophobia, and reinforced by the homophobia of others. If I had to identify one key issue for most of my gay clients it would be self-oppression, focused on their homosexuality. When clients disparage aspects of the gay world, other gay men different from themselves (effeminate men, drag queens, older gay men, etc.), I see this as a form of internalized homophobia, which may, on an unconscious level, reinforce the belief that homosexuality is wrong.

    The insidiousness of this kind of projection and displacement became clear to me when I recalled my discomfort as a Jewish little boy if Hassidic Jews would enter an underground carriage. I felt embarrassed by their funny clothes and full beards (this was the 1940s, remember) and squirmed in my seat, wishing to disassociate my Jewishness from theirs.

T: Certainly, I agree that internalized homophobia is a core issue which is underpinned by a deep feeling of shame.

N: Shame not just for something you've done, but shame for who you are!

T: As an example of my own self-oppression, I remember an incident in my own therapy group when I contracted to do some body work. The therapist asked me to remove my jewellery for safety reasons. As I was taking off my earring, neck chain, ring and watch I thought, 'If I were a real man, I wouldn't be wearing so much jewellery.' Needless to say, this became the work.

N: Considering what it is like for many boys growing up gay in a heterosexual world, it is not surprising that so many gay men struggle with self-esteem.

T: I think all gay men struggle with self-esteem no matter how seemingly accepting they are of their homosexuality. From the day of their birth, boys are programmed to grow up heterosexual. In the traditional nuclear family, in single-parent families, by their peers, by their teachers, in every aspect of society, the expectation is that the boy will be 'normal'.

N: But he secretly knows that he is not.

T: Yes, when he begins to suspect that there is something different about himself, and he may not know yet what that difference is, that is when he begins to feel acute shame about his very being. This can happen as early as four or five.

N: And clients report various incidents in their childhood and adolescence which reinforce this sense of shame. As the boy becomes aware of his attraction to his own sex, the shame becomes focused on this significant difference between him and his peers. He is bombarded with homophobic abuse, towards him if he is effeminate, or towards others, which he knows secretly is about himself. He reads in the tabloids about 'poofters' and 'queers', and struggles with the knowledge that they are talking about him.

Virtually every one of my clients had to spend a good portion of their childhood holding a shameful secret. And of course many gay men who are fully or partially in the closet still do.

T: But don't forget that it is not only what the boy experiences from the outside world that oppresses him, but his own decisions about himself, that is, that parts of himself are not acceptable.

N: Yes, and I usually find that these decisions are still based on the environment's rejection – for example, fathers who cannot accept the boys' timidity and fearfulness, and insensitively reject them because they are not interested in stereotypical male activities.

T: And it is not only fathers. One of my clients recently told the group about his mother organizing the neighbourhood boys to teach him how to play football (he believes she suspected something was not quite right about him). He was bored. On the way home from the football lesson he picked some wildflowers for his mother, and she didn't know how to react.

N: Considering what most gay men have gone through, in their childhood and adolescence, it is remarkable how healthy they are. I still resent the fact that until recently the psychiatric and psychotherapeutic establishments automatically categorized homosexuality itself as pathological.

T: And some still do.

N: Not to mention some religious leaders, politicians, journalists and anyone who needs someone to despise, since it is no longer acceptable to be openly racist, sexist or anti-Semitic.

I want to come back to the subject of shame, or more specifically the shameful secret that lurks behind the decision to come out.

T: Most of my clients have already come out before coming to see me, however I am sure I have an opinion or two on the subject.

N: My experience is a little different. While many of my clients are out in some aspects of their life, and may have a circle of gay friends, they may still be in the closet at work, or with their family.

T: I noticed that I just said to myself, sometimes not coming out at work seems the only option to a client, because, realistically, they might lose their job.

N: This might be true, but I wonder at the emotional cost to the individual who believes he has to remain in the closet, day after day, week after week, month after month. These gay men in this situation eventually have to decide whether the job is important enough for them to live with the tension of holding such an important secret, and having to worry about being found out. In my experience this can lead to high levels of stress and paranoia, and feelings of low self-esteem. During the course of therapy many clients either decide to come out at work (often to increased respect from their colleagues, who had already suspected the truth) or to change their workplace to a friendlier environment.

T: When I was a kid in the fifties, coming out meant admitting to yourself that you were gay. Nowadays it practically means putting a notice in *The Times*.

N: More likely the *Guardian*.

T: Seriously though, for young, politically correct gay men there is peer pressure to be 'in your face' out.

N: I love it! I have become much more up-front militant in my old age. I must confess I enjoy some heterosexual discomfort at my up-front attitude towards who I am. The other day I was looking at wedding bands . . .

T: Are we getting married after 37 years of living in sin?

N: If it becomes legal, why not? There are enormous legal and financial benefits. For example, when one of us dies, the other would not have to pay some of the death duties until the surviving spouse dies. He wouldn't have to sell the house to pay the death duties, etc.

T: I accept your proposal.

N: Good, but back to my story: I said to the ring salesperson, 'I will need two matching rings.' She said, 'his and hers?' I said, 'No, his and his.' I enjoyed the expression on her face.

T: However, coming out to families is almost always a more emotionally laden event, because in this area lies the potential risk of rejection by persons of great importance to the client.

N: Yes, and this possible loss of love can seem life-threatening to the more archaic parts of the individual. One client's mother's reaction to her son revealing his sexual orientation was to exclaim, 'I wish you had never been born.' While this extreme reaction is not that common, the risk of some kind of rejection is very real. On a more optimistic note, most parents come to accept the reality of their son being gay. In fact, this very mother now has a loving relationship with my client, because of his insistence that she accepts him for who he is.

T: Well, you know, whenever we have an argument, I usually threaten to go home to mother . . . your mother!

N: Coming out to parents is not necessarily the most difficult. Married gay men, if they decide to come out to their wife and children, can find this extremely traumatic. Issues of which of the relatives to tell complicate the problem, but often the most frightening is the prospect of being rejected by their children.

I remember a poignant moment in one of the therapy groups when a member read out a letter from his teenage daughter, where she called him a 'dirty queer' and never wanted to see him again. On the other hand, another gay client has become much closer to his two children since coming out. He can now be open with them, and the older one told him she had suspected for a long time.

A great tragedy is the gay man who had AIDS and has not come out to his parents. Just when he is the most vulnerable, regressed and needy he is afraid to ask for support from his family. Some clients with AIDS, who have already come out to parents, have to go through the same trauma of possible rejection again when deciding to tell their families about their condition.

T: Before we go further on the subject of AIDS, I'd like to mention coming out to friends. It's usually easier in my experience, gay men shed those friends with whom they do not feel safe to be themselves. There are exceptions, however, with individuals who are not at all on the gay scene, and who lead a 'straight' life. The thought of possibly being rejected by their friends can be quite devastating. Though, for me, it is a false premise as they are leading a life that denies a huge part of themselves.

N: I can't imagine having a homophobic friend any more than an anti-Semitic one. I wonder, though, whether we have been out and up-front about our sexuality for so long that we have lost sight of just how terrifying it can be for our clients to come out in various aspects of their lives.

T: I don't think so, I have worked on this issue with many clients.

N: Of course, I have as well. Most of my gay clients are pretty much living an openly gay life in London. What often emerges is the fact that their parents and family in the North still do not know, and going home at Christmas is very anxiety-producing. Sometimes there are further complications in the family dynamics, where one parent has been told (usually mother) and there is collusion to keep the secret from the other. I have even had several situations where one parent has told their son not to come out to the other parent because it 'would kill them'. The message, of course, is that their homosexuality is so shameful that it is potentially fatal to their loved ones.

T: And imagine what effect this could have on the more archaic part of the individual. Nowadays, homosexuality is also seen as potentially fatal to the gay man himself. AIDS has added to the burden of shame that so many gay men carry. They are now seen (by some) as carriers of a fatal, dangerous and disgusting disease, which brings us to the topic of AIDS.

N: It is such a powerful subject for me, as we have lost so many friends.

T: It was the loss of a very dear friend that started me on my journey to becoming a psychotherapist. Briefly, it was while visiting Bob in the hospital, shortly before his death (this was in 1985) that I noticed there was a guy in another room who had no visitors. I attempted to make eye contact with him and he didn't respond. While intellectually I understood it might be his choice to have no visitors, I was horrified, and I decided that I needed somehow or other to find some role in being with men who were alone and dying of AIDS.

I volunteered to become a buddy with the Terrence Higgins Trust, and also decided to do some counselling skills training. When we were discussing our future plans, I came out with, 'I want to do a little light counselling.' My psychotherapy colleagues have not let me forget this naive remark to this day.

N: Well you have gone from a little light counselling to a lot of heavy psychotherapy.

T: I don't necessarily see it as heavy, but certainly I experience it as wrenching and painful.

N: Watching a client you have come to love, slowly die, is pretty difficult. With clients in the terminal stages of AIDS I usually relax the usual boundaries and see them in the hospital or at home. The character of the therapy subtly changes from the possibility of change to simply being with them.

T: For me, one of the most bizarre aspects of working with people with AIDS has been to sit with them and blithely, calmly, and cold-bloodedly discuss their funeral. This kind of discussion can demonstrate that the client has made an existential acceptance of their death, and this can be a result of long hard work.

N: I am not sure about that, I thought I was working existentially with a man with AIDS and I indicated that he needed to accept the reality of his death. He replied, 'You want me to accept the unacceptable.' I am not certain that doing therapy with individuals with a fatal disease must involve helping them to accept their death. In fact, I am beginning to realize that denial may be a perfectly reasonable solution for some individuals, and that I, as their therapist, have no right to impose on them preconceived theoretical notions of how they should deal with death.

T: Working with PWAs (persons with AIDS), sometimes I find my counter-transference both difficult and painful and it can get in the way of being with them. I have learned the hard way that I have to be extra vigilant in keeping my own issues out of the counselling room (as much as possible). With one client, I overreacted to his accidentally cutting himself in my bathroom. I am experienced in the AIDS field, and know the facts, and only with supervision did I realize I was influenced by undealt-with grief over a close friend who had just died.

N: I keep looking for survivors' guilt in my counter-transference, but I cannot really find it.

T: Sometimes I feel twinges of it and wonder, 'Why them and not me?' But mostly I just feel grateful that we have both survived.

N: AIDS has certainly brought up other issues besides illness and death – suicide, for example. As a psychotherapist I used to take an extreme view that suicide is never an existential choice, but one made from a regressed position of neurotic influences, which can be modified through psychotherapy. With clients who are dying, and whose quality of life had deteriorated to the point where there was no hope it could ever get better, I had to rethink this position. For them, it did seem like a genuine existential and mature choice.

Having watched several clients slowly deteriorate and die, I can still only imagine what it must have been like for their partners.

T: Sometimes I find working with the partners of people with AIDS more excruciatingly poignant than with PWAs themselves.

N: The counsellors I supervise at an AIDS organization, often find it especially painful working with the partners of PWAs.

T: We have been talking about working with clients with AIDS, but this topic has permeated my work with all of my gay clients. One would not expect to find death and illness in the psychotherapy of young men very often, but it would be a rare gay man who would not, at some stage or another, bring up the subject of AIDS.

N: And not surprisingly, death can become associated with sex. Obviously this can feed into existing issues of guilt and shame, and an unconscious fear that perhaps 'they' are right that homosexuality is wrong. More sinister is the seductiveness of the forbidden, unsafe sex. While I am not a Kleinian, I sometimes wonder about the existence of the death instinct when a client reports, 'I don't know what came over me, but I had unsafe sex last night.' This is not a rare occurrence among gay men who are usually very careful to remain safe, and I have really struggled to explain it theoretically. Clearly I have a need to make some sense of what seems to be a senseless act. In addition to *thanatos*, I have thought about Fairbairn's 'internal saboteur', Berne's idea of the 'demon' (destructive parental introjects) or simply retro-flected anger suicidally turned against the self.

T: Perhaps they were just sick and tired of wearing a condom, is it necessarily pathology?

N: If it is a form of suicide, I think it is. They certainly do not describe it as a cold-blooded decision to have unsafe sex but more as an eruption of frightening uncontrollable dark forces.

T: That would depend on the client. I certainly believe that for some men it is clearly self-destructive behaviour. For others, I understand their reluctance to think of disease and death when they are having healthy fun. Nevertheless, as their therapist, I feel some responsibility to remind them of the possible consequences. I find that I need to redo my safer sex lecture from time to time. It is as though they just don't want to hear it.

N: I know that some individuals would say that unsafe sex, like any form of suicide, is an existential choice. I have never been able to accept this, and define it as a serious problem with pathological underpinnings. I would treat it like any other form of self-destructive behaviour (like drunk driving).

T: Let's not forget that unsafe sex, like drunk driving, can kill someone else too.

N: Yes, I can remember saying to a client who was letting his partner (who was HIV positive) penetrate him, without a condom, 'Why does he want to kill you?' He was shocked by my confrontation, and replied, 'I never thought of it that way.'

T: I am aware that we sound like parents talking about our naughty children.

N: Frankly, I unashamedly use aspects of the therapeutic alliance *in loco parentis*. I think it is naive to deny the regressive aspects of the psychotherapeutic relationship, and I hope to use them responsibly.

On this issue, first I address the archaic child, attempting to protect him from immediate danger (it is not safe to run across the street). Then in our adult relationship we would explore the dynamics and aetiology of this behaviour. I have found from my TA (transactional analysis) background, that a contract, to stay safe, can be effective while working through these issues.

T: I would do it slightly differently. I wouldn't work with the archaic child but in our present relationship, using my reaction to his revealing that he is having unsafe sex.

N: That is not so different from the way I work. I remember when a client disclosed that he had been unsafe, I blurted out, 'How could you be so stupid.' He sensed that my rage was loving, and did not repeat this behaviour.

T: One of my clients talked about having unsafe sex while experiencing an Extacy high. He was mortified, and extremely upset, that he had let himself lose control like that. We discussed it for weeks in the group. Clearly this situation can come up with alcohol and other drugs.

N: I remember when 'boy was I drunk last night' was an excuse to oneself when struggling with unacknowledged homosexuality. Now in the era of gay liberation and HIV it sounds much more sinister.

T: What complicated the situation with him was that he was emotionally involved with the other man. Not only did this make it more difficult for him to say no, but he had the illusion that sex without a condom was more intimate.

Talking about our clients' sex lives, I would like to bring up the subject of casual sex, since a good portion of my gay clients lead a very active sex life.

N: I am glad you did not use the judgemental word 'promiscuous'.

T: No, I didn't. For me a definition of promiscuous is someone who is having more sex than me.

N: Is having a lot of casual sex pathology then, is it sexual acting out?

T: Some people would say it always is, but I strongly disagree. For me it depends very much on how my client presents it. If he comes to me and says, 'I am worried about the amount of anonymous sex I am having', I take his concerns seriously and explore them, and it doesn't mean that they are pathological.

N: Yes, it needn't be pathology, even if the client is distressed about it. I remember when homosexuality was automatically defined as an illness. When I was 17, I revealed to my parents that I was gay (and I was distressed). They promptly sent me to a psychiatrist who tried to cure me of my affliction and make me normal. Of course, it didn't work (hallelujah!) and I realized that my sexual orientation was not an illness, but just who I was. They had the problem, not I.

T: So was it your 'gay gene' or did you choose to be homosexual?

N: Often I think that this is not a legitimate question. Do we ask our straight friends why they are heterosexual? I hope that the term 'homosexual' used as a noun, eventually becomes obsolete. Perhaps in an ideal world one's sexuality, including orientation, will be only one part of a person's identity.

T: Just what do we mean when we say a person is a homosexual? Does it mean they only sleep with men, mostly sleep with men, occasionally sleep with men but prefer them to women? Never sleep with men but fantasize about it all the time?

N: In our current society, I think of the word homosexual as a noun describing a man who would use the term to define himself. A long-term prison inmate, whose sex life is exclusively homosexual, might be offended if you described him as a homosexual. He would say his preference is for women, but he is simply being expedient, and this could be true. There are many variations of people's sexual practices (both past and present), fantasies and emotional attachments, which complicate labelling their sexuality. If this must be labelled, the only definition which makes any sense to me is the person's self-definition.

T: In other words, homosexual should only be used as a modifier. For example, someone might say, 'I have homosexual fantasies', 'I'm in a homosexual relationship', etc. The current term homosexual is used to denote a sexual identity.

N: The only time straights use the term heterosexual is to show that they are not the dreaded other.

T: Yes, because they are an overwhelming majority, the assumption is that heterosexuality is normal, and therefore we are by definition deviant.

N: The word deviant should be simply a neutral mathematical description, but it has judgemental overtones. Is left-handedness described as deviant?

T: Is homosexuality just another human variation like left-handedness?

N: I used to be interested in theories of the aetiology of homosexuality. The psychoanalytic literature has just about every variation of possibility of introjection, identification, reaction formation, castration anxiety, reverse Oedipus complex etc., etc. Frankly after reading all these ideas, some of them superficially plausible, I now pretty much reject them all. They are very well summed up in Lewes (1995).

T: My clinical experience of several hundred gay male clients is that virtually all of them believe that they were always gay.

N: I think that this is very important. My experience is the same, and in spite of the unscientific basis of our conclusions, our combined clinical sample of hundreds of gay men has to be seriously considered. Most theories of the origin of homosexuality have been based on a handful (or less) of patients, usually unhappy about their sexuality.

T: So where does that leave us with the gay gene?

N: The evidence is not conclusive, but Le Vay (1996) discusses much of the current evidence, and, combined with my own clinical experience, I believe that homosexual men are born that way, or at least with a strong predisposition. This may not be necessarily true for women, but that topic is beyond the scope of this chapter.

T: I am inclined to agree that homosexuality in men is probably inborn. This would refute the notion that being gay is a lifestyle choice. Earlier you used the word deviance in relation to left-handedness. I can remember when children who were left-handed were forced to write with their right hand. Also, don't forget that being left-handed was considered being 'sinister'. Nowadays it is simply seen as an acceptable minority variation. Isn't it about time that homosexuality is viewed in the same way?

N: Ask the fundamentalists! I have worked with a number of distressed young men who had been through a programme of attempting to convert them to heterosexuality. These self-righteous fanatics (see Peck, 1983) only succeeded in adding another layer of guilt. Not only were these unfortunate victims bad, evil and sinners, but they did not even have the willpower to overcome their affliction.

T: And what about the medical, psychiatric and psychodynamic fanatics? It was not so long ago that some gay men were given aversion therapy or even brain surgery in an attempt to cure them. The rationale was that they were unhappy with their sexual orientation.

N: My guess is that it was the doctors who were unhappy! In a society where it is still acceptable to hate homosexuals, I can understand that some men might want to change their orientation. Of course, aversion therapy didn't work any more than religion, except where men chose to simply repress this intrinsic part of themselves.

T: Yes, and these poor souls become the married men who end up disgraced in the local newspapers for 'gross indecency'.

N: Gross indecency is a law that has been stretched to persecute gay men for offences which would be ignored in a heterosexual couple (like having sex in the back of a car in a lovers' lane).

T: And what about Clause 28? Shall we extend it to forbid promoting left-handedness as an acceptable lifestyle? We don't want the right-handed kiddies to be tempted to convert.

N: But what if left-handedness is not simply a lifestyle choice but inborn? We have only hinted at the implications of the real possibility that homosexuality is genetic.

T: So what about the theory, started by Freud, that a too-close relationship with the mother, combined with an absent, distant or hostile father, makes a boy homosexual?

N: If absent fathers were a factor, we would find an explosion of homosexuality among the offspring of single mothers. In the US there is a whole culture, in the black community, of boys brought up exclusively by their mothers. I have not heard any evidence of an increase in homosexuality among this group; if anything, the culture is very macho and homophobic.

T: Nevertheless, in my clinical practice it is quite common for my gay male clients to have unusually close relationships with their mothers, and they often report distant or hostile fathers.

N: I have found this to be common in my practice as well. However, I don't believe that this is the cause of their homosexuality, but the result of it. Isay (1989) makes a convincing argument that the fathers of boys who become gay, realize that their little boys are different (timid, effeminate, sensitive, etc.) and might also sense that the boy has primitive sexual feelings for him. This might cause the father to withdraw from his son which could result in the little boy clinging to his mother and forming a closer relationship with her. These same characteristics might also be especially attractive to her. I know that this is an oversimplification but it seems to me to be essentially true.

T: Many, but by no means all, of my gay clients were mother's special little boy.

N: We certainly have digressed from the topic of casual sex and is it pathology?

T: This brings up, for me, the whole question of what is pathology, and should we even think in terms of an illness model for any of our clients?

N: Even floridly psychotic or clinically depressed ones?

T: I need to think about it, I am not sure.

N: Well then, let's go back to the subject of casual sex. There is a continuum from a regular casual partner, to one-night-stands, to completely anonymous encounters in parks, toilets or backrooms, where not a single word might be exchanged.

T: It is a continuum of greater and greater depersonalization of the other.

N: I want to go off on a theoretical tangent about this very common behaviour among gay men, and many psychotherapy theories have a common thread, the relieving of anxiety.

T: What do you mean by anxiety?

N: I won't answer directly, but I will talk about different experiences of feelings which could be termed anxieties.

T: Go on.

N: I feel a bit cornered. I reject the Freudian concept of castration anxiety. That would be seen as an Oedipal regression to an earlier phase (oral, anal or phallic) as a defence, with the compulsive sexuality a desperate attempt to prove that he has an intact penis.

T: My clients rarely bring castration anxiety, even in dreams.

N: Mine don't either. It is my heterosexual clients who bring Oedipal issues. As we have alluded to already, many of my gay male clients seem to have won the battle for mum's affections long before the Oedipal phase.

T: That reminds me of the old joke, 'My mother made me a homosexual.' 'Really, would she make me one too?'
OK, carry on.

N: From a Kleinian perspective, I would look for unconscious envy and greed. For example, one of my clients expressed strong feelings of envy and greedy (oral) desire towards good-looking men. If he can seduce them he fantasizes that he thereby spoiled their beauty. He wants to possess them and destroy them at the same time.

T: I have had clients who wanted to seduce straight men for similar reasons.

N: When working with men who usually relate to partners as part objects with extreme depersonalization, I may also think in terms of Kleinian theory. Many gay men seem stuck in the 'paranoid/schizoid position', splitting love and sex as a defence. A familiar pattern is for a gay man to start a relationship with enthusiasm, but when it becomes more intimate and loving, he loses sexual interest in his partner and ends the relationship.

T: Or they seek couples therapy . . . but this is not uncommon among hetero-sexuals as well.

N: Don't they usually wait until the children are born and the woman changes from lover to mother?

T: What does this have to do with casual sex?

N: Many gay couples who want to stay together but encounter this problem decide on an open relationship.

T: Yes, but the deal is usually that intimacy and love are reserved for the primary relationship, but casual sex is okay.

N: In my practice of couples therapy with gay men, this is usually the presenting problem. Often one wants to change the rules and make the relationship an open one, or has been discovered to be cheating. The partner may secretly want to be able to have sex with other men as well, but is afraid of this resulting in the relationship breaking up.

T: It is not the only problem gay male couples have to struggle with. After all, we are dealing with two men, with no role models of relationships. Power is often the issue. Some couples attempt to imitate traditional heterosexual marriages.

N: Didn't you tell me about a friend whose boyfriend expected him to have his dinner and slippers ready when he came home from work?

T: Yes, and he didn't want his 'wife' to work. My friend soon tired of that.

N: Most gay male couples, however, need to find their own methods of dealing with two careers. For example, if one is offered a good job in another city, it is not automatically assumed that the other will follow, like the traditional good wife.

T: I am willing to make a generalization about the difference between male and female sexuality here. Dealing with two men is so different than working with two women or a straight couple. The easy availability of casual sex in the gay world is part of the problem these couples have to struggle with.

N: More theory about casual sex, especially if it has compulsive elements. As an integrative therapist, I find it fascinating how many ways there are to explain the same behaviour, especially as so many of them seem to be (at least partially) true.

For example, Stoller posits an anxiety which is a fear of loss of gender identity, not through castration but because of incomplete separation from the mother. In other words, masculine sexual activity in order to deal with fear of remerging with mother, and losing one's gender.

T: I agree. My ordinary gay clients do not have significant gender issues that I can discern.

N: I do find Stoller (1975) more useful in his emphasis on the hostile elements in this kind of sexual activity. He subtitles his book on perversion (I hate that word) *The Erotic Form of Hatred*, and certainly in much of impersonal sexuality there are elements of hostility, envy, spite, role playing, dominance, submission, domination through submission, manipulation and various sexual forms of hostility. Stoller talks about turning childhood trauma and frustration into adult triumph. Sex becomes an unconscious drama of revenge on parents.

T: It sounds a bit far-fetched to me.

N: Even if there is some truth in it, and I believe there is, I still think of the most impersonal forms of sexuality as a desperate attempt at human contact . . . yet, a search for love. In the only way they can. Perhaps in the only way that feels safe.

T: It sounds like you are pathologizing casual sex. Can't it just be a bit of fun?

N: Of course, and that doesn't exclude the possibility of other things going on at the same time. For example, they might also feel guilt and shame about their sexual activities. Alice Miller (1981) talks about sexual shame as an introjection of mother's original disgust at the child's natural sexuality.

T: Are you finished with your theory lecture?

N: Not quite. If compulsive cruising is presented as a problem, when I dig deeper we usually find anxiety again. Here I find Kohut's ideas about frantic activity as a defence against depletion or fragmentation of the self useful.

T: It doesn't have to be sex, excessive working or compulsive jogging can serve the same purpose.

N: True. As a last gasp of the ways I might think of compulsive sexuality: a defence against death anxiety (Yalom, 1980), excitement as a substitute for intimacy, sexualization of dependency needs, sexual conquests as a means of self-esteem regulation, as a defence against depression, etc.

T: That is all very interesting, and some of it seems correct at times, but do you really find it that useful in your practice?

N: Sometimes it helps me to make some kind of sense of what is going on for the client.

T: I confess sometimes I think along those lines too, but isn't it for the client to make sense of what is going on?

N: Yes, but I might make an interpretation to help the client to understand.

T: I would rarely do that.

N: The subject of the more exotic aspects of gay men's sex lives brings me to the subject of gay men working with straight psychotherapists.

T: I don't feel as strongly about it as you do. I remember a man I co-led a men's therapy group with who insisted on being referred to as 'non-gay'.

N: I know I have already written about this (Leitman, 1995), but I still wonder if most heterosexual therapists can be non-judgemental about some gay men's sexual practices.

T: And what about our counter-transference and possible collusion with the client?

N: Touché. That could open the proverbial can of worms.

T: Is the danger that we will collude with the client and the gay sub-culture, that certain behaviours are an acceptable and normal part of being gay?

N: Yes, but equally we could collude with the greater society's condemnation (or even disgust) with these behaviours, by agreeing with the client's super-ego condemnation and self-loathing.

T: Hang on, let's not get carried away with what are considered extreme sexual behaviours among gays. There are very few, if any, of these variations which have not been tried by men and women with each other.

N: Oh really? . . . my clients seldom have issues about their actual sexual practice, or even the frequency and importance of sex in their lives. What they usually bring is, 'Why can't I find (keep) a lover?' Being able to talk about sex is not the only advantage of a gay therapist working with gay men. Recently some writers have talked about 'gay affirmative therapy'. This is subtly different from a straight therapist accepting a client's sexual orientation. I have not met many heterosexual therapists who believe that a homosexual lifestyle can be just as fulfilling as a heterosexual one. We have come a long way from the days when most therapists would characterize homosexuality as sick and try to cure it, but for the most part the attitude seems to be, 'Well, that is the way you are, so you have to make the best of it.'

   I expect that this statement might result in some outrage among the readers of this chapter. I invite them to examine their liberal attitudes, to ascertain whether they really consider homosexuality equal to hetero.

T: Okay. Let's lay it on the line. How would they feel if their son/daughter was gay?

N: Or if they had three children, and they were all gay.

T: I'm sure they would have no objection if all three were straight!

N: Which brings me back to the subject of gay affirmative therapy. I hope that I can convey to my clients the possibilities of a rich, loving, useful and rewarding life as a gay man, which is not a compromise or second best.

T: And the possibility of a long-term relationship, if that's what they want. Over the years my experience has been, when clients are finishing therapy with me, they almost always comment on how important the knowledge of our relationship has been to them.

N: Yes, I am comfortable with being a role model for our clients. Some of the younger gay men I have worked with have never personally known two gay men in a long-term relationship.

T: Long ago I made a clinical decision to be more personally transparent and revealing with my gay clients than is the usual accepted practice.

N: I am as well, it is much easier when you work at home. I even have a picture of you in my consulting room (I can imagine some analytic therapists wincing here). I can assure them that in spite of the fact that I am hardly a blank screen, I still receive lots of transference projections.

T: I remember that I said that I don't work differently with my gay clients. I withdraw that statement.

N: Not only do I work slightly differently, but the quality of the relationship is different.

T: Yes it is, and I value the relationship, above all, in therapy.

N: So how do you see the relationship as different?

T: Well, first of all, we are both attracted to men.

N: A heterosexual male therapist and heterosexual male client are both attracted to women.

T: And both of them believe that this was the way it was meant to be.

N: Gay men usually take some years before they feel that way.

T: And some never do.

N: There are many other aspects of being gay which the client and therapist have in common. They almost always had to struggle with their sexual orientation before accepting it. They usually encounter some hostility in their family, virtually always in their peer group, and in society in general.

Many of my gay clients have expressed enormous relief to be with an out gay therapist where they do not have to pretend.

T: It is like a kinship relationship, we belong to the same clan.

N: Those gay men in the closet, who have no gay friends, don't have that kinship feeling and can feel very isolated. They may move in straight circles, but don't feel that they belong anywhere.

T: I recently returned from a trip to San Francisco. When I was there, I went to the Castro district (the gay neighbourhood) with a lesbian friend, and we were both delighted not to be in the minority for a change. To be in a milieu where heterosexuality was not the accepted norm.

N: That is one of the reasons I have always led therapy groups for gay men. I have found that the members express great relief in being in a group of their 'brothers', and much of the therapeutic work is in the sharing of similar experiences. Bringing gay men of different ages and cultural and economic backgrounds together in a safe therapeutic setting has turned out to be a profound medium for healing and one of my main reasons for being an up-front gay therapist.

T: On this point I agree with you completely. For many of my clients in group therapy the greatest revelation has been that others have the same difficulties and have had similar experiences in their lives. 'I am not the only one.' For me, group therapy is the therapy of choice most of the time.

N: I like to combine group and individual therapy at the same time (in spite of the complications). Usually my clients start in individual therapy, then join one of my groups, and eventually finish the individual sessions, but continue in group. I see it as a weaning process from dependency on me to a bonding with their peers.

T: On this I differ slightly. Usually when a client, in individual therapy, and I decide that he might benefit from group therapy, the individual sessions stop.

N: Why?

T: Because I think that having both individual and group therapy at the same time dissipates the work, and I prefer that he brings everything going on for him to the group. In fact, when a client in group requests individual sessions, I question why he can't discuss what is on his mind in the group.

N: You haven't mentioned envy and sibling rivalry between group members, especially if some are also in individual and some not.

T: That is another reason I don't like to combine individual and group.

N: Group therapy with gay men has inspired and moved me to see how bravely and creatively many of these clients have found ways of leading valuable and fulfilling lives in a society which is reluctant to fully accept them.

T: Yeah! And dear God is it different from when I was a teenager! Society was more than reluctant to accept homosexuals. It actively wanted to eliminate them. Gay was illegal, and there were periodic purges when gay bars were closed down and gay meeting areas were harassed. Gays were arrested and jailed, and even forced to have psychiatric examinations and aversion therapy. While most gay men managed to escape active persecution by the law, the threat was always there.

N: Also, of course, the threat of blackmail. Most gays had to remain, at least partially, in the closet as the exposure of their sexual orientation would have led to their dismissal from their jobs, or even being run out of town. When I was an undergraduate at university, I was very careful to conceal my sexuality. If the university had found out, I would have been expelled immediately, without question. I am envious of current undergraduates in many universities who have gay societies they can join. It was very lonely being completely in the closet at that vulnerable age. I knew I was gay, and yet, in a very large university, I never met another gay man. I am sure they were there, but they must have been as scared as I was.

T: My experience in the Air Force was similar, I went to great lengths to hide my homosexuality. Unfortunately, in the services I don't think much has changed.

N: What has drastically changed since the fifties is the position of older gay men. I can remember when gay men were either young or 'sad old queens'. Of course, there were older men living quiet satisfying lives, but any older man who dared to appear in gay bars was an object of derision.

T: In this regard, gays had lagged behind the straight world; older men have always been considered attractive to women. But now we have come of age, so to speak.

N: Many of my gay clients live an out gay lifestyle at work, with family, friends, etc., which would have been inconceivable when we were young.

T: Well I'm glad that we can live that way now.

N: I have been gratified how accepting and respectful the psychotherapeutic professional community has been to me as an out gay psychotherapist. Personally, I have never encountered any overt hostility.

T: As a sort of peroration to this chapter, I want to ask a question. Why are heterosexuals so terrified of us? There seem to be endless amounts of studies, attempts at cures, fixes or change methods. Why can't they just accept what is, is?

References

Berne, E. (1972) *What Do You Say After You Say Hello?* New York: Grove Press.
Fairbairn, W.R.D. (1952) *Psychoanalytic Studies of the Personality*. London: Tavistock.
Isay, R. (1989) *Being Homosexual: Gay Men and their Development*. New York: Farrar, Straus, Giroux.
Kohut, H. (1984) *How Does Analysis Cure?* Chicago: Chicago University Press.
Le Vay, S. (1996) *Queer Science*. Cambridge, MA: MIT Press.
Leitman, N. (1995) 'To the point', *Counselling News*, December: 3.
Lewes, K. (1995) *Psychoanalysis and Male Homosexuality*. London: Aronson.
Miller, A. (1981) *The Drama of the Gifted Child*. New York: Basic Books.
Peck, M.S. (1983) *People of the Lie*. London: Rider.
Stoller, R. (1975) *Perversion: The Erotic Form of Hatred*. New York: Delta.
Yalom, I. (1980) *Existential Psychotherapy*. New York: Basic Books.

5

The lessons from group therapy

Ian Craib

As a registered and fully paid-up member of the United Kingdom Council of Narcissists, I found it impossible to refuse an invitation to write about politics and therapy drawing on my own experience; my problem is to stop writing about myself and say something interesting. I will allow myself a brief summary of and one story about my political and therapeutic history and then move on to what I hope will be the crux of this chapter: I am interested in what might be called the psychological pre-conditions of a democratic and egalitarian society and what might be learned about such an enterprise from a psychoanalytic understanding of group processes. I am also interested in developing a critique of contemporary political discourse. You might think, rightly, that this is an easy task, since most political arguments seem to start in the gutter and move rapidly downwards. The worrying thing is that there seems no alternative on offer.

Background

Politics have played a central part in my life from around the age of 15 or 16. My mother in those days was a deferential Tory voter and I took over her views without question as, I now see, a way of getting at my stepfather who was just on the borderline between what used to be known as the respectable and the unrespectable working class (or at earlier times the deserving and undeserving poor). The change which took me away from my parents and towards the rest of my life was a casual comment from, of all people, my divinity master on the pointlessness of Britain maintaining an independent nuclear deterrent. I remember laying awake for most of the night after that comment arguing with myself about a number of things, not just connected to nuclear weapons. The upshot was that I joined CND and undertook my first political battle – against the headmaster's ruling that only sixth-formers could wear CND badges. This battle provided me with the only unproblematic political victory that I can remember.

Having joined CND I moved rapidly to the far left and I was in and out of the Labour Party until the early eighties. From my present position I feel I wasted a lot of time on sectarian politics but I remain pleased and proud about my involvement in CND and later the anti-Vietnam War movement, and more generally the student movement of the late sixties; if a sizeable number of adolescents and young adults are not involved in political rebellion, then I think the future is likely to be grim.

By the mid-1970s my life seemed to be falling apart and I went into psychotherapy, taking the same course, without realizing it, as a number of my comrades; there seems an inevitability about the way in which my experience as a patient led to my training as a therapist, but I am surprised, even now, that I trained as a group-analytic therapist. Somewhere in this process I discovered what I can only call a love of groups, of watching them, participating in them and talking about them. Politically I have not undergone any great change in my views and I would still put myself on the far left. I have a gut sympathy for those like the South American anarchists who, in one possibly apocryphal story, went on strike for a two-hour working day with an hour's lunch-break. But I can no longer *live* in politics – there is no space and I feel claustrophobic.

My story is about psychic claustrophobia. My move to the far left was to what was then called the International Socialist Group (IS), which some years later was to become the Socialist Workers' Party. It was a Trotskyist cum anarcho-syndicalist group for those to whom such labels mean anything. In those days it was an intellectual powerhouse. It boasted the philosopher Alasdair McIntyre, Michael Kidron the economist, Paul Foot, then at the beginning of his journalistic career, Peter Sedgewick who became a significant writer on psychiatry, as well as Gus MacDonald of *World in Action* fame and, strangely, Roger Protz, later of the Campaign for Real Ale. The ideas around at the time took me through my A levels and on to a sociology degree, a Ph.D. and the academic career that is still my main source of income.

I cannot now remember the exact dates, but some time in the early mid-sixties – '64, '65 or thereabouts – I became the rather naive editor of a youth paper called *Rebel*. We were at that time pursuing entrist tactics in the Labour Party Young Socialists and we had a reasonable circulation and were technologically innovative – I think we were the first on the left to use the offset-litho methods used by *Private Eye*. Yet among the many orthodox Trotskyist groups we were regularly vilified – it sometimes seemed that throughout the country smoke-filled rooms full of comrades spent their evenings composing and passing resolutions condemning our modest enterprise.

If these critics knew the editorial board there might have been some reason for their condemnation; the politics were moving towards what the orthodox Leninists called the infantile left and there were experiments with various illegal substances. But the reason for all this condemnation was that we published *jokes*. In particular, we published a strip cartoon, *Supertrot*, in which Trotsky in a singlet emblazoned with a large ST, and his faithful sidekick Rosa (Luxemburg) with long blonde hair, thigh-length leather boots and a mini-skirt, raced around the world saving the Fourth International. It seemed that we were guilty of everything from anti-Semitism to what, in a different organization, would have been called blasphemy.

The cartoon was signed ASOF. I can now reveal to an expectant world that ASOF stood for Anarchist Sons of Freedom, and although I never met them I understand the Anarchist Sons of Freedom were a couple of public schoolboys from Woking. As befits adolescents, those of us on the editorial board who supported the cartoon were well aware of the absurdity of it all, and I remember a number of evenings sitting around in pubs honing our sense of absurdity. One statement from a friend struck me as a real truth: 'People who really believe what they say are one step away from madness.' As proof of the validity of the statement I would offer the fact that one of our 'hard-line' critics emerged some 20 years later as a political advisor to Dame Shirley Porter and Westminster City Council. It would be nice to present this insight as the product of three decades of hard-won experience, but I'm afraid I have known it for most of my life. I had already discovered that it was true of Christians, and since that time I have discovered that it's true first of sociologists and then of psychotherapists and psychoanalysts.

Faith and belief

Obviously this idea requires some elaboration. We all believe things. Belief is different from knowledge: knowledge is always tentative, open to revision, and the accumulation of knowledge is subject to strict rules of testing and evidence.

Knowledge is developed by the sciences, the natural sciences, and less spectacularly the social sciences. Bowlby's developmental psychology and his immense research work is one area of psychoanalysis which deserves the status of 'scientific'. Belief does not necessarily depend on such evidence and procedures, and perhaps many of our 'clinical' judgements are based on something closer to belief than to knowledge. Those who accept the existence of recovered memories seem to be engaging in an act of belief – everything we know about memory points to it being part representation and part construction, and if this is true of 'normal' memory it seems to me to follow that recovered memories are likely to be more construction than memory. But it often seems that we hold beliefs more firmly than we hold to knowledge, as if we have to compensate for a lack of evidence by the intensity of our convictions.

There are in fact different ways of holding beliefs. One can hold them in the same way that one accepts knowledge but more so. They are provisional, perhaps even a matter of personal idiosyncrasy. I like to think that my cat has an expressive face and uses it to communicate certain feelings to me, but I think it is unlikely. In this sense my belief is what I like to think and I am aware of that. But I could believe with certainty that my cat was communicating to me and I could find him more pleasant company than my family and colleagues and spend most of my time with him. This is closer to what I mean when I suggest that people who really believe what they say are one step away from madness.

Another way of formulating this is that a belief in this latter sense fills psychic space in such a way that it is difficult to take a questioning distance from it, to reflect upon the belief in oneself, to accept, in my story, a humorous look at what is sacred, and perhaps more importantly to accept that others may believe differently. To really believe what one is saying is a denial of internal space and of external difference.

When I trailed these ideas before psychotherapists at St George's Hospital in London, it was suggested it was belief that was urgently needed in western societies. Since then I have been wondering about a distinction between belief and faith partly as a way of trying to make sense of my own relation to Christianity. Here, I want to use 'belief' to describe a cognitive commitment backed by an intense emotional commitment which is at the centre of the believer's perception of the world. The Nicene Creed is a statement of belief, in God, Christ, the Holy Ghost, the resurrection, heaven and so on. My understanding of the development of this Creed is that it had much the same status as Labour Party policy – an agreement between arguing factions, open to manipulation by various leaders. However, at various times during history and in the contemporary world, some variant of these beliefs has driven people to kill and torture their fellows and I imagine produced a breakdown in the ability to empathize with others, to feel compassion; belief in this sense fills the inner world, leading only to condemnation and ruling out understanding. Although I call myself a Christian, I am, in the sense of belief that I have just described, a Christian atheist; I do not believe that Christ was born of a virgin or that he returned from the dead, nor do I believe in anything recognizable as a Christian God. On the other hand, the Christian story as a metaphor is something I find central to making sense of the part of my existence that I would call spiritual, and the Christian ritual offers me a connection with others and with myself that I find profoundly satisfying.

This is where faith appears. I should acknowledge that the idea came originally from my wife, Fiona Grant, in a discussion about personal relationships but I have been pondering it in relation to other areas. By faith I mean the experience we have of being in relationship with ourselves and others, caught up in a network which is larger than any one, two or three people and which will remain whether we love or hate each other; or perhaps, more accurately, will remain when we love each other and when we hate each other. Part of this is the faith in oneself to be able to make connections with others and maintain those connections through troubles. I guess I am talking about something close to what Erikson (1965) talks about as basic trust. Of course it is never complete – only a fool would have complete faith in the world, and there are always internal conflicts. Faith in the sense I am trying to develop here involves tolerating a question mark about one's ability to tolerate a loss of faith or a betrayal of faith.

In a group context I would refer to faith as the trust that the group will be there from week to week, even if the personnel are changing, or even if the therapist changes. Of course groups do not last forever, but a sense of continuity and a sense of there being a history and there being a future is important. I have noticed that in my longest running slow open group* – now approaching its 12th birthday – the arrival of a new or departure of an old member is marked by a period of reminiscing and a passing on of the group's history. Recently this group was talking about gardens and one member mentioned some small statues in his garden. I made a transference comment about my being the group's statue. The group then pictured me covered in bird shit, then their shit which they loaded on to me. One member who had likened me to a large rock said that in fact the group was the rock, that was there all the time though members came and went. I agreed with this and pointed out that the group would remain (or could remain) even if the leader were not there. There is something about the continuity of the group over generations of members which is not there in individual work, and which can enable a sense of this supra-individual continuity which for many thousands of years must have been the most profound human experience. Indeed Durkheim (1915) suggests that such a necessary experience lies at the root of all religion.

I am not of course suggesting anything quite so grand for the experience of group therapy, but it must always be remembered that the creature we think of as 'the individual' is a fiction which has developed only over the last few centuries and it is a fiction in the same sense that a baby was a fiction for Winnicott when he commented that there was no such thing as a baby, only a baby/carer pair. There are only relationships, and I suspect that it will be in the movement towards theories of intersubjectivity and dialogue that psychoanalytic group analysis will be able to define its relationship to psychoanalysis (Diamond, 1996; Pines, 1996; Zinkin, 1996).

Psychic space and the political culture

I will return to the notion of faith at various points in what follows but for a while I will concentrate on belief. I have already described a belief, or rather people who believe what they say, as filling internal space, as not having any distance from themselves. I want to suggest that the dominant form of political culture is a culture of belief rather than a culture of knowledge or faith. I suspect that this must always be the case to some degree in political democracies where arguments may be pursued with more or less freedom.

---

* A 'slow open group' is a group of 6–9 members. When somebody leaves he or she is replaced and the group can keep going for many years.

Arguments push people to opposing positions and this is a necessary part of a progressive dialectic. There will always be times in such a process when people will *really* believe what they say but the dialectic – or the dialogue – should progress and something new emerge, not necessarily a synthesis but a change, a modification, to both, or all, sides of the argument. But clearly this cannot happen if there is no internal space. My argument is that in the current political climate people cannot appear to think or argue with themselves: they have at least to *appear* to really believe what they say, or what is worse, they really do believe what they say.

An idea of what I mean can be gained by listening to any of the major radio news programmes on BBC Radio 4, to both the interviewing and the political arguments that take place. If there were a learning process involved in political argument one would expect politicians to express doubt and reservations about what they say, to change their minds fairly regularly as more information and more points of view are fed into the arguments, to concede some points and to maintain others. Yet under questioning, all these ways of behaving appear weak, vacillating, if not actually shifty. There are certainly implicit, and I think more often than not clearly explicit, expectations that there be clear answers to most questions, and answers that bring satisfaction, while hints of doubt that bring unease, or dis-ease, are very difficult to tolerate. Arguments between politicians tend to be attacks upon each other without any careful consideration of what might really be the case; statistics are quoted without any thought as to what they might really mean, facts are swapped and discounted, and nobody seems to understand what is involved in putting an argument together. Argument seems to mean 'row' rather than discussion. Disagreements within parties, or even within governments, which since such groups are made up (just about) of normal human beings one might expect to be a normal feature of life, are considered a dangerous weakness. The image of 'good leadership' which our political system currently promotes seems to be one of strength, narrow-mindedness, closedness. Any demonstration of internal space is a weakness to be exploited.

As a result of this, political discourse is 'moralized' rather than 'rationalized'. At the time of writing, within months of the next British general election, morality itself – family values, communitarianism, religious belief – is becoming a political topic, but I think the tendency has been noticeable for some time. I might be displaying my own paranoia at this point, but it seems to me that the moralities that are urged upon the population are not the broadening moralities which encourage tolerance and diversity, but rather the restrictive moralities which say 'don't' and are often aimed at weaker groups – single mothers, beggars, asylum seekers, benefit claimants; in other words, we are witnessing a form of moralized scapegoating. There is more to this process than urging moralities on to people: issues are not seen in realistic terms as practical problems which are always to some degree or another insoluble, but as moral problems for which somebody must be to blame if things go wrong. And if somebody is to blame then somebody must be punished and this creates the usually mild, sometimes intense, climate of fear that seems to haunt many contemporary organizations.

The sociological background

Before turning to group psychotherapy I want to talk for a while about the sociological background to this closing down of the individual's psychic space. It is, of course, a form of social control, a closing down of horizons individually and collectively. If we find it difficult to experience internal space, it is difficult to imagine the possibility of an external space in which the world could be a different place, in which we could bring about change.

There are long-term processes at work behind what I have described and more recent processes. Probably the best account of the longer term processes can be culled from Christopher Lasch's *Haven in a Heartless World* (1977) and *The Culture of Narcissism* (1980). From this point of view the beginning lies in the separation of home and work which comes with the Industrial Revolution. The father departs from the home and the family ceases to be a basic unit of production; if there has been a decline in the role of the family, it has been going on for 250 years. As the nineteenth and twentieth centuries develop, so the organization of work changes; it is increasingly governed by technology and organized bureaucratically, denying the male worker any significant degree of autonomy. The crafts, the skills which might once have provided the basis of independent judgement, and moral agency, and therefore also of a healthy political democracy, disappear.

In the home the basis for paternal authority (as opposed to paternal power) disappears. The father as a figure who has skills and knowledge to pass on to the child and whose authority can be accepted because it is demonstrably effective becomes less common, if not extinct. The speed of technological change, which has been accumulating since the Industrial Revolution, now means that conditions of life change so quickly that parents have very little to pass on to their children, and the role of the state in socialization and in family life generally has been increasing throughout this century. Generally, Freudian social analysis sees the role of the state as varying inversely with the role of the super-ego, or at least of the Freudian super-ego as an internalized and accepted authority to which a critical attitude may be adopted. We are left with a punitive, irrational Kleinian super-ego. Lasch (1980) talks about the impoverished inner world that this produces, the omnipotent infant on the one hand and the punitive figure of power on the other. I have argued elsewhere (Craib, 1994) that many forms of modern psychotherapy seem geared to feeding the omnipotent infant.

The more recent changes are those that have occurred since the 1960s and the best analysis that I know is provided by David Harvey (1989). From the 1960s onwards there has been a steady shift in the western world away from large-scale industrial production as Third-World countries, particularly in the Far East, have been able to produce the same goods more cheaply, largely through cheaper labour. During the eighties this was compounded by the development of computer technology which enables the transfer, at short notice, of large sums of money to wherever the rate of profit is highest. This has led to the economic changes with which we are becoming increasingly familiar. First there is an emphasis on short-term returns – producers no longer build up large stocks of goods but seek products that have a comparatively short life span. The service industries that produce commodities that are used up immediately on production – restaurants, taxis, hairdressers, psychotherapists – fare best. The emphasis on the short term spreads throughout the culture, producing what George Ritzer (1993) calls in his graphically named book '*The McDonaldization of Society*'. It seems that all organizations need at least to appear to be producing new products – hence the constant reorganizations in the health and education systems.

The labour market also changes – there has been a decrease in male full-time employment and an increase in female part-time employment, and a particularly pronounced increase in short-term contract working. The economic stability which marked the first 30 years after the Second World War has disappeared, at least at an individual level, although the stability of multinational organizations in the process that sociologists call globalization has not been affected in any significant way. So at the time when the individual psyche is internally weakened, the individual finds him or herself under increasing pressure from external forces, with comparatively little social support. Family relationships are becoming less stable and the organizations which make up what used to be called civil society – community organizations, political parties, trade unions – have been weakened and increasingly faced with comparatively distant and threatening organizations beyond any possibility of control.

This takes us a long way from psychotherapy of any sort, and it is in fact a very brief and crude summary of the main lines of contemporary social change and to some degree a one-sided description of what is happening around us. There is still more tolerance and individual freedom than there was a century or even half a century ago, but my sense is that this is under threat from the processes I have described, and we are subjected to increasing pressure to conform not only outwardly but also inwardly. Hochschild's (1983) work on the sociology of the emotions, for example, shows how increasingly we are expected not just to behave in a particular way, but to *be* particular types of person. The danger is that counselling and psychotherapy become a part of this process, a way of producing the sort of crippled people who do well in a crippling situation. They become, in the title of Nikolas Rose's book *Governing the Soul*. The therapies described by Anthony Giddens (1991) are clearly geared to such a purpose (see Craib, 1994).

I think it is easy to see the way in which these social processes bring pressure to bear on internal and external space. What I want to do now is look at what happens in group psychotherapy, especially in group analytic psychotherapy, which I have come increasingly to see as a way of opening up internal space, often to a greater extent than in individual therapy.

Group psychotherapy and internal space

I am not suggesting that group psychotherapy can counterbalance or change the social processes that are creating our present difficulties, but I am suggesting that the group therapeutic process embodies certain – as it were – extra-therapeutic values on to which we need to hold in order to survive in a civilized way, and that they can be theorized into a useful contribution to contemporary critical political theory.

In the context of the last section, perhaps a good place to start is not with therapy groups but with the sort of experiential groups which are common in training courses and can best be described as to some degree Bionesque (Bion, 1961). The members' brief is simply to experience what it is like to be in a group, and there is a conductor who offers no guidance in any conventional sense, and offers occasional interpretations or comments. The anxiety at the commencement of these groups is immense, it returns regularly and it puts great pressure on the conductor. Such groups can in certain circumstances devote themselves to not learning – a process different from destructive attacks on the group which, I shall suggest below, are healthy signs (see Craib, 1997). Part of the refusal to think involves pressures which can prevent the conductor thinking (see, for example, Bramley, 1990; Craib, 1997) – his or her comments are met with incredulity, puzzlement, dismissal, often scorn. They cannot be reflected upon and agreed or disagreed with in a considered manner; in such groups the crucial dynamic is not so much emotions which are denied or suppressed (although they are there as well) as ideas which cannot be thought, or rather a thinking process which cannot be allowed.

The anxieties at work in such a situation are not unlike the socially generated anxieties I discussed above, and the pressure on the group leader to produce answers, to show concern and care for group members, and above all to relieve anxieties must be less intense than the same pressures experienced by politicians and civic leaders of all sorts. The pressures are simply mediated by the mass media – we cannot blame journalists, although perhaps we can point out that they do not have to become the puppets of such pressures which are created by society itself.

The intensity of group pressure is hard to resist and it inhibits thinking in the conductor and is experienced as a demand for decisiveness in the alleviation of anxiety, a framework which will allow the group not to have to think about the difficulties that generate anxieties. The group attempts to pressure the therapist out of thinking in order that he or she can relieve the group of the burden of thinking. Anxiety in this context may be the prompt to thought or the prompt to not thinking, and the strength of the group as a container, of which more shortly, tends to favour the outcome of thinking, although in some groups this is barely ever achieved.

In a therapy group this tends to happen more readily. It often seems to me the case – partly from my own experience which developed as I realized that Marxism did not supply the answers I wanted – that those who train as counsellors or therapists often desire at some level to close down their own psychic space, to find the answers. The best trainings are those that take students in the opposite direction, in this case towards the thinking that undermines the certainty that the group desires.

Patient therapy groups tend to be groups that start only too aware of their psychic space, and who believe that it is what is causing the trouble. They are troubled by ideas and feelings that they do not want, that they believe, rightly or wrongly, indicate that they are ill or mad, and with which they are not strong enough to cope. If the group works well they become more able to cope with their feelings and ideas; the group does not close their psychic space but strengthens its openness. This operates both through the group structure and the group process.

The therapy group is rather closer to life than individual therapy, at least from the point of view of the new member. At some stage the new group member makes a choice to join a group and possibly a very limited choice of a group therapist, but just as we do not choose our parents or our place of residence or our siblings and extended kin, so the new group member does not choose where to meet, the way the room is decorated, his or her fellow group members, or what will happen during sessions. Groups are very powerful tools and they bring out feelings and memories which often strike the new member as totally unexpected. 'I wasn't prepared for this', said a woman who was pulled into considering her parents' sexuality at her third meeting, simply by listening to other members of the group talk. Members have to react to the group events, just as in outside life we all have to react to life events, often with limited scope for initiative. The woman member I have just described had no alternative but to think and feel about her parents; her choice lay in whether to speak and what to say. A view of life as a process of reacting to events seems to be impermissible in contemporary political culture. When Harold Macmillan said that the greatest problem his government faced was 'events, my dear boy, events', I suspect he was stating an amusing truism. I am not sure any contemporary political leader would allow him or herself to seem so out of control.

This lesson, of life being perhaps a lot more to do with reaction than action, is closely connected with our ability to tolerate or extend psychic space. Returning to experiential groups, professionals often seem to work with fantasies of 'safety' and 'confidentiality' in which they collude together in their workplaces to persuade themselves that they are safe and that what they say is confidential. In fact, neither confidentiality nor safety can be guaranteed – none of us are that reliable. This fantasy too is a way of trying to close down psychic space, to exclude the painful consideration that other people may not be trusted or trustworthy, and that neither oneself nor any other adult human being can be completely reliable.

The ideology of modern capitalist society suggests that the individual own his or her self as his or her own property, an idea which is disputable on philosophical grounds (Cohen, 1995), but which is positively dangerous on interpersonal grounds. One can only 'take control' of one's own life, only achieve 'autonomy', or come into possession of one's self by trying to control the lives of those around oneself, attempting to close down one's own psychic space by closing down that of others. This emerges in several ways in a group: sometimes directly when one person in a group tries to achieve a personal satisfaction at the expense of others, for example by threatening to leave if a particular issue is pressed, or the attempt to monopolize attention on grounds of being in greater need. There has to be basic negotiation, not to mention struggle over time and space, which does more than enable the rerun of sibling rivalries: it allows the development of adult strategies for handling such situations. More often this happens through a group member talking about their relationships to partners, children or parents, with whom other members of the group spontaneously identify. The identifying member can reflect on his or her reaction in a way which is new and different from the first member. Over time, each member of the group begins to find a range of identifications, some of which are surprising: a man suddenly finding his rejected father inside himself, a passive member recognizing the rage of the angry member. It is tempting often to see the group as a theatre in which, when it is working at its best, members can each play a range of roles. In fact it is more limited and more serious than that.

It is more serious in the sense that it requires painful effort, pain to the point where people want to, and sometimes do, rush from the room. One of the most moving sights I have watched is somebody struggling against their most powerful feelings to understand what is going on in another person: the homophobic group member faced with another member's homosexuality, and of course the homosexual struggling with the homophobe. This goes further than the process of limiting narcissistic demands. It takes us into the area of taking back inside oneself projected parts of the personality, and I have become fascinated at the way this happens in groups. Often it happens under the surface: certainly I cannot see it going on. I think I first became properly aware of it two years into my first slow open group. A woman talked very early on in her time in the group, and apropos of nothing in particular, about how she thought prisoners had an easy time of it and prisons were really like holiday camps. I remembered it because it was one of those occasions where I had to put a metaphorical clamp on my mouth. She decided to leave after staying in the group for about 18 months and shortly before she left she said, again apropos of nothing in particular, how she would hate to be a prisoner and how awful it must be being in prison. There had been no discussion of prisons in between these two occasions. The statements are laden with metaphorical value for interpretation, but what

I want to draw out of it here is the way in which she had been able to take some part of her psyche back inside herself in her ability to identify with and feel an empathy for the wrongdoer who was being punished. This ability is an index of what I would call growing psychic space. It also gives a psychoanalytic meaning to Durkheim's comment (1984 [1893]) that the more developed a society, the more sympathy it is able to feel for the wrongdoer.

To return to the more open struggles for acceptance – for example, between homophobic and homosexual members of a group. This example is a dramatic one, and the clash can be over almost any issue. I have watched a five-year struggle between a member whose way of handling difficulties was to take time off work and act in a way which another, who felt he had to get on with it, thought attention-seeking and which would put him into a rage. Sometimes a group will split along the lines of who is worse off. In all cases, whatever the issue around which the conflict occurs, the energies on which it draws are very powerful, the sort of energies which one can hear being deployed in the political rows which in some circumstances can send me off around the house kicking furniture on the basis of an interview on a news bulletin.

In the group, just as in the outside world, there are no happy endings; people do not learn to love and understand each other, discover hidden and projected parts of themselves, and live happily ever after. What does happen is more interesting. First the members learn that they can sit with one another in the same room, or at least if they rush out they can then come back again, and for some people this is a major achievement. I have one example in my practice of a very angry man with a violent background who found it almost impossible to see beyond his own horizons or believe that others were capable of making contact with him. I do not know who gave most in the group, the man in question or those members who were terrified of him. I think the paradox of the situation was that he stayed there because of his concern for the more damaged members of the group. He managed to stay for two years before dropping out and I don't think he ever realized his contribution to the development of the others in the group, who discovered that they could sit in the same room and occasionally confront his limited certainties. I found his loss very painful because I did not feel he had taken from the group as much as he had given to it.

Sometimes it can go beyond this. People can discover that even if they do not like each other, they can still learn from each other, and to some degree understand each other. It is a mistake, I think, to believe that understanding leads to lots of 'goodies' like love, liking or forgiveness, but it does seem to add a little to tolerance. When I struggled with my own relationship with my parents when I first went into therapy, I think I hoped for a combination of absolution and restoration, as if everything could be made better. Over the years I came to think of it as a process of acceptance, and then more recently of there being such things as 'authentically bad relationships', relationships in which people feel more hatred than love, more hostility than friendliness, but which are still important because they are there; however angry and hostile I have felt towards my parents I have never wanted to break off the relationship. The *relationship* is of primary importance and its content can vary and often remain 'negative'; this seems to me potentially the most important lesson of group therapy and the point where faith becomes important.

I think the implications of this for one's internal space should be apparent: it becomes more spacious, but also more complex. Many years ago I came across an image in a novel by Gore Vidal, which sadly I cannot now trace, in which he used the image of a relationship being like a many-roomed mansion, in which there are rooms for love and for hate, for desire and intellect, friend and enemy, and so on.* I would argue that this is a desirable goal for psychotherapy: it does not lay down what feelings should be felt, it does not provide formulae for handling relationships, but rather tries to increase the register of emotions that are available and that people may allow themselves to experience and deploy in pursuing their chosen lives.

Such a mansion will have its dungeons into which the owner will desire not to look. I recently listened to man who, after a long time in therapy, plucked up the courage to tell the group what he would do to the man who had abused him as a child. It was a carefully honed fantasy, a work of art based, at least at first glance, on a hatred nursed over several decades and it took considerable courage not only for him to tell the group but for him to tell himself out loud that he had these desires. On one level, however, he already knew he felt this way. The process of unwanted identification works in less obvious ways. Men who listen to a woman describing a rape recognize the rapist in themselves, women listening to somebody describing difficulties with a mother recognize the bad mother in themselves, and so on. People who seriously set out on a self-exploration will find not only the 'inner child' about whom we hear so much these days, but also the inner paedophile, the inner torturer, the inner persecutor.

I am certainly not saying that this always happens, and some people go further along this path than others, but it goes on often enough to enable us to suggest that there is a sense in which each individual is also a universal: humanity is not made up of a series of species who are alien to each other, although individuals may often be alien to each other. But we all contain within us the best, the worst and the indifferent aspects of our humanity.The attempt to close down psychic space is a rejection of some part of our humanity. It might be, in fact I suspect it is, the case that no individual can include everything. There needs to be a division of labour in virtue and a division of labour in evil. The ideal world would not dispose of evil, but in an ideal world each individual might have the capacity to look at evil and

---

* I am grateful to Colin Feltham for pointing out the biblical association – 'In my Father's house there are many mansions', John 14.2 – spoken by Christ in a story involving the doubting Thomas.

say 'There but for the grace of God . . .' This might avoid the situation, which seems to be commonplace, where evil reproduces itself in the persecution of evil.

The internalization of the group

The group is stronger than the individual and can sometimes contain, or contain more easily, or with less difficulty, experiences that the individual finds overwhelming. To the extent that the group member can take on and take in the group as an object, so his or her psyche is strengthened. One feature of the group is that it can more readily survive attack and this is apparent to many members I think on a pre-reflective level. My experience as a patient and as a therapist is that the negative transferential feelings emerge more readily in the form of attacks on the usefulness of the group and on the therapist, as though the latter is invested with the group's strength. This is the vital function of what Morris Nitsun (1996) calls 'the anti-group'. The group can more clearly survive such attacks, although of course individuals will have fantasies that they have destroyed it. I think this is important: not only the therapist and the other members of the group become transference objects, but the group itself becomes such an object, a primitive, powerful maternal or paternal object which is both a terror and a security; in so far as this object can be understood and modified by and in the individual in the group process, the individual takes on some of the strength of the group. The internal function of this strength is to allow the individual to tolerate more of him or herself than was previously possible, including the toleration of suffering as a necessary part of life, change and growth.

Within this stronger psyche there is also, if things go well, an easier identification and acceptance of different parts of oneself as they have been refracted back through the complexities of the group process. I have seen it estimated that in a group of nine people there are several thousands of relationships going on at the same time: each of us in the circle will not only be related to each member of the group directly but to each of the myriad relationships that the other members have with each other. Within the strength of the internalized group there is a greater complexity.

I believe that this strength and complexity is profoundly different to that achieved through individual psychotherapy. In a group it is difficult to maintain notions of somebody being 'perfectly analyzed' or of issues being worked through to some sort of resolution, both of which are ways of describing the closing down of psychic space. One of many useful comments that my training therapist made came not only at the end of my training but at the end of that particular group. He said that he thought it was better that the group should end with relationships between members open and unsettled: this allowed us to go away with a creative task. This is certainly part of what I mean by saying that the group opens up psychic space: it sets problems that cannot be solved in the group and perhaps cannot be solved at all.

Such problems can however be lived with. I was struck by Christopher Bollas' essay 'The self as object' (Bollas, 1987), where he too talks of extending psychic space but in terms of allowing new or widened forms of self-management. What struck me was the instrumental language, the language of management and of control. My portrayal of the contemporary political culture suggests that there might be too much doing in the world. I would prefer to use the language of being, or living, preferably of being or living *with*. Greater psychic space involves a greater tolerance of self and of others; the strength that goes with it allows not only the tolerance but the pursuit of disagreements through internal disclosure and external discourse.

Back to political culture

This takes us back briefly to contemporary political culture. My earlier discussion described a situation which can be summed up as a public failure in processes of argument, understanding and tolerance, whereas my discussion of group processes described an increase in the ability to argue, understand and tolerate. Paradoxically, such an ability requires a firmer sense of one's own identity than is to be found among those who believe they are right. Going back to my earlier discussion, the group member learns not so much to believe in him or herself as to have faith in him or herself. The greater the pressures exerted through modern social changes the greater the requirement for such faith – particularly if we desire to maintain democratic procedures and a reasonable level of civilization.

One of the more interesting contemporary critical theorists, Jurgen Habermas, suggested that psychoanalysis could be seen as an emancipatory science, setting people free from constraints they do not understand and from distorted forms of communication (Habermas, 1972). I think now that this is too simple and conveys the idea that we can know what we are doing and free ourselves of internal conflict. In his later work, Habermas develops a distinction between what he calls the social system and the life world (1984, 1987). The rationality of the social system is an instrumental rationality, geared to persuading people into the activities that will maintain the social system in working order. The lifeworld, on the other hand, develops a communicative rationality which is geared to enabling people to develop and *collectively* control and organize their lives in the way they desire. It is the values of collectivity, of living together and arguing and deciding and continuing argument, which are contained within group therapy. For a while each week the group becomes a place where the possibility of a free society is stored. Perhaps it is appropriate to end with Habermas, the contemporary representative of the critical theorists among whom Foulkes began his work. But this is a downbeat ending. These ideas need to be preserved. They will not in themselves change the world, but they might sprout shoots that could be more effective.

References

Bion, W. (1961) *Experiences in Groups*. London: Tavistock.

Bollas, C. (1987) 'The self as object', in *The Shadow of the Object*. London: Free Association Books.

Bramley, W. (1990) 'Staff sensitivity groups: a conductor's field experiences', *Group Analysis*, 23 (3): 310–16.

Cohen, G.A. (1995) *Self Ownership, Freedom and Equality*. Cambridge: Cambridge University Press.

Craib, I. (1994) *The Importance of Disappointment*. London: Routledge.

Craib, I. (1997) 'Making sense of the anti-group', *Group Analysis*, 30 (1): 107–18.

Diamond, N. (1996) 'Can we speak of internal and external reality?', *Group Analysis*, 29 (3): 303–16.

Durkheim, E. (1915) *Elementary Forms of the Religious Life*. London: Allen and Unwin.

Durkheim, E. (1984 [1893]) *The Division of Labour in Society*. Basingstoke: Macmillan.

Erikson, E. (1965) *Childhood and Society*. Harmondsworth: Penguin.

Giddens, A. (1991) *Modernity and Self Identity*. Cambridge: Polity Press.

Habermas, J. (1972) *Knowledge and Human Interests*. London: Heinneman.

Habermas, J. (1984) *The Theory of Communicative Action Vol. 1: Reason and the Rationalisation of Society*. Cambridge: Polity Press.

Habermas, J. (1987) *The Theory of Communicative Action Vol. 2: A Critique of Functionalist Reason*. Cambridge: Polity Press.

Harvey, D. (1989) *The Condition of Post-Modernity*. Oxford: Blackwell.

Hochschild, A.R. (1983) *The Managed Heart: The Commercialisation of Human Feeling*. Berkeley: University of California Press.

Lasch, C. (1977) *Haven in a Heartless World*. New York: Basic Books.

Lasch, C. (1980) *The Culture of Narcissism*. London: Sphere Books.

Nitsun, M. (1996) *The Anti-Group*. London: Routledge.

Pines, M. (1996) 'Dialogue and selfhood: discovering connections', *Group Analysis*, 29 (3): 327–42.

Ritzer, G. (1993) *The McDonaldization of Society: An Investigation into the Changing Character of Contemporary Social Life*. Thousand Oaks: Pines Forge.

Rose, N. (1989) *Governing the Soul: The Shaping of the Private Self*. London: Routledge.

Zinkin, L. (1996) 'A dialogical model for group analysis: Jung and Bakhtin', *Group Analysis*, 29 (3): 343–54.

6

In search of meaning and sanity

Colin Feltham

Arguably therapy is an intriguing combination of all that is most subjective and idiosyncratic with rare possibilities of discovering meaningful objective truths about the human condition and clues for constructing a better society. In this chapter I allow myself to wander with relatively anti-academic abandon through personal reflections, professional observations and admittedly grandiose speculations in the belief that something of interest and perhaps use may be contained in such method and material.

Entry into the world of seeking and therapy

At around 16 I was an anguished person, writing poems about meaninglessness, reading books on Zen Buddhism and arguing with my parents about the stupidity of modern civilization generally and suburban existence particularly and of being educated simply to enter some deadening job. At 18 I was a timid drop-out, refusing to complete my stupid A level exams and flirting with soft drugs, yoga, meditation and all that. This was 1968: hippies, student revolts, LSD, Hermann Hesse, Aldous Huxley, Alan Watts, R.D. Laing, Timothy Leary, psychedelic anarchy, etc. I drifted from one dead-end job to another. Life was depressing, rudderless, and it seemed that only sex, or the pursuit of sex, saved me from worse depression. One American novelist – I cannot trace who – spoke of 'sex, that hung in the gloom like a chandelier'. At this time, like many others I would be reading either Henry Miller's zany, surreal outpourings – now, of course, almost completely out of favour – or something like Somerset Maugham's *The Razor's Edge*.

I took LSD on three occasions and each time the bad part of the trip got far worse. The heavenly part, as Aldous Huxley referred to it, was indeed heavenly – visual richness, inspired ideas, freedom from time and worry, reverence for life, access to innocent perception – but the bad was filled with paranoia, loss of mind control, and bleak, dark, ambushing depression. I vowed never to touch it again. It had confirmed for me that there was far more to the texture of everyday life than most people ever experienced but I can't imagine how people like Frank Lake and Stan Grof actually used it as part of therapeutic practice. During this time my best friend got into hard drugs, drug-related crime and imprisonment, which continued for many years. There but for the grace of God perhaps.

About this time I stumbled upon the writings of Krishnamurti and had several spontaneous mystical experiences simply from reading what he said about the narrowness of our lives and the need to face up profoundly and without gurus or leaders or methods to 'what is'. Mystical experience is not the best way to describe what were immediate and profound transformations of ordinary consciousness which, alas, did not and do not come (to me) very often. Krishnamurti's intolerance of false or self-deceiving religion, politics and psychology has always struck a deep chord in me. I had tried to read Freud, Jung and other psychotherapists but invariably found their language alien and their ideas fanciful. Similarly, I could never relate to the archaic symbolism and tedious historical preoccupations of the Bible, although I could relate to the angry, iconoclastic and insightful Jesus. Krishnamurti wrote and spoke simply, passionately and incisively and did not attempt to build an empire, although the redoubtable Masson (1994: 107) seems to find Krishnamurti as guilty of charlatanism as all other mystical and therapeutic gurus.

I was desperately looking for a meaning in life and for richer experience, but I also had to find some way of passing time, looking normal and making a living. I went to university and studied theology, rather aimlessly and facilitated by the clearing system which obviously needed to fill theology places at that time. I found the course difficult, against the grain, and took time out in the middle of it. At this time I met a woman with whom I became intimate and travelled around Europe. I was always looking for the right woman and the right career. She had a copy of *The Primal Scream* which I read and, like many other readers, I was immediately struck by it and converted to the idea, as I had never been by Freudian texts, that my misery lay in my emotionally deprived childhood (Janov, 1973). I read all I could get hold of on primal therapy and finally in 1978 went to Los Angeles to have it, shelling out £3,000 in advance as demanded. I now realize that at that time I saw this therapy as promising to confer a special status on me. I was going to be a 'primal man', someone with far deeper access to his feelings than others, one of a few in a perpetually superior state of consciousness. I suspect that many entering the therapy professions may have similar aspirations to specialness.

Primal therapy did not turn out to be quite the amazing transformation I had expected. Although I did recall and apparently re-experience many incidents and themes from my childhood, and perhaps even from my birth (a large 'perhaps'), and I did cry a lot and risk new behaviours (this was made easier by living in another country), I did not become a new person. I was still unable to find the right woman and the right career. I was still lost. However, I remained a kind of primal believer for a few years and continued to cry, or 'primal', with primal 'buddies' and with one or two top-up trips to the Primal Institute in Paris. Certainly, when my father died I was grateful that I was able to be with him and that I could grieve uninhibitedly at his bedside. To this day, there are certain films, sometimes depicting death or tender father–son themes, by which I am easily emotionally pole-axed. The emotional or spiritual triumph of innocence over oppression in the film *One Flew Over the Cuckoo's Nest* and the pathos of *The Elephant Man* (again, innocence and vulnerability against stupidity and brutality) makes these favourites of mine.

On reflection, that therapy and perhaps subsequent therapies did relatively little to sensitize me to other people's suffering and differences, reinforcing instead the sense of oneself as the centre of the universe. There are times when I watch the news or a documentary, or hear a client's story, or some music, that seem to pierce me and remind me of certain emotional truths that are deeper then anything ever captured in books. Since primal therapy, I have experienced various kinds of therapy, including psychoanalytically oriented therapy, and I still feel that something is tapped in primal therapy that is truer or deeper than in anything like psychoanalysis, person-centred or other therapies. I guess this is what Alice Miller has also felt by endorsing the work of Stettbacher (1991). However, perhaps powerful insights into and means of addressing human pain and suffering cannot and should not be colonized and possessed by any group of professionals or charismatics. And being truer or deeper does not necessarily equate with being true in any ultimate sense.

The sum of my experiences in therapy – primal therapy, primal integration, psychoanalytically oriented psychotherapy, co-counselling, couple counselling and intensive groupwork, as well as a familiarity with cognitive-behavioural, multi-modal and time-limited approaches – has left me convinced that none has the complete answer and that all have a degree of absurdity about them. Each has its strength but its absurdity lies in its stubborn self-promotion and lack of humility. No one approach adequately describes or explains the human condition, human suffering and folly, and the way out of it. I am more convinced than ever that many therapists deceive themselves, and therefore clients, into believing that they know more than they really do and that they can deliver more than they ever can. This is not the same as saying that therapy has no role at all, but to some extent we therapists are surely the blind leading the blind. We are the afflicted claiming to guide others away from affliction, or more subtly, allowing them to believe we are so gifted. Fish (1973), for example, suggests that much therapy is essentially placebo therapy – it works simply because client and therapist think it's going to work – and some researchers seem to agree.

Encounters with clients

I have counselled people in many settings: a probation hostel, a mental health agency, an alcohol treatment centre, a student counselling service, an employee counselling service and in private practice. Working in a residential setting with some of society's most deprived and disturbed people was an eye-opener for me. I had had a relatively secure background, however neurotogenic. These people, or many of them, had typically grown up in the care system, their parents being unknown, in prison or other trouble, or incapable of looking after them; they very often had had a pillar-to-post existence, sometimes being abused by the very people appointed to look after them. A few of them were convicted murderers, rapists, or robbers, but most were petty offenders, their offences being expressions of their anger against abusive caregivers and society generally, or their addictions, their inability to come by money honestly or their wish, in some cases, to return to the safety of prison or other institutions. My own therapy helped me, perhaps, to understand some of the depths of their pain sometimes. Mostly I probably had to suspend what I thought I knew in order to get alongside them and to help quite modestly.

I remember one young woman who had been sexually and physically abused for years by the lodger and several members of her family. The results appeared to include self-mutilation, a drink problem, substance misuse, depression and shunning all heterosexual contacts. Another woman who had been physically beaten by her father and brothers, had herself become a violent offender, and again a self-mutilator. There was something deeply engaging about both of them and at the same time they were unpredictable, sometimes threatening or self-harming. Their offences were obviously not calculated or profit-making affairs but the outcome of abuse, personal misery and helpless impulsivity. In their cases and most others there were traceable chains of causality: early intolerable abuse or neglect of various kinds, compounded through the years, leading to institutional life, stereotyping, dwindling chances for normal social and occupational success, leading to despair and distress which was often acted out. In fact I heard some years later that one was again in prison, this time convicted of murdering a man who had attempted to have sex with her.

Sometimes these clients (clients is not the right word; they were actually known as residents, and none of these terms is ever accurate) were affectionate, warm, insightful and easily warmed to. Sometimes they were frightening, unpleasant and lacking in many social skills. Many were young, so-called street people, living off their wits. A few were old lags, resigned to an endless succession of institutions or shelters. There was nothing essentially different about them, it was just that they had been through much more disruptive lives than most people. Even those who had had 'normal' parents obviously had mostly terrible parenting. Of course, you hear people saying 'I was an orphan, I had a terrible early live, but I've never broken the law', as if this is some sort of proof of free will or voluntary good character. By this argument, people simply choose to break the law, to be violent, because they are evil, weak or lazy. I do not recall clients who had *chosen* such a path but there were a few who I might describe as chilling, personality-disordered or psychopathic; people who had something seemingly unreachable and unlovable about them. (Other writers in this book have different reactions.)

A Simon and Garfunkel song contains the lines 'some folk's lives roll easy as the breeze, . . . [whereas] . . . some folk's lives never roll at all'. This accurately summarizes the lives and life chances of many of these people. Incidentally, I sometimes wonder how people like Carl Rogers, whose privileged lives apparently roll easy as the breeze, can think they can authentically extend their own experiences and insights to others far more troubled and disadvantaged than themselves.

Were my clients helped by residential care and counselling? Some, obviously not; some, very modestly or transiently; some, significantly; some, a very few, quite dramatically perhaps. In some cases the therapist or carer is a helpless witness to a cycle of violence or deprivation. A still-teenaged woman who grew up in care, is used by men, becomes pregnant, has her child taken into care, is caught shoplifting, becomes institutionalized, is used by men, becomes pregnant, and so on. She gets a break, a council flat, but then gets into debt (she cannot cope), shoplifts, ... Perhaps a money-management programme, contraceptive advice, social skills training, some psychodynamic therapy and ongoing supportive psychotherapy will all help? Perhaps. Help should be offered and probably has some positive effect but we should not fool ourselves into believing that our *theories* have much significance here. This woman needs support, pseudo-parental or community support.

Most offenders are men, however. Most violent offences are committed by men. At the time, I simply took this for granted. Now, I wonder. Now, it seems obvious that men create wars, men create uncontrollably polluting technology, men commit most crimes, men are bastards. On the other hand, men die younger, and young men apparently resort more and more frequently to suicide. This must be due to patriarchal factors; it must be due to the way boys are raised and socialized, runs fashionable argument. However, we overlook some important matters. Most offenders are not simply men but men from broken homes, from the lowest social strata, unemployed and often from the so-called criminal fraternity. Men generally are more likely to drink heavily as a form of self-medication against suffering than are women, and alcohol is heavily implicated in much crime and violence. Women very generally are more likely to self-harm in other ways and to internalize their suffering, perhaps. According to Fillion (1997), we should be wary of the now long-held assumption of female virtue.

I was glad to leave such work but still found myself working with difficult people (some might want to correct me here and insist on 'people I found or labelled difficult'), this time in a community mental health agency. Involved briefly in community care work, I witnessed the effects on people of long-term psychiatric incarceration. I also witnessed the absurd, if understandable, naivety of some workers who believed that the newly decarcerated would invariably turn into grateful butterflies; more often, they regretted coming out or lived chaotic, disoriented lives, exploited by each other and by petty criminals in their neighbourhoods. Although given access to dignity that should never have been denied them, for many it appeared almost too late. Within the same agency I saw for counselling many women on low incomes, with housebound lifestyles and little support, who attributed their depressions to themselves instead of to their obviously depressogenic circumstances (Pilgrim, 1997).

Having worked with employee counselling services, I have wavered between the belief that such services are a sign of humanitarian progress on the one hand, and subtle worker-control on the other (Newton, 1995). I heard many stories of bullying at work, of soul-destroying work routines, impossible workloads, heartlessly announced redundancies, and often felt that I myself was in an untenable position. In student counselling, many problems appear age-related and associated with separation from home and the surfacing of bad memories. But some problems are simply about loneliness, debt, psychological frailty and manifestations of the stupidity of higher education's stress on exams, cognitive achievement and ambition generally. Counselling within such organizations always affords frustrating insights into what needs to be changed institutionally but which will not be changed, or will only be changed when it is much too late to be of benefit.

As I think back upon past clients, fear and depression seem to be the predominant themes. We now typically use the term anxiety but fear is, I think, more honest because lack of courage is arguably epidemic. Courage might be the lost key to many problems we have come to regard as therapists' territory. Nobody wants to be crucified (or more likely fired, divorced, shamed or ostracized) and most of us conform. Most of us struggle to some extent to fit into our society or even sometimes to change it, but many of us as adults are already too hurt and confused to be effective. On top of this typically bad start, many experience either single dramatic traumas or clusters of shocks they cannot cope with. To work with people who have had a gun stuck in their face in a bank raid or who have helplessly witnessed a horrific death is to be reminded that we are all a hair's breadth away from life-changing misfortunes.

Writing in the late 1990s, I am aware of living in an increasingly uncaring society, made uncaring by political ideology which has promoted the fictions of efficiency and prosperity, which in reality are the lies of forcing people to work long hours until they burn out or accept early retirement, and fostering a myth of economic recovery always around the corner. Clients do not usually present with political problems but grinding daily economic worry is often implicit in their stories.

Human nature

This term is highly problematic but none the less has some meaning for me. Nothing has changed my view that there is something deeply flawed about human beings, whether it be called sin, ignorance, pain, alienation from our true nature, being fucked-up or anything else. (How about 'ontological disorder'?) Something collective, deeply programmed into us and barely affected by therapy continues to wreak havoc with the world. Perhaps we can think in terms of a species pathology or systemic flaw (Bohm, 1994; Stevens and Price, 1996). Very roughly speaking, I think we are trapped by our own stupid cleverness, our tendency to survive at all costs, to outwit, to constantly plan ahead, to fear and desire. Such tendencies run deeper than our familial pathologies and cultural idiosyncrasies and may be considered species injunctions perhaps. In broad terms, all religions have observed this phenomenon, but all religions fail – as I believe all psychotherapies ultimately fail – to correct this tendency, because it is stronger and more subtle than any system of human religion or therapy. Genuine mystical experiences and momentary breakthroughs in therapy show us the possibility of a way out of this dark side of human nature, but it still remains for most of us a possibility only, in spite of hopeful syntheses such as Symington's (1994) and the belief of many transpersonal therapists in therapeutic paths to genuine transcendence (Rowan, 1993).

Inspired figures like Jesus, Gotama, Krishnamurti and others appear to have had a large measure of sustained freedom from this tendency (there is no satisfactory single world for it), but I have met no therapists or clients of therapists who appear to be similarly free. Indeed, I have been disappointed to find that counsellors and therapists – however immersed in a noble struggle to cast off their own limitations, craziness or dishonesty – generally remain as vulnerable to vanity, greed, arrogance, unkindness, mediocrity, dishonesty, ruthless ambition and conflict as anyone else. I am occasionally aware of and depressed by my own layers of stupidity and hypocrisy (not necessarily lessening but sometimes deepening) beneath the persona of counsellor, writer and lecturer. It is commonplace to read in psychotherapeutic texts that practitioners must have lots of therapy themselves, that they can only take clients where they themselves have been psychologically, and so on. Jourard (1971: 157) went so far as to speak of 'the psychotherapist as exemplar as "reborn," in the Sufi sense, or awakened and liberated in the sense of the Zen masters'. But there are few if any Gandhis, Martin Luther Kings or Krishnamurtis among therapists.

I have been impressed by the sincerity and courage of many people in therapeutic groups who are obviously striving to be truthful and to push back the boundaries of human stupidity and fear. Perhaps what happens in such settings, however, is that aspirations to be unreservedly truthful are often converted into a parody of themselves; instead of setting the world alight, people so engaged tend eventually to wrap themselves in a closed, cultish therapeutic world, speaking therapy-speak and inadvertently merely promoting what Fay Weldon has called therapism.

I cannot easily subscribe to the belief among many humanistic therapists that human beings are essentially loving, self-actualizing, truth-seeking, and so on. Or, to put it differently, the tendencies towards self-deceit, self-protectiveness and self-promotion seem to exceed those towards discovery, love of truth and openness to change. Psychotherapeutic organizations, for example, closely resemble religious authorities which create and protect orthodoxies rather than welcome constant openness to new, living truth (Feltham, 1995; Thorne, 1997). I have seen this at close hand, in professional organizations which grow, expand their authority and increase their rules and regulations; this process does little or nothing to help the supposed benefactors, therapy clients, in spite of abundant professional rhetoric arguing that it does.

I have also seen individual therapists reaping the rewards of status and fame, becoming rather proud of themselves. I have certainly felt this myself, that with increased professional celebrity (as a biggish fish in a small pond) comes an increase in the temptation to think highly of myself as well as feeling, at times, curiously distanced from others and by others. The novelist John Updike has said that 'celebrity is a mask that eats into the face'. False prophets do not necessarily set out to be false; more often, they probably discover a little bit of truth, get admired because of it, and the whole process of distortion goes on from there. So I think of human beings as frequently succumbing to folly; this can be funny in a Bruegel-like way but is frequently tragic.

To listen to clients is certainly to find that to be human is apparently to have problems. To be human is to err and to suffer. Philosophers and priests have repeatedly pointed out that our thinking is crooked and our feelings are easily hurt. Loss, death and disappointment are universal – this is the human lot. Most clients are suffering, they are confused, they have layers and layers of bad memories and mind traps to deal with, and on top of that they believe that we therapists have some special insight that they do not have. This too is a powerful, perennial human belief: that others know better than we do. Priests, philosophers, politicians, psychotherapists, educators, scientists know better than others. Senior therapists know more, are more skilful, have plumbed more of their own psychological depths than junior therapists. Academics know better, are more rigorous in their thinking, than ordinary people – they *must* do, because they write books that the rest of us cannot understand!

When I was looking for contributors for this book, one therapist warned me that they should be highly experienced and wise, otherwise the results could be (embarrassingly) superficial and uninteresting. I worried about this for a while. Who is to be considered wise? Could someone point me in the right direction, towards the right people? Can the academic literature on research into wisdom help us (Sternberg, 1990)? When clients see therapists they tend to see them as more experienced and wise; they may initially idealize them and later denigrate them. But in the main therapists set themselves up as gurus who do not claim to be gurus, as cunning mirrors of others' souls. Also, although we deny it, I think we feel that if others bring their troubles to us, we *must* somehow be wiser, deeper, more loving or something special. By allowing ourselves to be thus regarded, endorsed by our prestigious professional organizations, we reinforce the sense of the indispensability of the experts. A cyclical deception is involved: I fool myself into believing that others know better; others, knowing deep down that they do not know better, none the less enjoy and profit from this ignorance. As the Woody Allen joke goes, 'My brother thinks he's a chicken; I'd tell him he's not, but I need the eggs.'

So, there is something tragi-comically wrong with us, but there's much more to us than that. Presumably the self-actualizing tendencies observed and passionately believed in by Carl Rogers are not simply a matter of naivety. As well as being ever prone to self-deceit, I think there is some core within us, or within most of us, that strives to be consistently truthful and to embody kindness, integrity and pro-social behaviour. It is not often evident in everyday life perhaps, but given the discipline of sustained work in groups or in therapy dyads, it is apparent that many people harbour a longing to be more honest than everyday social intercourse allows, and that many long for a just social order and a sane world. Therapists have underlined the pain of personal, emotional oppression but until recently little interest has been shown in the idea of a spiritual or political unconscious, an unheard cry for community, kindness, peace and truth. (See, however, Thorne (1997), Newman (1991) and Samuels (1993) for examples of therapists who partially address this.)

Before and during my own therapy I believed that children were oppressed innocents. After becoming a parent, I was and still am convinced that much of our personality structure is innate and that in general there is a great deal we do not know about temperament and predisposition. We probably naively believe that therapy, like religion, can undo the past or liberate us from all our most undesirable lifelong patterns (Steiner, 1974). I do not share this belief. The failures or very modest successes I have sometimes experienced as a counsellor have convinced me that certain genetic and collective forces are probably at work that override all conscious therapeutic efforts. Perhaps there are subtle constellations of genetic predisposition, intra-uterine, birth and post-natal factors that determine some of our lifelong problematic behaviour. Almost certainly, devastatingly bad early parenting sets us up for later failure to thrive and self-actualize. I regard the *language* of object relations therapists as unhelpful, but I am sure their *sense* of subtle early damage has merit. However, as yet we know relatively little about the precise cocktail of genetic, environmental and experiential components in human development (Plomin, 1994), and we should not allow our therapeutic zeal to prevent us from studying the views of those whose emphasis is on biology and evolution (for example, Gazzaniga, 1992).

It is tempting in passing to speculate on the role of the weather and external agents. We occasionally say 'I'm under the weather', signifying some residual belief in bad weather as causative in psychological dysfunctions. Or we say 'He just wanted to talk about the weather', referring to avoidance of psychological depths. Mostly, the view now seems to predominate that we must attribute our personal moods to ourselves and our own failures in psychological insight. Similarly, therapy has an unfortunate tendency to de-emphasize the role of economics, life chances, noxious environments and other external factors. The Freudian revolution, probably necessary in its time, has left a legacy of overemphasis on inner depths and corresponding neglect of outer deterioration (Bohm and Edwards, 1991).

It may be that the central, underlying dysfunction in human beings is overcorrectiveness, meaning that when we make necessary temporary adjustments at all levels, these adjustments inevitably become chronic, inflexible and problem-compounding. We continue to defend ourselves long after the threat has disappeared. And we continue to lean on Jesus and Freud (or Krishnamurti) long after their lessons have been useful and often to our own and others' detriment. Even existentialist therapists who warn us not to look to great psychologists as heroes, themselves appear often to worship the pantheon of their favourite philosopher heroes. Information and communication technology as a corrective to slow paper communication leads iatrogenically to information overload syndrome. And so on. We find the Buddhist middle way hard to follow, lurching always to some extreme from which we then suffer.

Spirituality and morality

I have little time for organized religion and indeed believe that in its fundamentalist guises it is one of the worst evils. The common suspicion that there is more to life is however another matter. Most of us appear to live very constricted, relatively fearful lives and those who look to counselling and therapy for help or liberation represent simply the tip of the iceberg of dissatisfaction, pain or ignorance. On the other hand, many people have experienced at least the touch of some richer way or moment of extraordinary fulfilment (Cohen and Phipps, 1979). I certainly concur with Symington's (1994) view that there are core values which we have lost touch with and that psychotherapy, in some way, has the potential to address. Jung and Frankl, among others, have attracted many readers and clients thirsty for spiritual meaning and direction. Recent texts by Friedman (1992), Rowan (1993), Brazier (1995) and Epstein (1996) also indicate renewed interest in a psychospiritual quest. Kirschner (1996), on the other hand, argues that contemporary therapies are simply the latest manifestations of the selfsame mysticism, romanticism and other movements into psychoanalysis and its derivatives.

During the 1980s I was involved in many groups of a therapy-like nature. Mainly in association with Tony Storey, formerly of the University of Cambridge, and Paul Mullins at Katherine Price Hughes Probation Hostel, the groups adhered to a disciplined yet apparently goalless contract. They were confined to here-and-now observations and required participants to concentrate hard on what transpired, even if the group lasted a whole day, a residential week or, in some cases, a marathon three weeks. People were asked to disclose their fleeting or persistent thoughts, feelings, sensations and images as freely as possible. Tony Storey had devised these groups from an interest in meditative techniques and essentially they were, indeed, a form of interpersonal contemplation. They did not aim at therapy but at enquiry. When we sit and watch and share our perceptions in as unguarded a way as we can, accepting silences, difficulties, emotional outbursts, misunderstandings and all manner of anomalous interactions, what is it that we experience? When we accept each person's experience, or statement of his or her experience, without deferring to the presumed expertise of the group leaders, facilitators or therapists, what emerges?

One of the main complaints people typically had about this kind of group was that there was no agenda and nothing was happening. Barred from everyday chit-chat and autobiographical exchanges, who are we and how can we relate to each other? The nakedness or rawness of this situation fascinated me. Participants sometimes included counsellors, psychotherapists, social workers, probation officers, police officers, magistrates, students, offenders and just ordinary people! Stripped of their roles and status, asked to speak only for themselves – in good, time-honoured, group therapy fashion – many struggled to articulate their present feelings without reference to some theory or past experience. The sheer sense of 'here we all are and this is all there is' rarely failed to inspire me. Admissions of sexual attraction, dislike, irritation, warmth, inability to understand or concentrate, fear of appearing odd, all served to expose the human condition.

Psychological simplicity and spiritual poverty are phenomena awaiting our attention in such groups. The more you expose, the more each preoccupation, each fear, looks like an illusion. My experience in these groups certainly confirmed for me the belief that most people contain vast reserves of good sense and spiritual striving (the truth shall set you free) that is, however, denied in most social situations. It doesn't necessarily require a therapist to unleash the forces of truth and love, but it does appear to require certain conditions or a context of permission (or perhaps oldfashioned courage and honesty, those relatively rare commodities!).

There is a pleasurable aspect to such experiences. Once I began to feel chaotic and described this in terms of an image of myself as a pig rushing round the room upsetting all the chairs. I talked in this vein for a while and realized that I had somehow entered a state of consciousness quite different from my usual one. I think I referred to it as resembling grace. I was momentarily freed from inhibitions, from all fears; my mind was extraordinarily alive, inquisitive, unafraid of others' reactions, unafraid of anything. This lasted for about an hour or so until I came down, back into normal fearful mode. Interestingly, one of the other participants said he had wanted to kill me, so arrogant had I seemed, yet he had also recognized that something else, something that was not-me, was at work.

Experiences in such groups are sure to inspire people to consider, if only temporarily, what a community ruled by honesty, enquiry and care might look like. Often at the end of groups there was a subtle but pervasive sense of love, of sharing in the same reality, facing the same problems. The morality of such an experience is about a commitment to truth-seeking, a faith in finding not solutions, but the possible dissolution of all phoney problems. Our bodily existence and our physical coexistence are more real than the phantoms of our minds. Thus, in intensive, disciplined group settings the possibility exists of learning profoundly that our fearful fantasies, carried over from family life and from cultural conditioning, can be let go of (de Maré et al., 1991). Presumably it is no coincidence that radical groupwork of all kinds declined from the 1980s as interest in problem management, stress management, self-improvement and other uncritically individualizing projects grew.

It is significant that in our time we seem enslaved to the gods of efficiency, evidence, success, professionalization and other chimeras. At the same time, New Age illusions appear to flourish in an underground or semi-commercial sort of way. The moral vacuum of postmodernism is defended or denied by some intellectuals, but I think it is plain that we have been living in dark, amoral times of fear, self-obsession and social irresponsibility. Perhaps this moral crisis expresses itself in the demoralization so many feel when presenting for therapy. Unfortunately therapists have no brief to reconstruct society, just as the clergy usually refuse to engage in politics and confine themselves so often to single moral issues, and usually from an anachronistic perspective. I think many of us are waiting – and waiting is of course a key problematic term, not something as close and achievable as Peck (1993) appears to believe – for a new social ethic and new leaders addressing our mental, spiritual and social health. Unfortunately we are also bombarded by theories of crisis and explanations for our postmodern predicament, which seem only to reinforce our paralysis (Sloan, 1996).

The future of therapy

The therapeutic scene is currently confused; there are too many competing therapies (Feltham, 1997) and too many competing therapy professions (James and Palmer, 1996). There is too much preoccupation with the minutiae of professionalization, with theoretical speculations and the search for infinitesimal clinical improvements. There is not enough concern for actually delivering a meaningful therapy to those who need it most, nor is sufficient attention paid to clarifying what therapy is in relation to other disciplines and cultural trends (Feltham, 1995). There is far too great a tendency for therapists to be enmeshed in sick professions and in hypo-critical compromises with iatrogenic institutions that ironically create the very distress they claim to be fighting.

Unlike some of my colleagues, I have been relatively heartened by the trend towards short-term therapy and counselling which, as I see it, goes hand in hand with the rejection of monolithic therapeutic traditions and extravagant outcome claims. The expansion of counselling in primary care is certainly welcome, and the work of Cummings (1990) and the idea of a community-based psychological general practitioner are appealing. What I would like to see in addition to this is an expansion in experimentation with groups such as those I have mentioned and with preventive and social-educational ventures generally. More and more, I regard counselling and therapeutic theories as of limited utility, as repetitious and often pretentious. This need not lead to the Masson-like conclusion that therapy should be abolished. Rather, I think in terms of a new, expanded vocation. Perhaps we might have mental health stewards (again, there is no good word for it), using the modest resources of therapy along with community groups and preventive and educational ventures of all kinds.

Indeed, if I were not an atheist I would see a role for myself and others as some sort of minister-cum-community facilitator and educator. To some degree, therapists *are* the new priests, bearing witness to suffering, hearing confessions and acting as intermediaries. I realize that in counselling sessions I often vacate my everyday self, somehow becoming a reliable, objective other for the client. That part of me which is not fucked-up temporarily overrides that which is, it is fallibly available to the client, just as that part of them that is not fucked-up reaches out fumblingly to me and to a sensed sanity beyond our common social madness. We are surely all battered by the traditional lies of politicians and by the deep social fictions which impinge on us from all sides. Many of us sense a need to explore or create a truly sane society. The work of Erich Fromm, Martin Buber, Maurice Friedman, Amitai Etzioni, M. Scott Peck and others seems to point in this direction. Differently but with similarly sensed ends, perhaps writers as diverse as Pearse and Crocker (1985), Bohm and Edwards (1991), Csikszentmihalyi (1993), Zohar and Marshall (1993), Goleman (1996), Albee and Gullotta (1997) and Newman and Holzman (1997) also capture aspects of the vision of psychosocial change I can barely articulate here.

The impossible vision

In his novel *Island*, Aldous Huxley depicted a sane society permeated by certain therapeutic and mystical ideas. Realistically enough, this society perished, the forces of darkness being too strong to allow it to thrive. I am aware that some psychoanalytic and other writers regard Utopian or even modestly wishful visions or preoccupations as neurotic projections of one's own unresolved inner (particularly psychosexual) conflicts (Chasseguet-Smirgel and Grunberger, 1986). But Utopias, whether the Christian Kingdom of Heaven, anarchist and Marxist visions, Skinner's Walden Two, Maslow's eupsychia, all have their positive and negative characteristics (Buber, 1949; Manuel, 1966). I am acutely aware that today one is not supposed to be idealistic. It is apparently acceptable to embrace currently politically correct causes and to privilege idealized fragmentation (post-modernism), but not global, perennial, transcendental aspirations. John

Rowan (1993: 197), for example, has pointed to the merits and dangers of visions and the problems of narrow, fixed visions purporting to contain truth claims. Writers such as Thomas Szasz have warned against the possible dangers of a therapeutic state.

Perhaps I am stuck in some 1970s time warp, perhaps I am searching for some unconsciously projected memory of intra-uterine paradise, but I still hanker – as I know many of my contemporaries do – for an existence, a society, that is radically different from the sick, brutal, stressful and dishonest society that I find myself in in Britain in the late 1990s. I believe that the proliferation of 'minority' political causes has ironically exacerbated matters by increasing fragmentation and drawing energy away from the kind of holistic and radical questioning associated with Krishnamurti, Bohm and others. (See, for example, Bohm's (1996) 'vision of dialogue'.) Vision can be extended in many directions:

> There is nothing like a United Nations of the Mind, designed to keep a finger on the pulse of the biosphere, ready to swing into global action when altered by tell-tale signs in the collective psyche. There could be. We probably already have the psychological expertise necessary to recognise the symptoms when we see them. All that is missing is the appropriate early warning system; an international network of analysts deployed to monitor sensitive places; paid to take what amounts to periodic polls of opinions prevailing at unconscious levels. And of course a willingness to take these measurements seriously and to act on the information provided. (Watson, 1980: 366)

It is easy to mock such sentiments and *perhaps* they are quite unrealistic or inflated. However, many of us probably realize that psychological insights do apply to societies, but are ignored. Technologically, it would be quite possible to have world leaders constructively quizzed on their destructive behaviour by psychologically informed and pro-socially motivated Jeremy Paxmans, for example! Prophets, priests, philosophers and therapists have always seen that we are both created and shaped by the world and that we create it. We all perpetuate psychological misery and we all have some power – so frustratingly elusive – to dissolve misery and suffering. The individualistic church of counselling and therapy requires a communal corrective. We need, I believe, a vision of community beyond the chronic suffering and folly we witness in the consulting room, and we need urgently to put aside the impoverished vision contained in the current professionalizing tide and in myths of efficiency.

Recently a client, breaking into tears as she recounted the stress she was under at work, said, 'It just doesn't feel safe to be human anymore.' She worked in a counselling agency where new, fictitious and impossible targets and criteria for success were being introduced (House, 1996). As she spoke and cried, I inwardly sighed heavily too as I reflected that it didn't feel safe for me either, in the institution where I worked, to be human, to show openly the stress, anger and illness in the making I was experiencing at trying to do the work (much of it soul-destroyingly bureaucratic) of two people. Some have suggested that therapy has recently been greatly oversold, but the products of managerialist ideology and commercialized higher education generally have probably been equally oversold.

If pushed to say what I most value about counselling and therapy it is not autonomy and self-actualization, but the promotion and restoration of humanity, of fellow-feeling, which has been seriously eroded by the psychological by-pollution of the worship of business values, erosion of community, uncritical competition and all manner of rhetoric about the goodness and inevitability of change and progress. Where therapists like Sidney Jourard in the 1970s stood for the corrective of autonomy, at the edge of the millennium we seem to need the corrective of social responsibility. Perhaps we are also the victims of our own success in the therapy and growth business, and have begun to be suffocated by our own theories. A new, atheoretical consciousness is needed as a corrective for these, something that cannot be appropriated by organizations of therapists, clergy or academics (Krishnamurti and Bohm, 1985; Newman and Holzman, 1997).

The only revolution, Krishnamurti suggested, is the radical, voluntary, deeply heartfelt, unmediated one which might change self and society simultaneously. At especially tragic times, such as the Dunblane massacre of schoolchildren and their teacher in 1996, some deep chord is struck in us as we momentarily realize (and then forget again) both the madness and evasiveness in ourselves and the responsibility we all carry for our society. Witnessing the triumphant election of the Labour Government in May 1997 engendered both a daring-to-hope and a world-weary readiness for disappointment. Partial, ever-preparatory psychological revolutions and individual therapies, however allegedly deep, are not enough. Only the holistic sanity of mental, spiritual and social health will do.

As almost a postscript to this chapter I feel a need for some sort of grand caveat. There is something about the written word that has a carved-in-stone distorting quality about it. Part of my own dialogical vision would mean that what I have said here could be responded to in ways which would change it. Indeed as I read over it myself I see contradictions, flaws and points for development. Just as clients' stories can be and frequently are forced into distorted linear moulds, so are our theories and observations distorted by the linearity of print and by the tradition of written soliloquy. Just as mystics find language inadequate to express direct experience, so must we perhaps realize that language is a constraint in therapy and in reflecting on therapy. A full vision must reckon with the limits of words and arguments and seek, somehow, to invite and create a communal intuition.

References

Albee, G.W. and Gullotta, T.P. (eds) (1997) *Primary Prevention Works*. Thousand Oaks, CA: Sage.
Bohm, D. (1994) *Thought as a System*. London: Routledge.

Bohm, D. (1996) *On Dialogue*. London: Routledge.

Bohm, D. and Edwards, M. (1991) *Changing Consciousness*. New York: HarperCollins.

Brazier, D. (1995) *Zen Therapy*. London: Constable.

Buber, M. (1949) *Paths in Utopia*. London: Routledge and Kegan Paul.

Chasseguet-Smirgel, J. and Grunberger, B. (1986) *Freud or Reich?: Psychoanalysis and Illusion*. London: Free Association Books.

Cohen, J.M. and Phipps, J.-F. (1979) *The Common Experience*. London: Rider.

Csikszentmihalyi, M. (1993) *The Evolving Self: A Psychology for the Third Millennium*. New York: HarperCollins.

Cummings, N. (1990) 'Brief, intermittent psychotherapy through the life cycle', in J.K. Zeig and S.G. Gilligan (eds), *Brief Therapy: Myths, Methods and Metaphors*. New York: Brunner/Mazel.

de Maré, P., Piper, R. and Thompson, S. (1991) *Koinonia: From Hate, Through Dialogue, to Culture in the Large Group*. London: Karnac.

Epstein, M. (1996) *Thoughts Without a Thinker: Psychotherapy from a Buddhist Perspective*. London: Duckworth.

Feltham, C. (1995) *What is Counselling?: The Promise and Problem of the Talking Therapies*. London: Sage.

Feltham, C. (ed.) (1997) *Which Psychotherapy?: Leading Exponents Explain Their Differences*. London: Sage.

Fillion, K. (1997) *Lip Service: The Myth of Female Virtue in Love, Sex and Friendship*. London: Pandora.

Fish, J.M. (1973) *Placebo Therapy*. San Francisco: Jossey-Bass.

Friedman, M. (1992) *Religion and Psychology: A Dialogical Approach*. New York: Paragon.

Gazzaniga, M.S. (1992) *Nature's Mind*. Harmondsworth: Penguin.

Goleman, D. (1996) *Emotional Intelligence*. London: Bloomsbury.

House, R. (1996) '"Audit-mindedness" in counselling: some underlying dynamics', *British Journal of Guidance and Counselling*, 24 (2): 277–83.

James, I. and Palmer, S. (1996) *Professional Therapeutic Titles: Myths and Realities*. Leicester: British Psychological Society.

Janov, A. (1973) *The Primal Scream*. London: Abacus.

Jourard, S.M. (1971) *The Transparent Self*, 2nd edn. New York: Van Nostrand.

Kirschner, S.R. (1996) *The Religious and Romantic Origins of Psychoanalysis*. Cambridge: Cambridge University Press.

Krishnamurti, J. and Bohm, D. (1985) *The Ending of Time*. London: Gollancz.

Manuel, F.E. (ed.) (1966) *Utopias and Utopian Thought*. London: Souvenir Press.

Masson, J.M. (1994) *My Father's Guru: A Journey through Spirituality and Disillusion*. London: HarperCollins.

Newman, F. (1991) *The Myth of Psychology*. New York: Castillo.

Newman, F. and Holzman, L. (1997) *The End of Knowing*. London: Routledge.

Newton, T. (1995) *'Managing' Stress*. London: Sage.

Pearse, I.H. and Crocker, L.H. (1985) *The Peckham Experiment*. Edinburgh: Scottish Academic Press.

Peck, M.S. (1993) *A World Waiting to be Born*. New York: Bantam.

Pilgrim, D. (1997) *Psychotherapy and Society*. London: Sage.

Plomin, R. (1994) *Genetics and Experience: The Interplay Between Nature and Nurture*. Thousand Oaks, CA: Sage.

Rowan, J. (1993) *The Transpersonal: Psychotherapy and Counselling*. London: Routledge.

Samuels, A. (1993) *The Political Psyche*. London: Routledge.

Sloan, T. (1996) *Damaged Life: The Crises of the Modern Psyche*. London: Routledge.

Steiner, C. (1974) *Scripts People Live*. New York: Grove Weidenfeld.

Sternberg, R.J. (ed.) (1990) *Wisdom: Its Nature, Origins and Development.* Cambridge: Cambridge University Press.

Stettbacher, J.K. (1991) *Making Sense of Suffering.* New York: Dutton.

Stevens, A. and Price, J. (1996) *Evolutionary Psychiatry.* London: Routledge.

Symington, N. (1994) *Emotion and Spirit: Questioning the Claims of Psychoanalysis and Religion.* London: Cassell.

Thorne, B. (1997) 'Counselling and psychotherapy: the sickness and the prognosis', in S. Palmer and V. Varma (eds), *The Future of Counselling and Psychotherapy.* London: Sage.

Watson, L. (1980) *Lifetide.* London: Hodder and Stoughton.

Zohar, D. and Marshall, I. (1993) *The Quantum Society.* London: Bloomsbury.

7

Suffering, evolution and psychotherapy

Paul Gilbert

The editor took the brave step of asking contributors to reflect on personal ideas of human nature, the human condition and the practice of psychotherapy. He is right, of course; our approaches to therapy are probably shaped by our responses to such questions. My own reflections have, I think, grown darker over the years, and I'm doubtful they go any further than most others. Still, the situation may be bad but not yet, I believe, hopeless.

The problem of suffering

The new Children's Hospital in Derby is full of colour and child-friendly equipment. Toys and pictures are scattered about the place. Many will pass through here and not realize that just a hundred years earlier their afflictions would have killed them. For the lucky ones, life-saving procedures will be conducted as routine. For others the story will be sadder. Some just a few hours old, others a few years old, will struggle in a losing battle against pain and death. For them life was an unfortunate mix of poor genes, infections, birth accidents and bad luck. A couple of blocks away both old and younger adults will be fighting unseen invaders. Those of a reflective mind might ponder how viruses and bacteria evolved such numerous ways to inflict pain and suffering – and on so many living things. For others, errors in some small gene yet to be discovered will signal an earlier than hoped for exit from this life. And for those who love them, and must now learn to live without them, life will never be the same. Diseases, be they viral, bacterial or genetic, obviously evolved over millions of years (Nesse and Williams, 1995) – indeed all of life evolved from bacteria-like organisms. For those who would take comfort in the idea of evolution as forward moving, we can recall the tapeworm, a recent adaptation that can only live in the human gut; and this is but one example of a parasite which evolved with its host. Viruses, bacteria and parasites also evolve. Spoken with dark poetry perhaps, evolution is not upwardly progressive but expands like a fungus – and we are but a vein on that fungus of life.

On the other side of the road lies the psychiatric hospital. That's where I work. And here live people persecuted by hostile voices, driven by delusions of grandeur, tormented by memories and emotions for which their only temporary release may be to open wounds in their own flesh. Today one of my patients wonders if she has the 'guts' to kill herself and give herself the dreamless sleep she so desires. She is my last patient and the day is already gone and the sky black. It is late autumn, the leaves of the summer are no more than a dull memory and sodden underfoot. The drive home is cold, wet and slow, clogged with other drivers doing likewise. The television news speaks of discoveries of new atrocities in Bosnia and Rwanda, reminders of the new famines in Africa and the preparations for Remembrance Day for the First World War.

These universal stories, of hatred of others or oneself, have haunted and hounded humankind through the centuries – so long and in so many places that they speak of archetypal themes. And when we look to other animals we see the seeds of these behaviours there too. Indeed, a quick map of the phylogeny of the mammalian mind will show how selective pressure gives rise to dominance hierarchies, ingroups and outgroups, cheating, deception, retribution (MacLean, 1990) and even war (Goodall, 1990). We can note the ease with which some of these archetypal patterns are recruited and inflamed by social contexts. Bosnia is but one recent example of all too many, where neighbours can end up raping and murdering each other over rather small differences in belief and allegiances to certain leaders. Disease, war and famine are all too common afflictions of life. We cannot blame evolution entirely for some of humanity's absurdities and outrageous cruelties, but we can to a fair degree.

Of course, humans are also capable of love and compassion. These are also evolved psychologies (Gilbert, 1989; Wright, 1996), and may well, as some claim, distinguish humans from other animals (Dalai Lama, 1993). None the less, I guess few of us will have avoided the conclusion that for many, life can be short and brutal. I want to start with this observation because first, be it consciously or not, our attitudes to suffering are probably paramount to how we conduct ourselves in therapy and the therapy we choose to practise. Second, not only may therapists be trying to work out their own forms of 'suffering', I suspect we choose to work with 'suffering' to make sense 'of life'. Be it conscious or not I suspect that for some at least, and I include myself here, there is a kind of anger at nature's injustice and (from our human point of view) blind stupidity, cruelty and wastefulness. All the things we find beautiful – from the gracefulness of the cheetah, to the sounds of the new birds of spring – each rests on the millions of poorer designs that didn't make it. Evolution hones things by 'weeding out'.

Whatever one's own beliefs on suffering, therapist and patient can be confronted with strong feelings in considering its cause. People who come to therapy are often full of such questions: 'Why was I abused?' 'Why didn't my parents love me?' 'Why do I suffer from schizophrenia, bipolar illness or cancer?' 'Why could I not have been as bright as Joe or Sue?' 'Why did I have to be born in Bosnia?' 'Why me?' 'Am I just another of evolution's drossum in the continual weeding out process?' The sheer misery, harshness, unfairness and traumatization of much of life for many people confront therapists daily. Sure, we rarely have the time to think about suffering in such mosaic terms, or in the context of 'the meaning of life', but the backdrop to our existential questions is always 'the process of life and death' (Yalom, 1980).

Therapists try various things to bring relief; there are over 400 schools of psychotherapy by some estimates. Sometimes these are efforts to remove suffering, sometimes just cope with it better. Some turn to religion. And so it is to religious notions of suffering I will turn in the next few sections. This is not only because I was brought up in a religious household and the 'discovery' of evolution theory was a major revelation and to some extent spiritual blow, but also because I doubt that questions of suffering are easily separated from spiritual or existential ones. However, it is not, I believe, until one has stepped outside orthodox religious pursuits that one can take a cold hard look at suffering.

The question of suffering and God

Few of us get past adolescence without coming into direct contact with religious beliefs, be these at home, in the school assembly or our first nativity play. I think I was five with I got to play one of the shepherds and was upset because Sally kept taking my crook. We soon learn that one thing most religions have in common is various ideals about morality (good and bad). Usually God is good and humans bad/sinful. The major problem with a concept of 'a creator' is the facts of disease, death and decay. Is this really such a good creation? If not, why not?

I came from a religious background, where there was no question as to the goodness of God the father, or that the world and universe were ultimately just – that everyone's suffering must have a cause, a reason in the grand design of things. So for me the gradual awareness of the power of evolutionary theory was staggering. It was as simple as it was elegant. No Gods or devils, no creators, no judges, no fathers in heaven. Suffering was basic to nature because this is the way it is. No reasons other than the basic story of gene replication need be given. Bleak it may be, but in its own way freeing. So many things that had not made sense as a child began to fall into place. Vestiges of a spirituality remain but of a rather different form to that I grew up with. Indeed, even spiritual approaches want to be evolutionary these days (Wilber, 1983, 1996). And I have often had an ironic smile at the gnostic idea that the creation of the physical domain was a mistake – some mistake! I have certainly not abandoned spiritual pursuits, and am appalled by the arrogance of some sociobiologists who believe they already know what happens after death. Of this we know nothing, and much depends on how we perceive consciousness (d'Aquili and Newberg, 1996; Goswami, 1993). All we can say is that we need no other explanation than evolution to explain the complexity and variety of life. For me then I believe that the deep spiritual yearnings (which may, of course, be related to fears of death of self, family and friends) need to go on. My spiritual quest is, like increasing numbers of others, a kind of make it up as you go – a vaguely Buddhism meets Star Trek type. A less romantic notion would be agnosticism.

Throughout history humans have confronted the major question of 'Why do we suffer?' This might be an even more ubiquitous question than 'What's the meaning of life?' Our attitudes and answers to this question affect what we will do about it. We have many answers. Atkinson (1993) has given an eloquent summary of some of the many ways we can construe both the experiences of suffering and 'the person who suffers'. I will begin by following her outline.

As noted above, suffering can be regarded as part of human nature, without any ultimate purpose or fairness. But this is a bleak view that can reduce hope and makes suffering and ultimate death hard to bear. Thus, not surprisingly, humans construct various other reasons so that they can imbue suffering with meaning. For example, suffering is often related to some kind of relationship – not uncommonly to God. Once placed in the context of 'a relationship' then archetypal themes to do with, for example, dominant-subordinate (punisher-controller, punished-controlled), father-child, or victim-saviour become meaningful constructs. Now if such beliefs do help people cope and reproduce then they are adaptive. Of course, people don't consciously know they are creating beliefs to help them cope and give hope which improves their genes' chance of survival. For a belief to work it has to be 'believed'. So self-deception can be helpful.

The history of the 'idea of God' and his or her supposed passions, desires, moral rules and social favourites have changed from one extreme to another (Armstrong, 1994). God can be anything from a tyrant to a benign loving energy. And many scholars now recognize that what we think about God is more a reflection of our inner-selves that we project, than any ultimate external reality. However, this is important because 'God as an archetypal idea' (Wenegrat, 1990) has much to answer for. The reason for this, it seems to me, is because God 'as an idea' and focus for emotional relating, can so easily recruit our evolved psychology of 'serving a leader'. And when this psychology is activated, and people take a submissive position within it, they are capable of the most terrible things, because they have given up their individuality and are now 'obeying orders' (Milgram, 1974). As Kelman and Hamilton (1989) note in their important work *Crimes of Obedience*, many religions are organized around hierarchical structures that legitimize grossly immoral acts on the part of followers but convince followers they will gain prestige. Indeed, people can feel it a duty to obey the most hideous orders of leaders.

Legitimacy from a higher authority works in other ways too. For example, people claim the authority of God when they enter the moral debate on abortion and euthanasia. And this is not a small issue because the question of suffering at the end of life demands our most urgent attention (Werth, 1996; Williams, 1997). To argue from a point of view of what 'God wants' is to privilege oneself with being close to the powerful authority. Historically, this is a very common way of approaching moral thinking (that is, trying to work out what 'the leader' wants), but it can lead to very unpleasant consequences – for example, the Crusades, fundamentalist states, etc. Even Hitler appealed to God for his policy against the Jews when he wrote: 'And so I believe today that my conduct is in accordance with the will of the almighty creator. In standing guard against the Jew I am defending the handiwork of the Lord' (Gilbert, 1987: 28). Whether people actually genuinely believe they know what God wants or whether they have any insight into the fact they are using the 'idea of God' to simply back up and give authority to their own prejudices is unknown. As in therapy, the depth of our self-delusions and deceptions can be hard to fathom.

Suffering as punishment   But we need to come back to suffering and consider how suffering has become incorporated into themes of dominant-subordinate, obedient-disobedient. In fact, for a long time suffering has, in some quarters, been seen as punishment for sins or violation of the rules imposed by authorities (such as God). For example, a patient whose child died in a cot death thought this was God's punishment for a previous abortion. In fact it is not that uncommon for depressed people to have a vague (and sometime acute) sense of being punished. Therapists may see this as projected super-ego, but the fact is people experience it as external to them – a punishing other as the reason for their plight. In this category God is typically punitive and vengeful. The up-side is that 'do the right thing' and one may not only avoid punishment but get rewards – entry to heaven. Perhaps the idea of the policeman in the sky has helped to maintain social order and cohesiveness – although the evidence for such is unclear. It has certainly helped the dominant few maintain order for their own interests.

Suffering as punishment for violation of rules has been used to explain all kinds of problem. Take, for example, the fact that most of us know we are not in some kind of paradise – but far from it. If you start with the idea that God must be good and he must have created paradise first, then something must have gone wrong. Many blamed Eve. Indeed, our relationship with God (at least in Judaism and Christianity) did not get off to a good start. There was the problem of the apples affair and seeking knowledge. Not only did God withdraw in anger, he was in a rather vindictive frame of mind that day and had it in for Eve and her descendants. As Burford and Shulman (1992) note:

> Unto the women he said, I will greatly multiply thy sorrow and conception; in sorrow thou shalt bring forth children; and thy desire shall be to thy husband; and he shall rule over thee. (Genesis 3: xvi)

So the pain and risk of childbirth is apparently not an evolved feature, hammered out by selective pressure and paid for by many millions who died in childbirth, but a punishment. The vindictive, authoritarian attitude was to pervade much early Christian teaching, so that St Ambrose (AD 340–397) writes:

> Adam was led to sin by Eve and not Eve by Adam. It is just and right that women accept as lord and master him whom she led to sin. (Burford and Shulman, 1992: 17)

The point here is that these people (males mostly) were trying to find out why life was so terrible; where did paradise go? Answer – we lost it because we were bad and angered the almighty. Women were seen as the cause of humans' fall from paradise. Other blameworthy villains are, of course, the devil. Indeed, the history of psychiatry is a history of, at first, doing battle with the devil (casting out of demons), and lately, ignoring the spiritual side of human yearning altogether in favour of Prozac (Zilboorg and Henry, 1941). None the less, the idea that we are born in sin is still surprisingly common – and it is someone's fault, but not God's.

Atonement or payback   Vengeance always involves making the 'other suffer'. So 'suffering as punishment' can be to allay vengeance – to atone, to be redeemed and accepted again. In suffering the person is somehow paying back something, repaying a debt and earning forgiveness. St Augustine was clear that only God's grace could redeem us for we are by nature sinners. His approach was an intensely submissive and 'pleading' kind of relationship with God. St Augustine's confessions may have inspired generation upon generation to fall on their knees seeking grace – and probably was a key text in giving rise to the darker side of repression of the passions. The point here is how powerfully the very ancient form of a dominant-subordinate relationship – a form of relationship that goes back to the reptiles – is projected into spiritual questions and how punitive it can be.

It is interesting that in many other religions, suffering and punishment are constantly juxtaposed. Even in Buddhism there is the concept of karma which arises from past sins. Suffering in this life is either to earn good karma, or work off bad karma from past lives (Harvey, 1990). Related to the idea that suffering somehow builds up Brownie points, is 'suffering as a test'. In other religious contexts God tests the faith of his people by making them suffer. They prove themselves by not defecting. This relates to the various trials and ordeals people are prepared to put themselves through to prove they are 'of the right stuff'. Again this is an archetypal theme which has little to do with spirituality. Tests of loyalty often require subordinates to make sacrifices and such behaviours can be found in families, political groups, the mafia and so forth. Sometimes conscious, sometimes not, this strategy is one of ingratiation – one humbles oneself, rids oneself of personal pride in an effort to win favour with the dominant.

Caring sacrifice For some, intense submissiveness can be associated with holiness. Indeed, it is common for us to confuse submissive behaviour with caring behaviour. One gives in to another's wishes and construes this as caring. It is the martyr complex. A variation on this theme is, 'I will suffer to save you.' This is the self-sacrifice idea and can exist in various hero complexes. Jesus, of course, was supposed to have suffered to take our sins away (and prove himself as a loyal, submissive son to his father). One view on this is that Jesus was required to do this because of a particular archetypal orientation to 'God as an idea'. The extraordinary psychology of a preaching of love with the brutalizing reality of crucifixion is (presumably) designed to activate the psychology of gratitude in followers. When gratitude is around guilt at disobedience is not far behind. This may work as long as one does not ask why one needed saving in the first place.

Spiritual maturation or advancement A favourite in my house was suffering to learn lessons. We are put on this earth to evolve in spirit. We do this by passing through countless incarnations and gradually learning various lessons. Suffering is part of growing insight and spiritual maturity. Why we need to learn these lessons in the first place was never explained. Nor was the reason for forgetting each previous life each time we touched down again. The idea of a cosmic recycling of consciousness has increasing appeal in our ecologically aware world, although for the life of me I cannot see what could be learned in schizophrenia or being born brain damaged. And at times some of the explanations are frankly psychopathic and sadistic. For example, a young man who became paraplegic following an accident might be seen as a spirit who has to learn humility or passivity etc.

Looking at the above, if suffering has purpose then it is rarely seen as the result of the incompetence, indifference or sadism of some distant creator. To give suffering meaning requires that the focus is on the victim, the sufferer, not the one who may cause it. This is common to all the above.

Psychological explanations

Psychologists and therapists, of course, are not immune to adopting similar attitudes to those who have a tendency to blame victims for their suffering – for example, AIDS sufferers are paying the price of a wayward sexuality. In this case there may not be some external deity who is inflicting suffering, but more the sufferer is 'getting punished' for irresponsible past actions. This is suffering in the service of retribution – or even envy (as when we see the wealthy fall from grace). And I wonder how many therapists have not been confronted with patients who have inspired the thought that 'they bring their problems on themselves'.

Psychologists and psychotherapists have their own explanations for psychological suffering and these depend on both personal philosophies and the chosen school of therapy. Most of us would, I suspect, feel that much serious psychological suffering can be traced back to bad upbringing and/or bad genes. Even so, we still think that it is the sufferer (victim) who will have to take action to make their suffering less.

Psychological maturation   The belief in a need to mature is as common in psychological therapies as it is in spiritual ones. We talk in terms of developmental difficulties, or a need to develop certain abilities or insights – we are lacking something, we need to grow and our suffering will change or reduce when we mature whatever it is we need to. More brutally, perhaps some people suffer (it is suggested) because they are immature and need to grow up – or, in more politically correct language, 'need an opportunity to grow'. Gut (1989) certainly makes an interesting case for the possibility that some depressed patients can actually use their depressions to grow and mature. I am never sure, however, how much the depression added to the process (apart from leading to the seeking of therapy) and how much the patient was simply able to use a therapeutic relationship, and could have done so, depressed or not. Still maturation does take place in therapy and Jung (1993 [1954]) was also of the view that at times people simply grow out of their problems. Derived from Piaget's theories, Kegan (1982) has given a fascinating overview on this point that with each maturational transition something must often be given up before something is gained.

Irrational thinking   Another source of suffering is negative thinking (for example, Beck et al., 1985). Cognitive therapists are keen on the old Greek adage that 'it is not things in themselves that disturb us but the view we take of them'. Like much else in life, this view is fair in small measures but should not be taken to extremes. Try the motto out in Bosnia in 1994 or Auschwitz in 1944. It remains theoretically sound, of course, but not necessarily useful or compassionate. In less polite terms, people suffer because they lose perspective and exaggerate.

Avoidance   Another view of suffering, shared by behaviourists and existentialists alike, is that we suffer because we engage in too much avoidance behaviour (Yalom, 1980). We live inauthentic lives, fearful to stand up for ourselves, are guilt- and shame-ridden, disowning our own feelings and desires, fearful to take on our anxiety, and hoping to cheat the fates by hiding away. Again in many ways this makes sense and patients can benefit greatly from a therapist's encouragement to confront and face (rather than run from) that which is feared. Indeed, learning to face our fears is a common antidote to neurosis in mythology, psychoanalysis and behaviour therapy.

Suffering and a science of things and mechanisms

Efforts to cure suffering come in many forms. One is via scientific means (for example, medicine). Here suffering is mostly related to 'errors in functioning'. Although humans have kept a wary eye on their deities, they have also tried to help themselves, to fix things. It has been obvious to many, for many hundreds of years, as we lurched from one holocaust to another, from one plague and set of famines to another, that if God had the power to do anything about our plight he could not or would not use it. We are on our own and have to work it out for ourselves. Of course, the hierarchy of the churches has not always been keen on this, and many a brave person was tortured or disposed of at the stake as a heretic for pushing such views.

But science did in the end prevail so that by the sixteenth and seventeenth centuries Europe was dowsed in a new fever of excitement. The Age of Enlightenment, as it became called, raised the hope that through the use of reason and science humans could begin to exert more control over the vagaries of destiny and fate. The Enlightenment was, according to Gay's (1977) brilliant historical account, the age when humans regained their nerve in their own abilities. Via reason, education, individual effort and inventions, by the accumulation of human knowledge and understanding, the world and the people in it could be changed. It was an age of the decline of mysticism, of a commitment to science and social reform, with a renewed belief in the value of human effort to improve things – an ideal that humans could be the masters of their own fate. This renewed optimism was captured by Descartes. According to Gay, Descartes was appalled by the suffering of the poor and the loss of life in childbirth. He believed that science would enable men to become 'masters and possessors of nature' and science, and was:

> to be desired not only for the invention of an infinite number of devices that would enable us to enjoy without any labour the fruits of the earth and all its comforts, but above all for the preservation of health, which is doubtless the first of all goods and the foundation of all other goods of this life. (Gay, 1977: 6)

This renewed scientific confidence did not emerge alone for it was a cousin and aid to the Industrial Revolution. In fact they fed each other. The invention of new mechanisms, from trains and industrial machines to clocks and mechanical toys, was seen as offering a path to a better life. The fact that this scramble to 'make things' was to sentence many millions to a life of factory work – of drudgery and sheer misery – was overlooked. Capitalism's foothold, gained during the Enlightenment, was to cast very dark shadows over the socio-economic lives it touched, even while it promised release from famine and disease. And now, of course, from the day we go to school to the day we retire we are encapsulated in a world created by competition, where losers and the less able are increasingly dumped, shamed or ignored. Our fight against world famine and disease seems as far away as ever, and the ideals of a free and just world are in tatters as the multinationals cruise the world looking for cheap labour. All this is a long way from the close-knit hunter-gatherer communities we evolved in for millions of years.

The type of science adopted was classical Newtonian science, as the Industrial Revolution dictated it should be – focused on mechanisms and inventions. And so it was natural to think that almost everything could be understood by understanding how 'mechanisms work'. This vision was to pervade not only much of science, but also medicine and psychology. And it has to be said, the understanding of the 'mechanisms of the body' was to offer big medical rewards in the fight against disease. Today we are at the threshold of a new age where the mechanisms of mind and body are understood as never before; neuro-imaging and the genome project are all distant offspring of Newtonian science. And like most things it will cast shadows as well as light. Not all are easy with the idea of our genetic code being read like a book, and the ethical issues it raises are increasingly complex (Kitcher, 1996).

Along with the industrial changes, medical sciences were at the forefront of the Enlightenment, promising freedom from some of nature's crueller tricks of disease and famine (Gay, 1977). Although some feminists point to the masculine language of the time, noting Bacon's famous phrase that nature should be 'put to the rack' and made to give up her secrets, this was not mere masculine posturing but an angry reflection on the suffering inherent in nature. Without awareness of the historical contexts in which the Enlightenment was born it is easy to see such sentiments as arrogant and misguided. The great hope of the Enlightenment was healing, to make things better, and indeed medicine became one of its champions, known as *the great art of healing* (Gay, 1977). It promised considerable relief to human suffering.

When, in the late nineteenth century, Freud and Nietzsche offered up new versions of human nature, of dark forces up to mischief out of sight, the first glimmerings of our disquiet resounded. A shimmer of doubt was felt not only about our creations but by the creators themselves – it was perhaps ourselves we should know better before projecting ourselves on to the world as inventors and improvers. Yet the mind was not immune to the 'fix it' mechanistic view. The idea that suffering comes from faulty mechanisms (the body) to be cured with new inventions (drugs) is still with us. Even Freud's theories were basically mechanistic, focusing on 'energies' dammed and repressed, and he believed that one day neurosis would be understood in terms of its chemical substrates.

Although born with noble ideals, the Enlightenment had many unfortunate and unforeseen effects. Industrializing nations choose to use much of their wealth to privilege the few, and develop and use increasingly destructive weapons to protect their interests. But in science, the Enlightenment was the age of splits. Biology, philosophy, psychology, sociology and medicine came to exist as separate disciplines with their own theories and methods, their own texts and heroes, and their own truths. Like blind men touching the elephant, their new information at times seemed to contradict that found by other groups. When people tried to reintroduce holistic medicine they were often forced to the fringes. 'Real science' was always mechanistic. To peer into biology, to study genes and neurochemistry, always seemed more like real science than the study of social attitudes or political beliefs. Efforts at the integration of 'the sciences' usually met with challenges from those whose territory one had encroached upon. And there were no good careers to be found here because science and research monies followed specific methodologies and the discovery of specific mechanisms. So serious has the split in our understanding of human behaviour become, that in 1986 Eisenberg could criticize psychiatry and psychology for developing two sciences: a brainless one and a mindless one, and never the twain shall meet.

We remain deeply split in our approach to suffering. Our understanding of, say, how social factors affect biology, is still in its infancy (for example, James, 1997; Kemper, 1990; Wilkinson, 1996). When we talk about the despair of poverty we should be able to think in terms of both 'loss of control' and low 5-HT (the brain chemical, Serotonin). To forget that people subjected to various stresses have changed biologies is to be too 'in the head' when the pain is very much in the whole experience of self in the world. As for multi-dimensional working, with some important exceptions (Lazarus, 1981) this is notable by its absence (Gilbert, 1995). As for me, I'm in favour of drugs, psychotherapy, social change, feminism and rock and roll. I have never felt comfortable operating purely in one domain.

Problems of the evolved mind

Freud noted that the (recent) developments of science had dealt humans three narcissistic blows. We have been dethroned from the centre of the universe – nothing but an insignificant outpost in one of many millions of galaxies; we have discovered that we are descended from apes and before them DNA sludge; and thanks to psychotherapists we've found out that we do not know, nor are in control of, our own minds (Slavin, 1985). And the pace of change is hardly likely to slow. Psychological therapists of the next century are going to have to come to terms with our growing understanding of neurochemistry, the role of genes in behaviour and emotions, an increasing demand for drugs without side-effects to 'produce happiness', and an increasingly individualistic approach (some would say responsibility) to self-fulfilment. We will, I believe, also need to be far more vocal in addressing the issue of social-environment toxicity – that some social contexts can seriously damage your mind (Belsky et al., 1990; James, 1997; Wilkinson, 1996).

The rest of this chapter will focus on Freud's second narcissistic blow – the discovery that we were not created *de novo* by God but are evolved creatures. I think we still have problems in coming to terms with our history. It is important because the human brain retains many vestiges of structures that stretch back to the reptiles (MacLean, 1990). At a simple level, anxiety, depression and paranoia can each affect us because we are biologically capable of these experiences. They are evolved potentials that in some measure serve adaptive ends (Gilbert, 1989; Marks, 1987). An animal with no capacity for fear would not survive long.

But the implications of an evolved mind extend well beyond our potential for negative emotions. Because the human mind is the product of a process of shaping and adapting for millions of years, it is made up of old and new structures. Bailey put it boldly when he said:

> . . . We must acknowledge that our species possesses the neural hardware and many of the motivational-emotional proclivities . . . of our reptilian ancestors, and, thus our drives, inner subjective feelings, fantasies and thoughts are thoroughly conditioned by emanations from the R-complex. The reptilian carry-overs provide the automatic, compulsive, urgency to much human behaviour, where free will steps aside and persons act as they have to act, often despising themselves in the process for their hatreds, prejudices, compulsions, conformity, deceptiveness and guile. (1987: 63)

The full impact of the implications of evolutionary thinking is yet to engage us (Dixon, 1987; Wright, 1996). The recognition that we have a reptilian brain in our heads and therefore should handle it with caution is still a novel idea. If we create societies of each against each, that speak directly to the reptilian brain, then, like some Faustian opera, we will summon the demons. And these will not be raging crazy people, but rational ones who believe that whatever harm they do to others or resources they grab for themselves, they are right, fair and justified in their actions.

The early psychoanalytic theorists were aware of the importance of understanding the mind in some kind of evolutionary context. Freud was keen on the idea of the 'primordial image' and Jung developed the ingenious idea of archetype, but few therapists recognized just how far back the structures in the human brain stretch (although see Janov and Holden, 1975; and more recently Gilbert, 1989, and Stevens and Price, 1996).

Archetype and the creation of meaning

Jung rejected Freudian libido theory because of his growing belief that the psyche was not made up of competing drives, as Freud insisted, but rather of various internal meaning-making and action-directed systems. These systems he called *archetypes*. Archetypes influence the unfolding of development (for example, to seek care, to become a member of a group, to find a sexual partner and become a parent, and to come to terms with death – Stevens, 1982). He believed the source of many of our passions and aspirations to be archetypal. He also suggested that many archetypal themes of human life are enacted in the rituals, stories and myths of all societies. The themes of grief, envy, shame, jealousy, guilt, deception, remorse, distrust, abandonment, exploitation, heroism, sacrifice and so forth will be known in all cultures.

Interestingly, Jung's friend and Nobel prize-winning author Herman Hesse, never really understood all the controversy about archetypes. He said that as far as humans are concerned, writers had known about them for centuries and if they could not feel them within themselves and connect with them, they could not write stories. In fact, story-telling is an interesting human activity for despite thousands of years and many differences in cultural styles and language, from the ancient Egyptian, Greek, Indian and Chinese cultures, we are able to understand the themes of all the stories humans have ever written. Whatever the textures of culture they are surface textures that do not cover the deeper meanings of human life.

Jung postulated that humans, as an evolved species, inherit specific predispositions for thought, feeling and action. These predispositions exist as foci within the collective unconscious and serve to guide behaviour, thoughts and emotions. He distinguished the *collective unconscious* from the personal by suggesting that the *personal unconscious* represented those aspects of personal experience that are rooted in real events. They had at one time been conscious but were either forgotten or repressed. The collective unconscious, however, is the realm of the inherited universal predispositions; the internal motivating systems that form the bedrock of species-typical behaviours. Jung suggested that:

> . . . The archetype in itself is empty and purely formal, nothing but a *facultas praeformandi*, a possibility of representation which is given a priori. The representations themselves are not inherited, only the forms, and in that respect they correspond in every way to the instincts, which are also determined in form only. The existence of instincts can no more be proved than the existence of the archetypes, so long as they do not manifest themselves concretely. With regard to the definiteness of the form, our comparison with the crystal is illuminating inasmuch as the axial system determines only the stereometric structure but not the concrete form of the individual crystal. This may be either large or small, and it may vary endlessly by reason of the different size of its planes or by the growing together of two crystals. The only thing that remains constant is the axial system, or rather, the invariable geometric proportions underlying it. The same is true of the archetype. In principle, it can be named and has an invariable nucleus of meaning but always only in principle, never as regards its concrete manifestation . . . (1972: 13–14)

So Jung was first and foremost concerned with those various universals common to humanity (Stevens, 1982). He attempted to articulate the internal psychic mechanisms that, across various cultures and time, brought into existence (into relationship) various universal life themes, myths, rituals and stories. These life themes – for attachments, seeking sexual partners, joining groups, forming social ranks, worshipping gods, etc. – arise, he argued, from some kind of pre-wiring, or preparation, of our psychology. Thus, Jung saw the mind as a mixed structure made up of various motives and modules.

Currently, the language used to describe the innate mechanisms that guide animals towards certain goals (for example, mates, territories and care of offspring etc.) is *strategies*. Strategies have built in 'calculators' that monitor signals and give an emotional value to them. For example, in a conflict situation, where there is going to be a winner and a loser, it is adaptive for the loser to give up before serious injury. So a strategy of 'submit to the stronger but challenge the weaker' might be a crude primitive strategy (Gilbert, 1992; Hinde, 1982). Whether we call them strategies or archetypes, the key idea is that humans come equipped with motivational systems to help them desire and seek out certain outcomes.

Evolution, motives and social roles

To outline how I consider suffering in therapy, I need to go on a brief tour of some evolutionary ideas. It is often because of our social needs for certain types of relationship that we feel so much psychological pain – be this because we feel unlovable, unwanted, inferior, rejected, in a state of grief or whatever. According to evolution theory, many of our basic social motivations (for example, for care, love, access to sexual partners, self-presentation, fear of shame, need to belong and social status) are linked to social outcomes and forms of social relating that are, or were, evolutionarily meaningful. For example, in general, we tend to feel good when cared for, when we have a sense of belonging within a group, have access to friends, gain respect and prestige, and find a mate. And we tend to work hard to achieve these things. Negative emotions, on the other hand, are often associated with not being cared for and feeling alienated from others – an outsider, losing or failing to obtain respect and not finding or losing a desired mate (Gilbert, 1989, 1995; Nesse, 1990); that is, feeling bad is often related to losing control over these evolutionarily meaningful outcomes and social roles.

The evidence is increasing that many social motives have been shaped via the solution of certain (interpersonal) problems – for example, care of the young, gaining sexual access, belonging to a group. The psychological mechanisms that help guide our motivational and evaluative processes can be seen as the deep structures of the mind (Barkow et al., 1992; Buss, 1991, 1995; Muran and Safran, 1993; Slavin and Kreigman, 1992). These in turn give rise to certain forms of relating – for example, attachment, friendship, sexual, dominate-subordinate – and although they may vary from culture to culture, they are none the less recognizable as salient forms of relating in all cultures (Fiske, 1992).

From a review of the literature on social relating, Gilbert (1989) suggested that some of our main biosocial goals are concerned with: *care eliciting/seeking and receiving, care giving, cooperating and sharing* and *competing/ranking and gaining status*. A similar classification has been empirically derived from research on interpersonal problems (Barkham et al., 1994). I didn't explore sexual relations as these can be integrated into

TABLE 7.1   *Core social roles*

	See self as	See other as
Care receiving	Obtaining inputs from other(s): care, protection, safety, reassurance.	Source of: care, nurturance, protection, safety, reassurance.
Care giving	Provider of: care, protection, safety, nurturance.	Recipient of: care, protection, safety, nurturance.
Cooperation	Of value to other, sharing, appreciating, contributing, affiliative.	Valuing, contribution sharing, appreciating, affiliative.
Competition/rank	Contestant, status/rank, inferior-superior, hostile-attractive.	Contestant, status/rank, inferior-superior, hostile-attractive.

Source: Gilbert, 1992, with kind permission of Lawrence Erlbaum.

relationships in different ways, but clearly they are important (Buss, 1995; Ridley, 1994). Evolutionists might consider the origin of these forms of relating using different language – such as kin altruism, reciprocal altruism (McGuire and Troisi, 1998) – but most agree that many of our most salient goals and ambitions revolve around *biosocial goals* and *needs for social success.* These derive from evolved social motives – for example, to form attachments, find a sexual partner(s), belong to a group, gain status and avoid being inferior/shamed/rejected.

Biosocial goals can be construed as *motivations to create certain forms of relating between self and others.* They may be experienced as something one is aiming for – for example, to gain status, sex, care for a child. They show themselves in particular types of *social role.* Birtchnell (1993), who takes a different approach to that presented here, makes the point that we need to distinguish between how we wish to relate to another and another may wish to relate to us (giving rise to either complementary or anti-complementary interactions). Another distinction is between active and passive forms of relating.

Leaving aside the issue of fulfilments of relating obtained via fantasy, biosocial goals can usually only be realized through social interactions and social roles. Thus, we can focus on evolutionarily meaningful, core (arche-typal) self–other relationships in terms of how the self and other(s) are construed and engaged. These are given in Table 7.1.

The inner world is thus made up of various models and ideals concerning self–other relationships – for example, wanting to be cared for, loved, be accepted by a group, to nurture others, obtain status, find a sexual partner who won't defect – and thus indicating needs and potential threats, frustrations and disappointments. And from a psychotherapy point of view these are the basic themes that patients seek help with.

Mentalities

Various roles require our internal mechanisms to be organized in certain ways. For example, to be sexually successful requires an individual to be attentive to possible signals in the environment (availability of a mate), to be motivated to engage in some action, to coordinate some kind of action plan(s) that begins with courting and ends in mating, and so forth. In other words, thoughts, plans, feelings, behaviours and, in humans, fantasies are all involved in the single goal of 'sex'. One can go through the same process for any type of relationship – for example, signal detection, arousal of motivation, action plans and feedback as to whether a plan is working (Oatley, 1992). Such internal co-assemblies, which operate for specific roles, might well be called archetypes, but in order to separate out the biosocial goal pursued from the internal mechanisms that are coordinated in its pursuit, I have called the latter 'mentalities' (Gilbert, 1989, 1992, 1997). The basic assumptions of mentality theory are given in Gilbert (1992: 335–6), and are (with minor word changes for clarity) outlined again here:

1 Core structures and predispositions for social interactions are inherited. As such they are part of a human collective set of potentials for social behaviour and experience. They are also subject to genetic variation, but are shaped and integrated in a personality via social experience.
2 Biosocial goals, like personality traits, represent various orientations to social life – to seek care, to give care, to lead, etc. Hence a biosocial goal is actualized via the enactment of a role.
3 Mentalities represent the various co-assemblies of affects, action tendencies and cognitive styles that are necessary to pursue biosocial goals and to operate successfully in given roles. They provide for our inherent meaning-making abilities or competencies. At any point in time these co-assemblies will be patterned by conditioned responses, memory systems, internal self–other models and so on.
4 Mentalities also act as signal detectors that allow the individual to track the environment and analyse information to see whether a role is being successfully enacted. For example, the crying of a child may activate in the parent the care-giving mentality, leading to a searching for the infant and a preparedness to comfort and sooth, or protect. The successful enactment of a role is associated with positive affect. Unsuccessful enactment is associated with negative affect.
5 Negative affect can then be seen as information that a goal has not been achieved, or that a role is not being enacted successfully or has been thwarted. This may lead to a change of strategy.
6 Like Jung's concept of archetype, biosocial goals and mentalities represent no more than a potential, and their exact articulation and interaction with each other depends on both genetics and learning (experience). These co-assembled linkages of thought, affect and behaviour can be considered as a mentality.

Mentalities are the internal mechanisms that enable individuals to pursue certain biosocial goals. At times, patients can present with what appears to be key components of a mentality missing. Consider, for example, a person who has no empathy for others. Be this acquired, genetic or both, this 'lack' leads to serious problems in caring for others, perspective-taking and so forth. It may also affect the preparedness to hurt others during conflict situations (Miller and Eisenberg, 1988). Other problems might present when a person is so fearful of hurting others, and being rejected, that they suffer from a lack of competitiveness and assertiveness.

This leads to the now-familiar idea, used by many therapists, that some forms of psychopathology are related to over or underdevelopment of certain key dimensions or functions within a person (see, for example, Beck et al., 1990). Because a state of mind often involves combinations of motives, affects and evaluations, referred to here as mentalities, it is legitimate to speak of, say, a competitive mentality (involving strong motives to gain status and win conflicts; thinking in terms of winner-loser, inferior-superior, dominant-subordinate), or a caring mentality (involving empathy, sympathy and compassion, and a focus on the needs of the other). In narcissistic people there is a high degree of competitiveness, noted in their motivation to be better than others and their being easily shamed and/or enraged by attacks on status (defensive responses to put-down), and an underdevelopment of caring and cooperation. Indeed, various approaches to psychopathology suggest that problems arise when a person engages in certain self–other relationships either too much or too little – for example, too much submission might be involved in depression, or, as noted here, too much dominance and too little care of others in narcissistic and psychopathic disorders (see Barkham et al., 1994; Beck et al., 1990; Birtchnell, 1993; Blackburn, 1988; Horowitz and Vitkus, 1986; Kiesler, 1983).

The social themes of psychological suffering.

For each of the social roles noted in Table 7.1, it is possible to identify certain types of themes in presenting problems. In a similar way to those who see humans as having many sub-personalities (Rowan, 1990), this approach suggests that humans are a mosaic of possibilities rather than single, uniform selves. The 'type of self' one experiences oneself to be at any particular time reflects deep archetypal themes. Different types of psychological problem are associated with different biosocial goals and mentalities. For example, people who are highly focused on needing others (care seeking) and see themselves as weak and incapable, tend to experience the self as vulnerable to abandonment, needing protection from others, and so forth. In contrast, those who are fearful of needing others, or find needing others an aversive experience, may present with themes of compulsive self-reliance or fear of being a burden. A summary of the typical kinds of themes that go with certain biosocial goals and mentalities is given in Table 7.2.

It can be noted that various themes relate to that part of self-experience that is either feared or absent. For example, those who fear being alone might become dependent and avoid facing being alone. Those who fear failure might become perfectionist or competitive and avoid gracefully

TABLE 7.2   *Relationship between mentalities and themes*

MENTALITY							
Care eliciting		Care giving		Cooperating		Competing	
Self	*Other*	*Self*	*Other*	*Self*	*Other*	*Self*	*Other*
Need	Provider	Provider	Need	Share	Share	Winner	Loser
				Exchange			

BASIC DEPRESSIVE THEMES

Abandonment	nurturer	outsider	aggressor
protection	rescuer	insider	avenger
emptiness	martyr	rebel	inhibitor
victim	guilt	moralist	special
compulsive self-reliance	protector	immoralist	excessive standards
burdener			subordinate
			defeated
		shame	shame
		envy	envy

Source: Gilbert, 1992, with kind permission of Lawrence Erlbaum.

accepting his or her limitations. Those who fear being excluded and shamed might become excessively compliant. Those who fear others having power over them might become individualistic and competitive etc. So this approach suggests that at times certain themes are compensations for fears of who or what the self might be. The point is that all of us have these as 'archetypal possibilities'; they are not, in themselves, evidence of pathology for they are very basic to the human psyche.

We can briefly consider a case: Mary was depressed and felt herself a victim to many people in her life. Her husband did not give her enough attention and she was very self-critical. Cognitive therapy worked a little, but it was also necessary for her to think about what she was avoiding. She was fearful of getting into a rage in case she lost control or became unlovable – for more than anything, she said, she wanted to be lovable. She was fearful of contacting her own wish for revenge and her desire to be boss and have other people do what she wanted. Considering some basic themes of human experience, and the fact that maybe more work was needed on those aspects of herself she would rather keep in the shadows, was helpful. It can be useful, I think, if people can loosen their personal identification with these inner themes and see them as 'part of the self' because we are constructed that way. The better we know them and own them the better we can cope with them. Jung called this individuation.

Of course, themes can only be rules of thumb, therapeutic concepts that should not be seen as evidence of actual internal schema, or entities in a rarefied form (Gilbert, 1992). All I am saying here is that we can think about ourselves in relationship with others in a number of describable dimensional ways. In other words, the origin of some of our most distressing and passionate experiences lies in the way our brains have evolved and how it engages a social world. It is our evolved brains that make possible different types of social relationships.

Going to extremes

Although there may be much debate on the precise types of biosocial goal, there is less debate on the general principles. Be it attachment behaviour (Bowlby 1980, 1988), our tendency to form ingroups and outgroups with a need to belong (Baumeister and Leary, 1995), or the ease with which we form hierarchical relationships (Gilbert, 1992) or even religious ones (Wenegrat, 1990), human relationships do typically take on certain patterns.

Humans, however, are also a species of extremes. At some point, nobody knows exactly when, we became self-conscious and highly creative. Neanderthals were bright, with bigger brains than we have, but they were not particularly creative. They did the same things for thousands of years. It is not to them that cave art can be attributed (Mithen, 1996). Some argue that it is language that made the difference and allowed us to think in special ways. Be that as it may, it is our creativity and ability to amplify on a theme that is crucial. But our restless creativity, linked to a brain of primitive strategies, can spell trouble. While animals can rely only on their own physical selves to deter intruders or defend status, humans can use knives, guns and nuclear weapons. While animals may be sexually excited by certain signals, humans can invent pornography – first in art and later on video. While animals seek out caves to protect themselves from the elements, humans build hotels, mansions and cities. What makes us the species we are is our creativity. But not only can this creativity be a source of wonder and change, it can also be a source of great distress and terror, for we can internally create representations of ourselves – to ourselves – that contain the worst archetypal elements. We can tell ourselves that we are losers, failures, damned and outcast. We can ruminate on vengeful thoughts and feelings – which may be directed at ourselves and/or others.

Humans can give new life to archetypal possibilities by the way they think and construe them. The fact that we can activate and amplify our internal archetypal 'selves' with thoughts and fantasies is of great importance. Let me use a sexual example. Suppose you break from reading this book and lie on your bed for ten minutes engaging in your own 'hot' sexual fantasy. What happens? Well, after a while you may note various stirrings in your body and you may begin to feel sexually aroused. If we could drop in on you and take a few biological measurements we would find various changes in your body. Not too surprising. You would not accept, I think, that these feelings are only your imagination. You would talk more about your internal experience, and this might include a mixture of feelings (in the loins), impulses, desires, memories and images, thoughts about who might fancy you and so on. The point of the story is that certain kinds of imagination bring to life, in our bodies and biological selves, response systems which are preparing for certain kinds of action – for example, to copulate, to fight, etc. So our imagination has access to biology. Our internal imaginations, our appraisals and so on can produce 'felt-experience' by virtue of the internal patterns they evoke and are associated with. We cannot pretend these are similar processes to a computer without a body. In old terms, we can summon angels or demons within ourselves. Not surprising then that in Buddhism the control of thinking and fantasies is central because it is so easy to activate the negative dimensions of the psyche.

There is another side to this example. Suppose you did go and lie on your bed as I suggested, and obtained the result indicated, this would mean that my writing (some months earlier) had affected your sexual system! What's interesting is that although we have a written and spoken language to convey meaning, most often this language aids in the manipulation of our affect and archetypal process. The origins of mass movements that can explode into violence or social change can be orchestrated by a few who manipulate the affect of followers via ideas and personal displays (Lindholm, 1993). If these ideas are focused on the need for specialness, the archetypal strategies for ingroup behaviour, with paranoia to outgroup, people may be activated into hate. Logic, compassion and reason step aside. People do not even recognize that they have allowed themselves to become driven by primitive limbic brain processes. They talk instead about being inspired, fired up, chosen, on a mission, etc.

Our capacity for amplification of the archetypal has given rise to many wonderful things: art, music and science. There is no doubt that although we share 99 per cent of the same genes as chimpanzees, chimpanzees are not 99 per cent human. The extra cognitive, imaginal qualities of humans, which allow for forethought and planning, are key to our success. But as Jung suggested, all light casts a shadow, and the shadow of these capacities is that they can be used for good or ill.

Retaliation   The suffering we bring to others is often called 'evil'. Evil acts are often socially defined – killing the enemy is heroic, killing your own side is evil. Evil is not some supernatural force or even (usually) a deformity of character, but is related to clear evolutionary (Watson, 1995) and social meanings (Baumeister, 1997). And those who bring suffering to others rarely, if ever, see what they do as evil or bad, but justified. If I were to pick one domain of functioning where our tendency to go to extremes is as sad as it is terrifying, it is in retaliation behaviour. There are many names for it including vengeance, a domain very under-researched yet of extraordinary importance for understanding the suffering we heap on others (Frijda, 1994; Scheff, 1994). Even in small measure the desire for vengeance, and lack of forgiveness, can be very destructive of relationships.

From an evolutionary point of view it is adaptive for animals to have a retaliation response. An animal who knows that a conspecific will retaliate against any violation of its control or domain is kept in its place (assuming that the violator does not believe it is stronger and can easily subdue any retaliation attempt). Fear of retaliation helps keep the peace. However, retaliations need to be seen to be credible and are common interactions in non-human primates, school playgrounds and (some) marriages. But humans can be obsessed with retaliation and the fear of retaliation, and in extraordinarily vindictive and sadistic ways. Retaliation is often seen as part of pursuing justice. Indeed, the words justice and justified have the same root. Not only can retaliation be an individual process (we can ruminate on revenge), but it can be a collectively shared ritual that conveys multiple meanings. Consider public burnings during the inquisition. Such public rituals were not only designed to rid the church of trouble-makers, but to act as a deterrent to others and a statement of power. To me it is a remarkable but sad fact that to this day there are some who remain terrified of some form of hell (God's retaliation and vengeance on disobedient subordinate sinners). From its inception hell has excited great sadistic fantasies, of burning, devouring, ripping and torture without end and there are many who are all too ready to threaten others with it. Even Jesus utilizes retaliatory vengeance. According to a recent version of the Bible (and there have been so many one loses count), Matthew 13 (40–43) talks about a parable based on sowing seeds and removing weeds. Jesus says:

> And as the seeds are pulled up and burned in the fire, so it will be at the end of the age. The Son of Man will send out his angels, and they will weed out of his kingdom everything that causes sin and all who do evil. They will throw them into the fiery furnace where there will be weeping and gnashing of teeth. Then the righteous will shine like the sun in the kingdom of their father. He who has ears, let him hear.

Jesus supposedly (I say supposedly because these words were written many decades after his death), repeats the threat in the parable of the net. To our modern ears we hear such threats and think them terrible (I hope). It was a fifteenth-century monk who pointed out that while there was one soul burning in hell his own soul could not be at peace until that one was freed. And we could go further and ask, while there is hell on earth (in the wars and diseases of humankind) how could anyone be happy in heaven? Yet according to Gascoigne (1977), by the Middle Ages one of the *pleasures* of being 'saved' was that one could look down on those in hell. Personally, I believe that monotheistic religions, with male-dominant gods, are always vulnerable to recruiting this master-slave, saviour-punisher archetypal psychology. So I'll stick with Buddhism and Star Trek.

It is not (only) our potential for compassion that marks us as humans, though this is important (but very poorly studied); rather it is the ways the human mind picks up archetypal themes and amplifies them. By a process of rumination (holding an image or thought in the mind) and creativity we can generate real inner and outer terrors. What an evolutionary approach helps us with is to understand what these basic themes are.

Therapy and suffering

The whole basis of cognitive therapy is to help people identify particular (negative) thoughts that lead to distress, and by challenging the basis of these thoughts, gain control over them. This is to try to help people stop dwelling on and recruiting negative emotions via negative thinking. Cognitive therapy 'works' to the extent that people can train themselves to do this, but if the affect from the more primitive brain is too great then there are problems with this approach (Linehan, 1993). We are both mechanism and not mechanism, in the same way perhaps that the piano is a mechanism but the music is not. The hope that by understanding the mechanisms of the brain we would solve psychological ills has proved naive. Violence and depression are not so rationally solved as smallpox. The reason for this is that many (but not all) forms of violence, depression and anxiety are not illnesses in that they are not alien to the system, but rather are very much part of its basic *modus operandi* (Nesse and Williams, 1995).

People often ask about the implications of evolutionary approaches to therapy. In many ways these are very similar to other therapies (see Gilbert, 1992, 1995). As Jung (1993 [1954]) points out, psychotherapy often involves various issues: sharing things that have been hidden because of shame; being educated into new ways of thinking and reasoning; developing understanding and insight about the self; being prepared to face fears and terrors; and maturation, growth and individuation. In regard to the therapeutic relationship, patients may want more than empathy. They want to be treated in a way that harks back to old archetypal issues – of wanting to be accepted and have a sense of belonging (Bailey, 1988; Bailey et al., 1992).

For me, two key ingredients of psychotherapy are: (a) to help people live with others more harmoniously – or leave; and (b) to have greater freedom to move within themselves; to be more self-accepting. This latter freedom comes in part from recognizing that what is in us, is not, in an odd sense, us at all. What I have inside me is the temperament I was born with, a set of archetypal potentials reaching back to the reptiles and a host of memories, emotional experiences, at times rather odd fantasies, and values that have been given to me. In large measure I (as I feel myself to be) created few of these things. Given this, freedom seems a most perplexing thing. If I am depressed or anxious my state (reflecting the arousal of some biological inner programme) controls my thoughts as much as my thoughts control my state. An extrovert man loves parties. One day he is struck by depression. When a party invitation arrives in the post he is filled with dread and anxiety. He does not go. His depression controls him.

Some patients are helped by what Jung called 'owning their own shadow'. People may need to recognize their own sadism, their own power games, their own martyr acts and their own cowardice, etc. I suspect that owning these things is easier if people don't identify with them. In other words, the sadistic part of me (which could be seriously activated if, say, anyone harmed my children) is there because evolution found it useful to put this system in. 'I' did not put it there or create it, but I can experience it working in 'me'. Thus, there is nothing bad about me for having this capacity, but I can choose to explore how much this capacity operates, in, say, my thoughts for vengeance when someone really 'pisses me off'. I can then choose to stay with such thoughts and ruminate on them, or give short shrift to my reptilian brain. If I feed this archetypal system it can get more powerful. In mythology we would say that we can summon demons. In the sci-fi movie *Forbidden Planet*, the doctor plugs into a mind machine and discovers that the Krill could 'summon monsters from the Id'. A wonderful phrase. In twentieth-century psychology we say that our thoughts and fantasies activate negative schema. However, it is well to recall that activation of some schema or archetypes in certain situations do become like demons. For example, we more or less know that the First World War was a war nobody wanted, but it came down to face-saving.

The competitive mentality thinks in terms of inferior-superior, winner-loser, etc., and this may be where our tendency to rate things comes from. In many ways we need to learn how to avoid rating ourselves, for this makes enemies of the inner self. From our earliest experiences we develop a tendency to rate ourselves, mostly in social rank and conformity terms. When individuals are depressed they often think of themselves as inferior compared to others. A depressed person may label or judge him or herself, and/or has judgements made by others that are not only negative but also suggest that he or she has been allocated a low rank and/or low status position. Personal and social judgements such as unlovable, worthless, bad, weak, inadequate, useless, etc. are in effect assignments of low status, rank and worth. In contrast, when people are hypomanic they often think of themselves as superior to others. But those who simply feel happy – say, on holiday – do not use the competitive mentality to think about themselves. This archetype is not active. So with depression, helping people recognize that thinking 'the self is worthless' is an old archetypal pattern and is no more a reflection of a real self than any other pattern, can be helpful (Gilbert, 1989, 1997).

It is now recognized that if patients can understand themselves, so that at least they are less self-attacking in their behaviour and thoughts, this can be helpful. There is some wisdom in the view that if, in the midst of this cruel and fickle world, people refuse to self-hate and instead try to act compassionately to themselves and others, then they might bring some kind of relief. Compassionate rationality is probably a key ingredient of change (Gilbert, 1997). Internal freedom (to own and explore one's own internal fantasies and feelings) may be increased by a reduction in internal shaming and global self-blaming. Healing may be dependent on the development of *compassion to self and others*. Rating the self 'good or bad' and rating parts of the self 'good or bad' only splits the self. Compassionate ownership allows a more integrative approach to the various different archetypal possibilities – for example, shame and pride, love and hate, etc. When people remove the global labels on self and others of bad, weak and worthless, and learn to loosen the tight control they put on themselves and others, their inner lives become less full of dread. In this way we can face ourselves and others as mosaics of complex rather than simple possibilities, and can come to know ourselves and others without shame. We become not ashamed to be frightened, not ashamed to give in, not ashamed of our sexual feelings, not shamed by our gender or colour, not shamed by our limitations and mistakes, not shamed by our needs for others' affection, not shamed by our hatreds. Whether we choose to act on them is a different matter but we are likely to have more control if we understand them. As the cognitive therapists say, a mistake is just a mistake, a sexual feeling is just a sexual feeling. Things are what they are but it is our judgements of them that make them shaming. And although our judgements of these inner things often come from the cultures we live in, still we can reclaim our right to be complex beings and refuse the one-dimensional spaces on offer. If we don't criticize and attack ourselves we can move within our minds without 'off limits' signs cropping up all over the place. We can learn to face what we need to face. And when we are more familiar with ourselves and more accepting of the complex of our different 'possibilities of being', we may be less shaming of others and more aware of how shame constrains, inviting concealment and deception.

Finally, although power, shaming, violence, exploitation and many of the horrors that are so easily released on the world all exist as archetypal possibilities, it is important to note that we are not powerless in the face of such archetypal forces. Indeed, the archetypes feed from the social signals presented to them. People who grow up in loving supportive environments are likely to become loving and supportive of others, whereas those who do not experience these environments develop different archetypal styles (Belsky et al., 1990).

If we want a caring environment/world then we must train our children for it, and not send mixed messages that say 'be nice to others but be number one'. Hoffman notes that the moral education of children should involve a greater focus on the other:

> One thing moral education can do is teach people a simple rule of thumb: Look beyond the immediate situation and ask questions such as 'What kind of experiences does the other person have in various situations beyond the immediate one?' 'How will my actions affect him or her, not only now but in the future?' and 'Are there people, present or absent, who might be affected by my action?' If children learn to ask questions like these, this should enhance their awareness of potential victims of their actions who are not present and to empathise with them to some extent. To increase the motivational power of empathic identification, children should also be encouraged to imagine how they would feel in the absent victims' place, or to imagine how someone close to them would feel in that person's place. (1991: 288)

Such education is on the feelings of the other not the self. And these principles might apply in therapy. For example, when we are looking at whether someone (say a violent person) can feel guilt, we are looking at whether they experience sympathy and empathy and can feel remorse. Guilt often involves sadness for the other in a way that shame and humiliation may not. Thus in treating anti-social behaviour therapists may need to find ways to help people to empathize and at times to acknowledge and work with guilt (Marshall et al., 1996). According to the model outlined here, this requires the activating of care-giving mentalities.

Conclusion

I started this chapter with reflections on suffering and noted how histori-cally our passion for 'a just world' has been encapsulated in many religious ideas. The down-side of this is beliefs that suffering must be a punishment, test or journey because bad things can't 'just happen'. Personally, I believe that in 100, maybe 200, years (I wish it were sooner), the indoctrination of children with certain types of belief – including fears of retribution, punishment and a dominant male ruler in the sky – will be seen as forms of abuse. But the power of projection is such that others will probably con-tinue to try to reinvent them – they are archetypal themes.

With the advent of science, however, we have had to increasingly con-front the issue that many people suffer from pure bad luck – bad genes, infections, being born in the wrong place at the wrong time and their social place, etc. Helping others depends on what we do and the resources we invest. So I am a believer in the Enlightenment and science. None the less, the idea that it is through our own efforts that we will prosper has not been without its critics. Ehrenfeld (1978), for example, wrote on the 'arrogance of humanism' with the view that the race to improve things simply destroys our relation with nature, our traditions and disconnects us from social communities and intimate relationships. Industrialization clearly does this in so many ways. But there does not have to be this trade-off. An evolu-tionary view would say the same – that humans evolved in close-knit communities, close to nature, and that many of us wish to get back to something similar (with a few modern comforts, of course).

By now I will have conveyed that to me the undercurrent of life is dark. There are great pleasures indeed if one is lucky enough to have the privilege of health and good parenting, but for many life is not so much fun. When it comes to helping troubled people, it helps me to remember that we are all caught up in human dramas that are millions of years old. Passions of love and hate are all part of our brain mechanisms. To the best of my ability I try not to bring any pre-judgement as to what will be helpful – for this person it might be a drug, for that person someone to talk to, for another it might be some highly technical therapy based on aspects of thought challenging (Gilbert, 1997). I do believe that we need to be more bio-psychosocial in our pursuits.

For the society in general evolutionary theory carries a warning, a warning that has existed in countless mythologies: this is to be careful what you create for you may summon the demons. Evolution theory tells us that we cannot create any social environment we like and expect people to prosper or behave morally. Once you give up the search for social justice and fairness, stop investing in the fabric and infrastructures of society, fail to see that harsh competitiveness often creates more and more losers, as the last 15 years of conservative government did, then you are indeed calling on the less savoury elements in all of us. The demons appear slowly at first, with increasing crime rates, rising ill-health among the poor, pollution and more fearful weapons, and abandonment of responsibility and segregation by the wealthy. The process can continue into sci-fi nightmare visions of social decay and despair – *Blade Runner* worlds. Evolution theory tells us what we are likely to be up to given half a chance; our social infrastructures can help us avoid the grosser aspects of our potential. To my mind the evidence is overwhelming; the social and political provide the stage and cloth for the archetypal and biological.

References

Armstrong, K. (1994) *A History of God.* London: Mandarin Books.

Atkinson, J.M. (1993) 'The patient as sufferer', *British Journal of Medical Psychology*, 66: 113–20.

Bailey, K. (1987) *Human Paleopsychology: Applications to Aggression and Pathological Processes.* Hillsdale, NJ: Lawrence Erlbaum Associates.

Bailey, K.G. (1988) 'Psychological kinships: implications for the helping professions', *Psychotherapy*, 25: 132–41.

Bailey, K.G., Wood, H. and Nava, G.R. (1992) 'What do clients want? Role of psychological kinship in professional helping', *Journal of Psychotherapy Integration*, 2: 125–47.

Barkham, M., Hardy, G.E. and Startup, M. (1994) 'The structure, validity and clinical relevance of the Inventory of Interpersonal Problems', *British Journal of Medical Psychology*, 67: 171–86.

Barkow, J.H., Cosmides, L. and Tooby, J. (1992) *The Adapted Mind: Evolutionary Psychology and the Generation of Culture.* New York: Oxford University Press.

Baumeister, R.F. (1997) *Evil: Inside Human Violence and Cruelty.* New York: W.H. Freeman.

Baumeister, R.F. and Leary, M.R. (1995) 'The need to belong: desire for interpersonal attachments as a fundamental human motivation', *Psychological Bulletin*, 117: 497–529.

Beck, A.T., Emery, G. and Greenberg, R.L. (1985) *Anxiety Disorders and Phobias: A Cognitive Approach.* New York: Basic Books.

Beck, A.T., Freeman, A. and Associates (1990) *Cognitive Therapy of Personality Disorders.* New York: Guilford Press.

Belsky, J., Steinberg, L. and Draper, P. (1990) 'Childhood experiences, interpersonal development, and reproductive strategy: an evolutionary theory of socialization', *Child Development*, 62: 647–70.

Birtchnell, J. (1993) *How Humans Relate: A New Interpersonal Theory.* Westport, CT: Praeger.

Blackburn, R. (1988) 'On moral judgements and personality disorders: the myth of psychopathic personality revisited', *British Journal of Psychiatry*, 153: 505–12.

Bowlby, J. (1980) *Loss: Sadness and Depression. Attachment and Loss*, Vol. 3. London: Hogarth Press.

Bowlby, J. (1988) 'Developmental psychiatry comes of age', *American Journal of Psychiatry*, 145: 1–10.

Burford, E.J. and Shulman, S. (1992) *Of Bridles and Burnings: The Punishment of Women*. New York: St Martin's Press.

Buss, D.M. (1991) 'Evolutionary personality psychology', *Annual Review of Psychology*, 42: 459–91.

Buss, D.M. (1995) 'Evolutionary psychology: a new paradigm for psychological science', *Psychological Inquiry*, 6: 1–87.

Dalai Lama (1993) *Power of Compassion*, Wembley Lectures (audio cassettes available from: Tibet Foundation, 10 Bloomsbury Way, London, WC1A 2SH).

d'Aquili, E. and Newberg, A.B. (1996) 'Consciousness and the machine', *Zygon*, 31: 235–52.

Dixon, N.F. (1987) *Our Own Worst Enemy*. London: Routledge.

Ehrenfeld, D. (1978) *The Arrogance of Humanism*. New York: Oxford University Press.

Eisenberg, L. (1986) 'Mindlessness and brainlessness in psychiatry', *British Journal of Psychiatry*, 148: 497–508.

Fiske, A.T. (1992) 'The four elementary forms of sociality: framework for a unified theory of social relations', *Psychological Review*, 99: 689–721.

Frijda, H.H. (1994) '*The lex talionis: on vengeance*', in S.H.M. Van Goozen, N.E. Van de Poll and J.A. Sergeant (eds), *Emotions: Essays on Emotion Theory*. Hillsdale, NJ: Lawrence Erlbaum Associates. pp. 263–89.

Gascoigne, B. (1977) *The Christians*. London: Jonathan Cape.

Gay, P. (1977) *The Enlightenment. An Interpretation: The Science of Freedom*. New York: W.W. Norton & Co.

Gilbert, M. (1987) *Holocaust: The Jewish Tragedy*. London: Fontana.

Gilbert, P. (1989) *Human Nature and Suffering*. Hove: Lawrence Erlbaum Associates.

Gilbert, P. (1992) *Depression: The Evolution of Powerlessness*. Hove: Lawrence Erlbaum Associates.

Gilbert, P. (1993) 'Defence and safety: their function in social behaviour and psychopathology', *British Journal of Clinical Psychology*, 32: 131–54.

Gilbert, P. (1995) 'Biopsychosocial approaches and evolutionary theory as aids to integration in clinical psychology and psychotherapy', *Clinical Psychology and Psychotherapy*, 2: 135–56.

Gilbert, P. (1997) *Overcoming Depression: A Self-Help Guide Using Cognitive Behavioural Techniques*. London: Robinsons.

Goodall, J. (1990) *Through a Window: Thirty Years with the Chimpanzees of Gnome*. London: Penguin.

Goswami, A. (1993) *The Self-Aware Universe: How Consciousness Creates the Material World*. New York: Simon and Schuster.

Gut, E. (1989) *Productive and Unproductive Depression: Success or Failure of a Vital Process*. London: Routledge & Kegan Paul.

Harvey, P. (1990) *An Introduction to Buddhism: Teachings, History and Practices*. Cambridge: Cambridge University Press.

Hinde, R.A. (1982) *Ethology*. Glasgow: Fontana Paperbacks.

Hoffman, M.L. (1991) 'Empathy, social cognition and moral action', in W.M. Kurtines and J.L. Gewirtz (eds), *Handbook of Moral Behaviour and Development. Vol. 1: Theory*. Hillsdale, NJ: Lawrence Erlbaum Associates. pp. 275–301.

Horowitz, L.M. and Vitkus, J. (1986) 'The interpersonal basis of psychiatric symptoms', *Clinical Psychology Review*, 6: 443–70.

James, O. (1997) *Britain on the Couch: Why We're Unhappier than We Were in the 1950s – Despite Being Richer*. London: Century.

Janov, A. and Holden, E.M. (1975) *Primal Man: The New Consciousness.* New York: Crowell.

Jung, C.G. (1972) *Four Archetypes.* London: Routledge & Kegan Paul.

Jung, C.G. (1993 [1954]) *The Practice of Psychotherapy*, 2nd edn. London: Routledge.

Kaufman, G. (1989) *The Psychology of Shame.* New York: Springer.

Kegan, R. (1982) *The Evolving Self: Problems and Process in Human Development.* Cambridge, MA: Harvard University Press.

Kelman, H.C. and Hamilton, V.L. (1989) *Crimes of Obedience.* New Haven, CT: Yale University Press.

Kemper, T.D. (1990) *Social Structure and Testosterone: Explorations of the Socio-Bio-Social Chain.* New Brunswick: Rutgers University Press.

Kiesler, D.J. (1983) 'The 1982 interpersonal circle: a taxonomy for complementarity in human transactions', *Psychological Review*, 90: 185–214.

Kitcher, P. (1996) *The Lives to Come: The Genetic Revolution and Human Possibilities.* London: Penguin.

Lazarus, A. (1981) *The Practice of Multimodal Therapy.* New York: McGraw-Hill.

Lindholm, C. (1993) *Charisma.* Oxford: Blackwell.

Linehan, M.M. (1993) *Cognitive-Behavioral Therapy Treatment of Borderline Personality Disorder.* New York: Guilford Press.

MacLean, P.D. (1990) *The Triune Brain in Evolution.* New York: Plenum Press.

Marks, I.M. (1987) *Fears, Phobias and Rituals: Panic, Anxiety and their Disorders.* Oxford: Oxford University Press.

Marshall, W.L., O'Sullivan, C. and Fernandez, M. (1996) 'The enhancement of victim empathy among incarcerated child molesters', *Legal and Criminal Psychology*, 1: 95–102.

McGuire, N. and Troisi, A. (1998) *Darwinian Psychiatry.* New York: Oxford University Press.

Milgram, S. (1974) *Obedience to Authority.* New York: Harper and Row.

Miller, P.A. and Eisenberg, N. (1988) 'The relation of empathy to aggressive behaviour and externalising/antisocial behaviour', *Psychological Bulletin*, 103: 324–44.

Mithen, S. (1996) *The Prehistory of the Mind: A Search for the Origins of Art, Religion and Science.* London: Thames and Hudson.

Muran, C.J. and Safran, J.D. (1993) 'Emotional and interpersonal considerations in cognitive therapy', in K.T. Kuehlwein and H. Rosen (eds), *Cognitive Therapies in Action: Evolving Innovative Practice.* San Francisco: Jossey-Bass. pp. 185–212.

Nesse, R.M. (1990) 'Evolutionary explanations of emotions', *Human Nature*, 1: 261–89.

Nesse, R.M. and Williams, G.C. (1995) *Evolution and Healing.* London: Weidenfeld & Nicolson.

Oatley, K. (1992) *Best Laid Schemes: The Psychology of Emotions.* Cambridge: Cambridge University Press.

Ridley, M. (1994) *The Red Queen: Sex and the Evolution of Human Nature.* London: Penguin.

Rowan, J. (1990) *Subpersonalities: The People Inside Us.* London: Routledge.

Scheff, T.J. (1994) *Bloody Revenge: Emotions, Nationalism and War.* Boulder, CO: Westview Press.

Slavin, M.O. (1985) 'The origins of psychic conflict and the adaptive function of repression: an evolutionary biological view', *Psychoanalysis and Contemporary Thought*, 8: 407–40.

Slavin, M.O. and Kreigman, D. (1992) *The Adaptive Design of the Human Psyche: Psychoanalysis, Evolutionary Biology, and the Therapeutic Process.* New York: Guilford.

Stevens, A. (1982) *Archetype: A Natural History of the Self.* London: Routledge & Kegan Paul.

Stevens, A. and Price, J.P. (1996) *Evolutionary Psychiatry.* London: Routledge.

Watson, A. (1995) *Dark Nature.* London: Penguin.

Wenegrat, B. (1990) *The Divine Archetype: The Sociobiology and Psychology of Religion.* Lexington, MA: Lexington Books.

Werth, J.L. (1996) *Rational Suicide: Implications for Mental Health Professionals.* Washington, DC: Taylor and Francis.

Wilber, K. (1983) *A Sociable God.* London: New Science Library.

Wilber, K. (1996) *The Atman Project: A Transpersonal View of Human Development,* 2nd edn. Wheaton: Quest Books.

Wilkinson, R.G. (1996) *Unhealthy Societies: The Afflictions of Inequality.* London: Routledge.

Williams, M. (1997) *Cry of Pain.* London: Penguin.

Wright, R. (1996) *The Moral Animal: Why We Are the Way We Are.* London: Abacus.

Yalom, I.D. (1980) *Existential Psychotherapy.* New York: Basic Books.

Zilboorg, G. and Henry, G.W. (1941) *History of Medical Psychology.* New York: W.W. Norton & Co.

8

Counselling with Holocaust survivors

Judith Hassan

I have often asked myself the question – why me? Why did I enter this world of extreme trauma with Holocaust survivors? After all there were many therapists who have a personal connection to the Shoah (word for Jewish Holocaust) and could have undertaken this task.

Looked at objectively, there were many issues related to timing which came together to contribute to my involvement. Some will be looked at in this chapter. Perhaps more importantly for me was my own search for meaning in the work I had undertaken, and which had been emphasized for me during my social work training. It was not enough just to be a technically good social worker. There needed to be some purpose in my work, as well as a spiritual component which gave meaning to my working in a Jewish organization.

My previous six years of working in the Jewish Welfare Board prior to my professional training had been a preparation for the real reason I had entered that organization. The re-emergence of the survivors' trauma over 40 years after the event, seemed to coincide with my need to engage in a challenge which kept my attention for the last 20 years. The unblocking and metamorphosis which had gone on for me during my training, had opened me up personally and professionally. It had given me the confidence to confront the incomprehensible.

Just as this entry into the world of extreme trauma turned on its head assumptions about human behaviour, it also threw me off balance in terms of my professional skills. While my chapter is devoted to 'counselling Holocaust survivors', the meaning of this is very different to our traditional understanding of this method of working. The redefinition of therapy emerges during the course of the chapter, and the final outcome breaks with many of the rules and boundaries which had governed my thinking.

Twenty years later I view the world through different eyes. I have witnessed the most unspeakable horrors as the survivors' stories have been told to me. It is impossible to remain the same, and hence my professional development had to mirror the adaptive processes necessary to survive. The chapter will reveal how this evolved.

The background – the beginning of the story

> Listen to survivors, listen to them very well, they have more to teach you than you them!
>
> Elie Wiesel (1982)

What I have to say is based on years of reaching out to survivors, sitting with them, struggling with them and with myself to find a source of healing and working together. There are no set techniques. I can only share the journey I have been on with survivors which began when I qualified as a psychodynamically trained social worker who entered this world beyond metaphor, the metamorphosis which had to take place for me to be accepted as a non-survivor, and how my way of working with survivors has evolved. Even after all these years, I feel a sense of humility, a need to learn more. This chapter will hopefully open up discussion among those of us concerned with survivors, so that we can reflect on our work and the approaches which seem to help survivors. The next ten years are crucial, as the older generation of survivors will be dying. Working with survivors demands courage and commitment, as we face with survivors the dark shadow of their Holocaust past. Such work is demanding, it threatens our professional complacency, and makes us look inwards on ourselves, our Jewish identity and our personal relationship to this most heinous event in history. Over the time I have been involved with survivors, it has been extremely difficult to engage counsellors, therapists and others from the helping professions in this special area of work.

Why this should be so gives a clue to the discomfort survivors often bring, not only to the general community – they have been called 'disturbers of the peace' (des Pres, 1976) – but also to the professionals. There have been attempts to fit survivors into existing therapeutic frameworks, particularly psychodynamic counselling and therapy models. Yet we find the fit is not quite right (Steinberg, 1989).

When we enter the world of the survivor we enter a world of chaos. The camp experience was a mad world, a world turned upside down in which the unimaginable happened. The abnormality and extremity of the experience is beyond the comprehension of those of us who were not there. The climate of the time when I began this work was very much influenced by a medico/psychiatric model of understanding the survivor, namely 'survivor syndrome'. To make some order out of the chaos, survivors were classified as suffering from syndromes and symptoms. The feeling expounded was that to have gone through the unimaginable, survivors must be damaged irreparably. The emphasis was therefore on diagnosis rather than understanding. The survivor seen as a victim was described as sick and psychologically unwell, and this view was compounded by the compensation claims procedure, which necessitated psychiatric assessment to find causal connections between the experience in the camp and the current situation.

Such classifications of survivors' suffering did not allow them to be seen as individuals. To protect themselves, some professionals erected defence mechanisms to ward off the uneasy feelings which survivors brought them. Professionals I have been in touch with at conferences we have held, have often said they felt deskilled by the survivor, and also isolated in the group of professionals they worked with. Sometimes they rationalized their brief involvement as a professional decision not to unearth the traumatic events which may have lain dormant for 40 to 50 years. Others would say it was too late to begin this work and it should have been done a long time ago.

For those survivors who were offered therapy, their behaviour was often misunderstood. For example, the processes which bereaved people go through while mourning have been well documented and are well known. There was some recognition of the need to deal with the 'unfinished business' related to the massive losses survivors had been through during and after the Holocaust. Loss of community, loss of family, loss of dignity, loss of identity and, for some, loss of childhood. These are but a few of the deprivations that survivors had to deal with. An opportunity to grieve, perhaps for the first time, may have brought some relief. However, what was often not understood by the professionals, was the survivors' need to go over what had happened again and again – to bear witness, so that it should never happen again. The survivor was speaking not only for him or herself but all those who perished. In this sense, there could be no completion of mourning. Instead of understanding this phenomenon, survivors were seen as suffering neurotic symptoms and a very pessimistic view emerged concerning the possibility of healing and recovery. This view was upheld by Krystal (1984) in his article on 'Integration and self-healing in post-traumatic states'.

With such emphasis on psychopathology, plus the intransigent role of many therapists, it is not surprising that my early entry into the world of the Holocaust was a difficult and limited one. The emphasis in my social work training had been on one-to-one psychodynamic counselling using primarily a psychosocial model. The expectation was to engage a client in a trusting relationship, and then to use and develop the relationship to address the problems the client was presenting. When I returned from my secondment to the Jewish Welfare Board (JWB), as it was then, I worked in a new area, which happened to be one in which a large number of refugees and survivors were living. Many elderly refugees were coming forward and asking for help often of a practical nature, for example waiting to go into sheltered housing or requesting a volunteer because of loneliness. Often their level of anxiety was excessive to the request they were making, and I began to pick up on an underlying agenda which was bringing them in at that point in time. There may have been a current loss – such as bereavement, loss of health or retirement – which seemed to be reactivating earlier losses which had not been mourned. I realized that many of these refugees were without family, and their asking for help was also related to a fear of dying alone and that no one would know what had happened to them. My earlier experience in the JWB had encouraged me to work with elderly people's emotional problems; chronological age was no reason for not engaging the client in this process – if the client was willing to undertake the work, so was I. Some were, as a result, able to die more peacefully.

There were no techniques to fall back on except my training and to follow my intuitive thoughts. I was fortunate at that point to meet Professor Shamai Davidson, a psychiatrist working with survivors in Israel who helped me to feel heard and understood when dealing with these elderly refugees. He helped me to look at my own inner world, at what effect these refugees were having on me in relation to my own mother's and grand-parents' experience in the Holocaust; what it meant for me as a Jew to work with people who had been persecuted as Jews. I began to understand why I had been drawn to working in a Jewish agency – I thought that as a professionally qualified social worker I could have worked in any agency. I cannot overstate the impact Shamai Davidson had on the course of events, and how the spiritual changes that were going on in me strengthened me to want to know more and to understand how I could help.

I became conscious of the fact that while many elderly refugees were able to come forward and ask for help and could accept counselling, almost no camp survivors came through our doors. I naively thought that as their suffering had been even greater than refugees', they would have more need for emotional support through our counselling services. I have learned since why survivors kept away. First, anger towards the Jewish community for not having done enough to help them when they needed it after liberation; then, the indifference of Jews towards their suffering; their feelings towards authority and institutions; their fears of weakness and vulnerability which asking for help would imply. Factors such as these meant that the organization became a fortress for me, with the survivor outside and myself locked inside.

The story – from intransigence to creativity

I would like to pause here, and illustrate by means of a well-known story (one which we used in our workshop in January 1992 on Creative Approaches to Working with Holocaust Survivors) how the adaptation happened which converted a possibly intransigent situation into a more positive, creative and meaningful one in relation to my work with camp survivors in particular.

The story is the one which separates heaven from hell. In hell people stand around a pot of food using spoons which are so long that they cannot feed their hungry mouths. Consequently, the people starved and died. In heaven, we see a similar situation of people standing around a pot. Instead of feeding themselves, they feed each other, and are nourished and so live.

There is considerable evidence from the literature that prisoners in the concentration camps began to form themselves into pairs or groups to help each other to survive. Elie Wiesel (1982), among many others, maintained he would not have survived alone. Shamai Davidson (1984) in his paper on human reciprocity amongst Jewish prisoners in the death camps; Victor Frankl (1978) in his book *Man's Search for Meaning*; and Terrence des Pres (1976) in his book *The Survivor*, all emphasize the therapeutic value of the group in helping survivors pass another minute in the camp. This mutual support and social bonding allowed the survivors to 'feed' each other. Though hell was all around them, aspects of goodness remained in some form and sustained them during moments of despair.

As I immersed myself in this world of the survivor, I came to realize that my tools (training and experience) were often ineffective in reaching survivors. Despite the spoon (tool) I was using being beautifully made and well constructed, if I could not feed the empty mouths it was of little value. The spoon was straight and did not bend. It could only be used in a certain way.

Survivors suffered, but could not be reached. The community was dying without being heard. A wasteland had developed between the professional and the survivor. Somehow I had to translate the adaptation process to the current situation in practice.

A turning point in my work came when a camp survivor (not a client) came to see me, having heard my name through an organization in Israel (ELAH). This survivor asked me to help her set up a self-help group for some camp survivors who wanted to come together to meet socially. They did not want therapy, but to help each other mutually. They would not need to explain why they were there. In this self-help group I was an honorary member (a non-survivor).

My usual professional role was not functional in this situation. As the survivors shared their experiences with each other in this informal social setting, in a venue of their choice, I could hear the hidden agendas but had no authorization to deal with them. I observed, I listened, I learned – survivors came to know me personally. Not only was I individualized to them, but I began to see each one as having gone into the Holocaust, experienced the Holocaust and adapted after liberation to what had happened in quite a unique way. This was not a homogeneous group – they both shared with each other, but also fought with each other. My willingness to cross the professional boundary and act as a facilitator for this group to happen played a major part in all the subsequent work which followed.

What I realized from that experience, which lasted over two years, was how this approach was much more meaningful for the survivors (who now numbered about 40 in the group) because the mutual support aspect of it mirrored the camp experience. Many survivors in other groups have felt 'outsiders' and that they did not belong. In this group they did belong. The non-clinical, informal atmosphere in which we had refreshments together, and shared in parties, was a more acceptable environment for the therapeutic work to take place, and the group members felt 'normalized'.

In this group there was music, there was laughter and enjoyment. They celebrated being together but at the same time their Auschwitz numbers were clearly marked on some of their arms. What it taught me was how amidst horror and adversity it was possible to sing, to share a joke, and this had helped pass one more minute in that hell they had been through. What had worked in their past experience in the camp seemed to have relevance today. The past was acknowledged particularly in the first two meetings, but subsequently the focus shifted to being actively involved in this group and having a collective voice, for example in opposing fascism.

The survivors were not only strengthened themselves, but they gave me the impetus to look for the creative side of the survivor that had helped him or her to cope. The spoon (tool) was starting to take on a different shape and form. I was learning from them how to 'feed' them, and how they could thrive. Their individuality and their strengths which they had used for so many years unsupported by professionals, taught me how to free both them and myself from the incarceration in psychopathology.

Thus emerged the image of the survivor free from the 'victim' label. The empowerment which the mutual support generated in the first self-help group laid the foundation for the philosophy for the Holocaust Survivor Centre (HSC) which subsequently opened in London in January 1993. In this centre survivors are not merely recipients of services, but are actively involved in its fund-raising; its public-speaking programme, which involves going into schools and talking about their Holocaust experience to children; its users group; befriending each other; and recording their testimonies for posterity. This is a social centre in which the most popular events are playing cards and eating together, as well as celebrating the Jewish festivals. Together they commemorate Yom Hashoah, and together they warn others where fascism leads. Again, as in the earlier group, there are power struggles, but it is in this very dynamic that survivors feel alive.

How could such 'feeding' and 'nourishment' then be translated into a therapeutic setting such as Shalvata*? I believe there are no short cuts – the many years I spent in building up trust with survivors opened up the possibility for some of them to come forward and ask for individual, family and group work.

---

* Shalvata means 'peace of mind' in Hebrew. Shalvata was opened by Jewish Care in 1990 to offer a specialized therapy service for those who went through the Holocaust and may be suffering from long-term effects of severe trauma.

Shalvata – peace of mind

I would like to dwell here on the setting of Shalvata compared to my earlier work as a social work team leader at the Head Office of Jewish Care (formerly Jewish Welfare Board). The thought that went into Shalvata has been an essential ingredient to the possibility of developing this special service. The decor reflects a non-clinical atmosphere. It is light and airy, which is often commented on, especially by those survivors who were hidden in small rooms or those crowded in barracks. Nothing in Shalvata smacks of institutionalization – even a small detail like using china cups not plastic ones. The creative work which goes on means that art materials and musical instruments are visible, and this encourages us to think beyond talking as the only therapy. The multidisciplinary staff have developed an openness to work with me, whereas formerly I had often felt quite isolated in my work with survivors. They are very committed to the Jewish content of our work, which is symbolized by the choice of name of the centre. This naming of the centre is also a memorial to Shamai Davidson, whose own medical centre in Hod Hasharon bears the same name.

Jewish Care have always backed this work with Holocaust survivors as a priority for a Jewish Social Service, and this has enabled the work to develop. The non-statutory status of our organization means that we do not have the power that statutory workers have. The social work focus of the agency encourages a range of responses, using group and community approaches, and not just one-to-one counselling. As a voluntary agency we can act as a pressure group, and consequently empowerment as a concept and a focus for social change is in keeping with our voluntary role.

Shalvata as a system within a system provides the catalyst for our model of therapeutic work with survivors. With the development of the HSC next door to Shalvata, we have an ideal opportunity to overcome the organizational barriers which had imprisoned me before.

The separate entrances to the two centres means that survivors can make their first entry point through the non-threatening door of the social centre. They can join the varied social and educational programmes in the HSC, and for many this input is enough. Many have described it as a lifeline for them during their declining years. They feel at last they belong, and the HSC serves as some form of replacement for the lost communities in Europe, which many feel was their greatest loss. Their ability to enjoy themselves is perhaps their greatest victory over the Nazis.

I make it my job to sit with the survivors and have tea with them, and I encourage my staff at Shalvata to do the same. When there is a bereavement in the centre they offer support as a replacement family. Some of the survivors who know me from the earlier group take pleasure in showing me how much they enjoy this centre. Sometimes one of them takes me by the hand into the centre and shows me how she has prepared the tables for one of their many parties. The pleasantness of the surroundings reflects the dignity we wish the survivors to feel.

Since the HSC opened next to Shalvata, an increasing number of survivors feel at east to come forward and ask to see a member of the Shalvata staff. One recommends the other. The two centres running side by side means that the survivors can continue to 'feed' each other, but at Shalvata the 'dark shadow' of the Holocaust can be addressed through a range of different approaches. Some of these survivors have previously gone from therapist to therapist without their Holocaust experience being addressed. At Shalvata they begin to feel heard and understood.

The therapeutic tool is reshaped to 'feed' survivors

When a survivor asks to see me, I want to know who this person is, which journey have they been on, and which route are they currently on which has brought them to me at that moment in time. I have come to realize that no two survivors are the same – their experiences as children prior to the Holocaust have to be taken into account; also, what age were they when the Holocaust began; whether they were with their family during the war; which camp were they in; what support they got from others during this incarceration; what happened to them after liberation; what subsequent losses they experienced. These are but a few of the variables which differentiated the survivors from each other and affected their adaptation after liberation.

Survivors whom I did not meet through the self-help groups I have been involved with, have sometimes questioned how I could understand what they have been through – I was younger than they were and had not gone through a comparable experience. My answer to them is that I could not possibly know what it would be like to have gone through the hell of the death camps, but I would like them to teach me. Seeing the survivor as my teacher and my guide enabled a different relationship to be established. I would share with the survivor personal information about my own link to the Holocaust. They are not patients or even clients, but individuals whom we engage in a process which may lead to some healing. Robert Krell (1989), who himself is a survivor as well as a therapist, points out that, 'in therapy with Holocaust survivors and/or their children, the therapist may be sought out for precisely these reasons that make them feel some degree of intimacy is possible'.

Using the metaphor of a journey helps the therapeutic process to begin by looking together at a map of Europe as it was during the Second World War. This encourages the process of communication. Robert Krell supports such an approach and finds it an excellent tool to convey interest, and it helps to involve both the survivor and the worker in a joint venture.

Having engaged the survivor in a therapeutic process, it then becomes important to look at which route to take. Does the survivor want to go back to the past to work through some of the unfinished business, or does he or she want to look at strategies to help him or her to deal with the present? The more involvement the survivor feels in making choices as to which approach may be most meaningful to him or her, the less vulnerable and dependent the survivor feels, and this avoids the re-creation of the powerlessness of his or her victim past.

The survivor teaches us as professionals to be creative in our approaches. Sometimes the reality of reliving the trauma is too great and we have to find other ways of working through the emotions which the survivor has carried with him or her. In the camps there was ample evidence of the survivors' ability to transcend the horror of what was going on through their creative imagination. For example, a survivor told me that when she was starving, she could imagine eating a slice of bread. Another said that when he was exhausted from working, he could imagine he was asleep. We also have literature on how music, art and story-telling helped some survivors cope with their adversity.

Jews are often natural story-tellers, and if this had helped some to cope in the camps, perhaps it would have relevance to our current work. The testimony, for example, as I use it in practice, is not just a factual document of the survivor's life history. I encourage the use of metaphor and creativity to convey the unimaginable. I would now like to demonstrate how I have used such an approach with a survivor I have worked with.

Work with a camp survivor

Mrs E came to the Jewish Welfare Board originally at the point when her husband died. She was seen by a social worker who offered her bereavement counselling and wanted to help her to mourn. However, Mrs E could not make use of this counselling and terminated her contact. I then met Mrs E six years later in the original self-help group for camp survivors. We got to know each other informally, and she later asked if she could come and see me as she would like to write down what had happened to her during and after the Holocaust. She had never been able to tell her children what had really happened to her in Auschwitz-Birkenau and she wanted them to know.

We met regularly over several months and she would talk to me about her life before the camp, during the incarceration and after liberation. She thought her English was not good enough to write it down herself, so she would speak and I would write it up for her in the first person. Her imagery was vivid and contained the essence of her experience.

One day I was ordered to search through some clothing and chanced to find a diamond hidden away in a shoulder pad. Yet I could so easily discard it – it had no usefulness for me – it could not get me what I needed – the food that would sustain me. The diamond had no value in that world. The beauty of the diamond only reflected me as I really was – dirty and full of lice. (Survivor's testimony)

As well as the detail of the recording, it was also the process which was therapeutic. Mrs E was able to give something to me – she was helping me understand the incomprehensible. My recording seemed to demonstrate the success of her teaching. We shared the painfulness of what was recalled, and for the first time she felt heard. As a result, Mrs E was able to go on a trip back to Auschwitz with her daughter and a group of young people. The willingness of this group to listen to her in the watchtower in Birkenau gave meaning to her survival in that she had not survived in vain.

Mrs E's ego had been strengthened sufficiently through the self-help group and informal contact with me for this journey to be able to happen. By bearing witness to me and the group of young people as well as her daughter, some healing had taken place. Mrs E now participates in the HSC – she is one of the survivors involved in the public-speaking and education programme; she participates in the art class and enjoys the festivities as well as playing cards. I turn to her for advice about the HSC – I tune in to her strength and sense of justice and humanity. I owe a great debt to what she has taught and continues to teach me about survivors and surviving. Her dignity conveys a much more hopeful message to professionals than the pathological image referred to earlier in this chapter.

Mrs E, however, felt that she held on to her 'humanity' in the camp because her home life and early childhood experiences had been very positive for her. Indeed, the memory of her home and her parents helped to sustain her at times when all seemed to be lost. She was also together with her sisters, and they helped to keep each other going. Mrs E maintained and still keeps her orthodoxy, and her belief in God also strengthened her. These were the factors which 'fed' her during her incarceration.

Others I have worked with, however, went into the Holocaust at a much earlier age and had no memories to hold on to during the trauma and afterwards. These child survivors lost their childhood years as well as the other major losses they experienced. They have become 'missing years', and the sense of deprivation and abandonment for many I have been in contact with has at times been overwhelming.

If counselling were the only tool on offer, I am not sure whether we could have reached so many of the child survivors as has in fact been the case. I had encouraged a self-help group of child survivors to begin meeting at Shalvata even before the HSC began. I had felt that the Holocaust as experienced through the eyes of a child was very different to that experienced by the older survivors from the camps. There have been descriptions of children 'playing' in the crematoria, and Spielberg's film on Oskar Schindler creates an image of children using the spades for burying the dead as a see-saw. These children had to grow up fast, usually without parental models, and without the luxury of toys and a full stomach.

The overwhelming trauma has, they would agree, clearly scarred them. Nietzche once wrote, 'He who has a why to live for can bear almost any how' (quoted in Frankl, 1978). Was it possible to find meaning in a life so deprived and traumatized? I had to remember that most of these child survivors had coped, had worked, had raised families and many had become very successful active members of the community. These child survivors are, however, now reaching middle age and coming up to retirement – a major loss for anyone, but for a survivor possibly life-threatening because work meant survival in the camps.

My own belief in the possibility of healing when a child survivor turns to me at a time of crisis, seems to convey itself. The 'feeding' I receive from my consultant, Sonny Herman, as well as the organizational backing, sustain me to make some positive interventions.

Work with a child survivor – a hidden child

Again I would like to illustrate the process from my practice and show how feelings of helplessness can be contained. This survivor came to see me about 20 months ago. She had been a member of the self-help child survivor group which met at Shalvata, and I had met her informally. She therefore knew Shalvata as a setting which welcomed survivors and she felt comfortable being there.

I met her by chance one day when I happened to be in the area in which she lives. She spoke to me in the street and seemed very distraught. She told me her daughter, now in her early thirties, had been admitted to hospital and she feared for her life – she is a drug addict. She asked to come and see me at Shalvata and I encouraged her to do so.

As she came into my office, I noticed her smallness of stature, her very young appearance (she was in her early fifties). Looking at her, there was no evidence physically of her suffering – clearly this outward appearance had helped her to function until now, but something inside her was crumbling.

Much of the early work focused on her presenting problem about her daughter, and also her grandchildren. There seemed to be no boundary between herself and her daughter. It was her sense of powerlessness in relation to her daughter – watching her killing herself and not being able to do anything about it – that I tended to focus on.

There was considerable ambivalence about whether she wanted to look at herself, and there was never any pressure to do so. She then made a decision to continue seeing me to deal with the 'other Rachel' – the one who she was having difficulty controlling, the other side of herself which was now beginning to overshadow her. She said that she trusted me – she also knew another child survivor in the group who was seeing me and who had encouraged her to come.

As she began to talk about herself, it emerged that she had been a two-and-a-half-year-old child when she and her sister were placed in a convent in France. Her mother was deported to Auschwitz and she never saw her again. Her father had come to England but did not look for Rachel and her sister until after the war was over. In the latter part of this hiding experience Rachel's sister was placed somewhere else, and Rachel was entirely on her own in a cellar. The nuns only came in to feed her.

Once in England she was in a boarding school, which she felt were the best years of her life. She was with other children and enjoyed this new experience. However, tragedy struck again when her sister died of a brain tumour. Subsequently, years of both verbal and physical abuse by her father, and the unhappiness of home life with her stepmother, prompted Rachel to leave home when she was 18 years old. Her marriage was brief and not a happy one. She worked, looked after her daughter and found ways of coping. She dealt with the trauma of her experience by following hedonistic principles.

Rachel, therefore, had no stability in her life. She missed her childhood both in the convent and with her father, and constantly seemed to want to recapture it by having 'fun'. The sense of deprivation, abandonment and loss which she experienced were all suppressed in her mind, only to surface when the powerlessness of her current experience with her daughter served to act as a trigger to her earlier memories.

To go back to the past as a way of working through the trauma was discussed with her. She had to regulate what she could cope with. We looked first at what had helped her to deal with the trauma, and one way seemed to be through her art work. Quite early on in our weekly meetings, she brought me in some of her work. One painting depicted her and her sister in the cellar, and the drawing was as though it were done by a child, compared to her other works of art. This painting had been hidden away in her cupboard at home – she could not bear to look at it. She had brought it out of 'hiding' to bring to me, and we shared the experience of having it in the room. She then asked if I would keep it for her at Shalvata until she was ready to take it back.

Her ability to be creative and use her imagination to deal with the trauma has been encouraged during our work together. She stopped work and stopped looking after her grandchildren for her son-in-law, so that she could maximize her time and energy to confront the issues which were now more difficult to keep out of her present. In hiding, she had to keep silent so she would not be discovered – now she was finding her voice. She also began to write as well as paint.

She increasingly socialized with other child survivors who helped to 'normalize' what she had been through. She began to participate in some of the celebrations of the Jewish festivals, and gradually began making links to her Jewish roots, which she had lost contact with in her life. She commented to me one day 'whenever I come and see you I buy a kosher chicken'. We laughed together about this, but clearly her identity as a Jew was clarifying itself for her again. The integration of this part of herself has in my view helped the process of healing. Interestingly, her former attachment to a spiritual guru began to lessen, particularly as we began to focus on the ritualistic aspect of mourning and the 'burial' of her mother.

To reach this stage took one year, during which I focused on the nurturing side of our relationship: strengthening Rachel is how she took control over certain events in her life; supporting her by phone when she needed it; helping her make a claim to the German Government to increase her 'pension'; going with her to the German psychiatrist who needed to make the assessment; and getting financial help for her from World Jewish Relief to pay for some of her bills as her income was reduced during this time of our work together.

I was giving her an opportunity to become attached to me and to experience the security of an ongoing relationship. On the other hand, her involvement with other activities in the HSC meant her dependency was not solely on me, and consequently this reduced the vulnerability factor. The importance of working as part of a team, both with the Shalvata staff as well as with the coordinator of the HSC or associated therapists, is an essential part in helping the survivor to feel more integrated and contained.

This first year strengthened Rachel so that we could then move forward. As she became more attached to me she also became more angry with me at times of separation. The closeness she felt brought with it fears of loss and abandonment. Nevertheless, as Ornstein (1985) wrote: 'Feeling understood by the therapist fosters the development of self-object transferences . . . only when such a rehabilitation of the self has occurred can the process of mourning begin.'

Reconnection with an uncle from Israel (her mother's brother) opened up the subject of what had happened to her mother – had she ever had a Jewish burial? We began to look at the possibility of putting her mother's name on her sister's grave, and saying Kaddish for her mother. First we had to find the sister's grave in the East End of London. Here again we went out of the office setting and visited the cemetery. Sonny Herman, who is both Rabbi and psychotherapist, accompanied us. The sister's grave was unmarked and unidentified. Sonny got the sister's name printed out and marked out the grave. Rachel stood between us and Sonny said Kaddish. The symbolism of this reunited 'family' standing in the cemetery was very powerful.

In the sessions that followed Rachel said a great weight had been lifted off her shoulders. She felt as if she had been carrying her mother on her back all her life. We spent time choosing the inscription on the stone which would join her mother's name with her sister's – she said her sister had always been waiting for her mother to return from the camp. Instead of the helplessness of the earlier feelings about her being unable to save her mother, and her sense of inadequacy in looking after her sister, she now felt there was something she could do, and this strengthened her. Again the spiritual aspect of this and the integration of the Jewish ritualism took on meaning for her. She said that this was the moment of her liberation, not when she was let out of the convent. We identified this time between the visit to the cemetery and the setting of the stone as her mourning period. The time limit of this she felt was helpful to her.

The work shifted much more into the present, and our current work focuses on her relationships, and how she attempts to prevent the patterns of the past repeating themselves in the present. Clearly she has internalized something from me which helps her reflect on rather than just react to a situation. There is always a strong pull back to the hedonistic principle which kept her going before. As she grows older her looks may change, and may not be the same source of power as she previously experienced. The props of smoking and drinking as a way of easing pain are now being seen as of limited value even though they may be enjoyed in the moment. Each time she puts herself in control of events she frees herself from her victim past. Her father's words that 'she will never be any good and she will turn out like her mother' no longer have to be a self-fulfilling prophecy.

The work is not finished, but a process has begun. As Rachel moves away from being a helpless victim, she has become involved in helping to set up and run an assertiveness training course in the HSC in conjunction with Jewish Care's training department.

My work with Rachel illustrates how my psychodynamic training provides a framework for the transference and countertransference processes which inevitably go on. However, this is not a one-way process of client and therapist – the one asking for help and the other offering it. We embarked on this work together. It is not a 'pure' approach – it allows survivors to meet socially and for child survivors, in particular, to have a peer group which they may not have experienced before as their childhood and adolescence were taken away from them. It is not 'pure' in the sense that the office setting is not the only setting for work, and the practical approaches are also central to what we offer. It is not 'pure' in the sense that professional boundaries may need to be crossed in order to convey trust and a sense of immersion in and commitment to the unique experiences of the survivor – personal details and more informal approaches need to be incorporated as well as the more traditional skills of the professional relationship. It is not 'pure' in the sense that the therapist does not work in an isolated way with the survivor – spiritual (Rabbis), social (self-help and the HSC), recreational (outings), group (both therapy and self-help), and creative (art, music, writing) approaches can all be part of the healing process which allows integration of the part into the whole. The complexity of the subject demands a complexity of response. In my view the only therapy of any value is the one in which the person we are working with feels helped. I would argue that therapists who stick too rigidly to traditional psychoanalytical models are less likely to be able to reach out and touch the needs of Holocaust survivors whose world was changed through the Shoah.

I could illustrate by many more cases how the liberating effect of finding new ways of working with the effects of extreme trauma have resulted in helping the survivor feel dignified and understood, rather than a case to be diagnosed. Sometimes a survivor would say to me, 'It is enough to know you are there should I need you.'

When suicide and depression haunt the survivor we have to think openly about which range of interventions will assist. We struggle together, we take some calculated risks, but gradually the survivor may begin to take control again, and the strengths which have helped him or her survive are reinforced. Victor Frankl's (1978) words are almost uppermost in my mind when he reminds us that it was the environment in the camp which was abnormal, the survivors' reaction to it was normal. This is a concept of optimism, and strengthens the worker to give hope to the survivor when the dark shadow of the Holocaust threatens to engulf him or her.

Reflections – witness and vision of the therapist

My chapter ends with hope. It is this hope, this belief in some possibility of healing so long after the trauma, which is perhaps encapsulated in the words of a child survivor when she recently told me, 'I not only trusted you and your being able to help me, but you trusted me. For the first time in my life someone believed me and listened to me.' For those who have undergone extreme trauma, it is not enough for them to bear witness. Something needs to be conveyed to the therapist which is not stored away in records or archives, but becomes a living process which involves the therapist as witness in his or her own right.

Being there with the survivor, being touched by the horror of each one's story, allows for the transmission of the experience and the possibility for it to be memorialized. Many survivors want to protect their own children from hearing the atrocities they have been through, while others may flood their children with such memories. Our therapeutic work in the future is to build bridges between the first and second generation of survivors, for a communication process to take place. This however takes time. As each second passes, the survivor grows older and comes nearer to death. If their message is not transmitted, the meaning in their survival is threatened. The therapist therefore, as witness, becomes the temporary bridge for the survivors, or as Dina Wardi (1992) puts it, 'the memorial candle'.

The therapist works alongside the children of survivors in sharing the weight of remembering for the future. Because we came into this work relatively late there has already been some transmission of trauma from one generation to the next. However, in a similar way to the one we adopt in working with survivors themselves, we underline the strengths and coping side of the second generation, rather than emphasizing any pathology. We are currently reaching phase two of our work with the long-term effects of the Holocaust, and this will include the development of both social groups for children of survivors in the HSC as well as facilitated discussion groups in Shalvata. We will appeal to children of survivors to take an active part in fund-raising, befriending and generally volunteering in the HSC, as well as perhaps becoming the future educators of schoolchildren when the eye-witnesses are no longer alive. The apparent transmission of trauma to the second generation can therefore be converted more constructively into action which, hopefully, will obviate the same transmission to a third generation of holocaust survivors.

The witnessing of extreme trauma by the therapist through the eyes of the survivor reveals a complexity and discomfort which we may prefer not to look at. How do we incorporate in the same image a vision of the Nazi as a mass murderer by day, and at the same time the family man who can enjoy evenings at home with his wife and children? How can we comprehend a situation in which kapos meted out punishment to fellow prisoners? What indeed would you and I be like in a situation of starvation, degradation and brutalization? Survivors confront us the therapists with the 'Nazi' within us. They also teach us about the possibility of maintaining dignity and humanity in an environment of bestiality. The split between victim and oppressor is not a clear-cut one. The capacity for goodness may be present alongside the capacity for evil. It is a dynamic that is around when we enter this world of extreme trauma, and an acceptance of this phenomenon means it can be looked at in the therapeutic work. This means that the rage which may have been repressed during the incarceration and later can be addressed, as well as an acknowledgement of the human acts of kindness which went on in the camps between one prisoner and another.

This complexity can be illustrated by the account given to me by one survivor when he was emphasizing that he survived by putting himself first rather than thinking of anyone else. However, in the same breath he told me the story of his journey on a train with many other survivors who were taken out of Auschwitz with no food or water near the end of the war. The man next to him was dying and he wanted to give up his life. The survivor told me how he kept this man alive by talking to him and encouraging him to survive. Today they are still in touch with each other, and this man owes him his life. However, against the overwhelming horror this story had little significance for him.

Carefully balanced against this awesome task of listening very closely and witnessing events from the past, is the therapist's vision of a future. Without the vision, the overwhelming feelings associated with listening to extreme trauma would submerge the therapist. There have been many times along the way when I came close to relinquishing my involvement, but my vision of what needed to be done was kept on track by the support networks I was fortunate to establish. The crucial timing of events such as my meeting with Shamai Davidson and later Sonny Herman (my professional consultants), restored my faith in a healing process. This mirroring of the survivors' journey through their work with me and my own professional journey, is the key to the development of these new ways of working. Counselling Holocaust survivors is therefore seen as the culmination of a learning process I have been privileged to undertake with survivors who advise me about what seems to help them.

The survivors' vision is that in the future such horrific events should never happen again. Their task is to ensure that lessons are learned from the past.

The therapist's task is to translate this into our work with survivors. Vision is built on the concept of 'liberation' both for the survivor and the therapist. The ageing survivor wishes to be set free of the memories and nightmares that haunt him or her – not to forget but to lay the ghosts to rest. To achieve this goal the therapist needs to work on devictimizing the survivor through the strategies suggested in this chapter. This rests on the liberation of the therapist from working in a limited framework and the development of new and innovative approaches.

The liberating effect of such development in my work has had consequences on how I respond to other traumatic experiences in my work. For example, the work we undertake with some 120 Bosnian refugees is based on my learning from survivors about what they wished they had been offered when they first arrived in this country. The approach again, however, is not to offer counselling as a first response for traumatized people. Instead I work through a Bosnian community worker to involve members of their group in supporting each other through social, recreational activities. Focusing on work helps to counteract the sense of depression related to the trauma and uprooting. The professional role is to outreach through non-threatening, non-institutional social groups to build up the trust necessary to develop therapeutic services. Counselling would come quite low down on a scale of priorities for severely traumatized people. Use of creative approaches such as art work, music and writing are often more meaningful interventions once basic needs have been met. We are not lulled this time around into believing that all is well because people are trying to get on with their lives, because we know how long term the effects can be if no help is offered.

Though survivors believe their experience of suffering in the Shoah is unique and not comparable to other genocides, it has nevertheless alerted me to the needs of displaced people more generally, and made me respond with a sense of urgency rather than complacency.

Witnessing the experiences of persecuted people has underlined my perception of the role of therapists as agents of social change. Being active in my work – fighting on behalf of claims for compensation, challenging medical attitudes towards survivors, ensuring survivors' voices are heard through public-speaking, training and education programmes – challenges the more passive role of the therapist and that of bystander.

To ensure that changes come about not only within the individual but in a wider context there needs to be the possibility of influencing events, and this depends on the role one has and the authority that is attributed to it.

I have two roles – that of therapist and that of manager of the services for Holocaust survivors and refugees. My day-to-day contact with survivors and the pain of surviving reminds me of my task as manager, namely to ensure that the needs of the survivors are represented in the organization. The witnessing of the trauma inspired in me the vision of a service which would maximize the potential for some healing of these deep and festering wounds. To be a therapist would not have been enough. My role needed to be one in which I had the possibility of ensuring the implementation and development of our current services – the HSC and Shalvata. A process of change and development was inextricably linked to my becoming central to the organization's infrastructure. The transference of powerlessness in situations of extreme trauma had to be converted into action. My role as manager was the tool whereby this could happen. As time went by, the team of therapists I work with took on more of the role of witnessing the survivors' trauma. As manager I needed to constantly keep the vision of devictimizing and empowering survivors and keeping them central to the consciousness of the whole community. As manager I needed to ensure that the HSC does not become just another day centre or a friendship club for the elderly, but that the programme has to remain meaningful to the needs of survivors. A balance constantly needs to be maintained between a collective remembering and the memorialization of the Shoah, in addition to providing a place in which survivors can enjoy themselves and forget for a while the horror they have been through.

As manager I can maintain sufficient overall perspective to implement new and creative ways of working therapeutically with survivors, and to fight for the necessary resources to achieve this. My status in the organization enables me to promote our work, both nationally and internationally, for the needs of survivors to be recognized. This also involves regular contact with the media, lecturing, writing and publicizing our work. All raise the profile of survivors, as well as the therapeutic work we undertake. The better our service is known, the more powerful the impact it has.

However, this powerful role as the manager of the services for survivors also brings with it a link with authority. This role could only have emerged for me having built up trust first with survivors, as well as regularly maintaining personal contact on a daily basis. Some may see my role as therapist as well as manager as a conflict point. In fact the two have been able to coexist and have kept me on course in terms of bringing the vision of the future into reality.

I remember very clearly when I was asked by Jewish Care to present the case for a centre for survivors to their Executive Committee. It was a time of recession and there were limited funds. Some of the survivors themselves were not optimistic that I would succeed in getting the necessary resources to develop the centre. However, my own conviction spurred me on. I had prepared a short paper for presentation at the meeting.

I was asked to address the meeting, and found that my own certainty about the needs of survivors being met at that moment in time strengthened me to convey a clear message. Any later would have been too late. Somehow this urgency got transmitted to the people I was speaking to. I was pleading not for myself, but for the survivors, and also for those who had been murdered and could not speak. I too was bearing witness – what I had heard from the survivors about their suffering and their present and future needs had to be heard by others who had not had the opportunity to listen. The words flowed freely from my mouth, and there was complete silence in the room as I spoke. The outcome of the meeting was a unanimous decision to create the Holocaust Survivor Centre.

As messenger for the survivor to the larger community my task is at times an isolated and lonely one. It can be seen in one of two ways. There is some sense of relief that someone is prepared to speak up for survivors, and consequently I can ease the conscience of the community by my insistence that we provide these unique services. On the other hand I, like the survivors, am a constant reminder of the Shoah within our midst, a source of discomfort and distress which would best be forgotten.

To compensate for this weighty responsibility, I like to reflect on our achievements. I walk into the HSC and see the survivors enjoying themselves, whether playing cards, eating together in the café or celebrating one of the Jewish festivals. Seeing a survivor in therapy pull out of their suicidal thoughts, seeing families opening up to share and communicate their trauma, gives meaning to the struggle to carry on.

There is still much to be done in partnership with the survivors. We are constantly working against time, listening and responding, adapting and changing our therapeutic interventions, and working towards a future in which the survivors' experience will be part of each one of us. When this has been achieved, the survivor will be able to let go more peacefully. There will be a sense that the lessons of their experience of extreme trauma will have been internalized by those who were not there and did not witness at first hand the horror of the Shoah. This chapter is part of a process through which the testimonies of both the survivor and the therapist are recorded for posterity.

References

Davidson, S. (1984) 'Human reciprocity among Jewish prisoners in the Nazi concentration camps'. *The Nazi Concentration Camp Proceedings of the 4th Yad Vashem International Conference 1980*. Jerusalem: Yad Vashem.

des Pres, T. (1976) *The Survivor – An Anatomy of Life in the Death Camps*. New York: Oxford University Press.

Frankl, V. (1978) *Man's Search for Meaning*. London: Hodder & Stoughton.

Krell, R. (1989) 'Alternative approaches to Holocaust survivors', in P. Marcus and A. Rosenberg (eds), *Healing their Wounds – Psychotherapy with Holocaust Survivors and their Families*. New York: Praeger. p. 224.

Krystal, H. (1984) 'Integration and self-healing in post-traumatic states', in S.A. Luel and P. Marus (eds), *Psychoanalytic Reflections on the Holocaust: Selected Essays*. New York: Ktav Publishing House. pp. 113–34.

Ornstein, A. (1985) 'Survival and recovery', in D. Lewis and N. Averhahn (eds), *Psychoanalytic Inquiry 5*. Hillside, NJ: The Analytic Press. pp. 99–130.

Steinberg, A. (1989) 'Holocaust survivors and their children: a review of the clinical literature in healing their wounds', in P. Marcus and A. Rosenberg (eds), *Healing their Wounds – Psychotherapy with Holocaust Survivors and their Families*. New York: Praeger.

Wardi, D. (1992) *Memorial Candle*. New York: Routledge.

Wiesel, E. (1982) 'The Holocaust Patient'. An address to Cedars-Sinai medical staff, Los Angeles.

9

Deeper dungeons, deeper insights

Bob Johnson

'Do other minds exist?' This question will strike working therapists as odd, if not superfluous – since they spend their lives struggling to untangle little else. Yet if there is one topic to which therapists can bring most benefit to the wider world from their everyday experience, it is this. Strange as it may now seem, this was among the most central questions for serious debate among my philosophy professors at Cambridge University only 40 years ago. And given the ethos of the times, they bungled it, as so many of our leading theoreticians still do today.

Nowadays, of course, I would regard any individual who doubted that other minds existed as seriously mentally or emotionally handicapped – but that is to draw on four decades of ever-increasing confidence in exploring human emotions, culminating in five years intensive 'education' in Parkhurst Prison's Special Unit with Britain's most dangerous criminals, including many who were regularly categorized as too dangerous for Broadmoor. But the question itself strikes at the very root of conventional methodology – and though working therapists may find it hard to believe, it must, on present conventional, objective scientific wisdom, be invariably and unavoidably answered in the negative. Minds, for the orthodox, do not exist.

This chapter falls conveniently into three sections, covering:

1. mind and emotion,
2. 'truth, trust and consent', and finally
3. psychopaths.

Mind and emotion

I now see the problem of mind as being at a very similar stage to the controversy regarding the circulation of the blood in the 1600s. When Harvey first suggested this novel idea, only 350 years ago, all the material and objective evidence was against. Clearly the heart was working very hard doing something or other. What it did was not at all obvious, except that when it stopped so did we. But the notion that blood actually went somewhere, and then came back, was just not borne out in physical practice – there was quite simply nowhere for it to go.

So though the concept that blood went round and round, in a matter of minutes, was a highly intriguing idea – without which clinical medicine could merely fumble when dealing with the most vital physical organ a human has – there was no concrete evidence to support it. Harvey's problem was that before microscopes came on the scene, the capillaries, which turned out to be the missing link between arteries and veins, were invisible – they could not be seen, they could not be observed. So to concrete-thinking 'scientists', there was not a shred of evidence that they existed. Speculation was all very well, but heretics had to bear in mind that medical practice was aimed at saving lives, not dabbling in novel, and possibly highly dangerous, ideas which could not be borne out by obvious physical proof. Passions would undoubtedly have run high, promotions would have been barred, research funds denied and publications side-lined – yet all the while the blood did circulate, and more lives could be saved by placing this fact at the centre, if not actually at the heart, of clinical practice.

Essentially the same now holds true of the mind. Clearly the brain is very busy, circuits are humming, synapses are firing, and a great deal seems to be going on which appears to be vital to who we are, or quite simply how we 'be'. But there is nothing concrete. No one has yet come up with the equivalent of a microscope which can visualize the definitive function, the *raison d'être*, of all this hectic cortical activity. What does it mean? Here, we have to draw a blank. Everyone now knows without a second thought that the purpose of the heart is to push the blood round and round. But what on earth is the brain for? Is it too engaged on some mysterious, and literally invisible, 'plan' or even, perish the thought, 'purpose'? If so, what could that be, and how are we to discover it? And once discovered, how are we to publish it abroad, unless we can winkle out some tangible, objective and measurable proof?

So, though 'Do other minds exist?' might seem innocuous enough – or indeed of perishable relevance to practising therapists – it points up a dilemma which has not gone away, which haunts our very civilization from the most eminent theoretical physicist down to the humblest church-goer. It turns centrally on what human beings actually are, and indeed what they mean as a whole, to say nothing of what they are actually for. Many confine these prickly questions to spiritual or religious considerations – but, for all the range of opinion and prejudice you can find there, the fact remains that these 'value' considerations apply in full to this topic – which of course makes it all that much harder to resolve.

Where Harvey was contending with the presence or absence of invisible 'channels' or 'passageways' that no one had ever seen, or was ever likely to see with the naked eye, the question of minds contends with a whole ethos of how we view the world, and in particular, how we investigate it. For whatever else may have been achieved by the objective scientific method, there can be no doubt at all that it has proved itself a complete dud when faced with mental phenomena. Progress in what we might call the 'real' science of consciousness will be paralytically slow until the status of subjectivity is re-established.

I speak with especial warmth on this topic, having endured a year taking an Objective Experimental Psychology degree at Cambridge University, under the eminent professor Oliver L. Zangwill. You might have imagined that it was hard to make the most fascinating phenomenon in the entire cosmos boring – but that is what this undergraduate course succeeded in doing to human consciousness. I even remember verbatim a question from my BA degree exam, which itself must be something of a record since it was posed to me precisely 39 years ago. The question stated, 'The study of emotion has not advanced since Aristotle – discuss.' In my answer, I cheerfully argued that this was a correct statement – thereby falling somewhat short of what the examiners anticipated, and radically reducing the chances of any golden laurels settling congratulatorily upon my heretical brow. I remember a redoubtable professor of psychology from Oxford no less, who could scarcely contain his disgust at this response. Challenges to the established status quo are never welcomed by it, especially not from undergraduates. However this may be, we remain as fundamentally ignorant today of the underlying purposes of the brain as were pre-Harvey clinicians of the heart.

Objectivity, like motherhood and apple pie, sounds universally desirable, and yet it is not quite as laudable as at first appears. The world around us, and the way we think about it, indeed the very fact that we *can* think about it, snooker it beyond redemption. The key to 'reductionism' is that bigger things are composed of lesser things, and lesser things of smaller things, and so on *ad infinitum*. And though it sounds eminently desirable that by breaking complex items or events down to their smallest component we can 'understand' them ever more clearly, the truth is that really complex events simply do not survive being 'broken down' or 'anatomized'. Just as hearts could be dissected forever without once revealing how blood was gloriously pumped, so too the human brain can be sliced into ever-more microscopic detail, while all the time what is really going on can only be found out elsewhere.

This is not the place for a full-blown expedition into epistemology, though it is quite essential that practitioners in this field are aware of supportive philosophical arguments to bolster their case. The damage first began with David Hume in 1739, who suggested that just because one cause followed another today, this was no justification for assuming it would do so tomorrow. We all work on this 'sceptical' principle in our daily lives – who could ever 100 per cent guarantee that turning the ignition switch will invariably start the car today just because it did so yesterday? We all know that in the 'real' world effect does not necessarily and absolutely follow cause. But this does not stop us craving intellectual certainty, so when Hume doubted we could ever achieve such an ideal, even in principle, he received rather more brickbats and decidedly less eulogies even than Harvey. His scepticism is still valid, even after Kant's monumental efforts to repair it – if Kant could not do so, then no one can. But too many prefer to ignore this black hole in our structure of knowledge, and cover it with verbiage, cobwebs or establishment opprobrium.

The upshot is that those who acknowledge we can only 'know' things with very short 'causal chains' will make more practical progress in our curious cosmos than those who insist that we can still think on a level playing field, not to say a Euclidean plane. Similarly, it is absolutely essential that we adopt a holistic approach – if you want to know what minds are for then take a step back and watch the whole organism in operation, and see how the thing works in practice. The more you cut it up, the less lively it tends to be. But by standing back and observing, then it is possible to trace through a single golden thread, and by doing so to bring more relief to mental disorders than is otherwise remotely possible.

I have a fascination with fundamental philosophical issues, driven home so hard during that benighted year in 'Experimental Psychology', so perhaps I might indulge one further blast in this direction. Physicists 100 years ago were thrown into consternation by the clear fact that, unlike anything else in the universe, light travelled at the same speed however fast its source was moving. This problem remains. Einstein 'solved' it by assuming that space and time were malleable and bent them round the supposed constant speed of light. He declared that nothing travelled faster than light. He has since been proved wrong – 'tunnelling electrons' do – but as with all items upsetting the status quo, even eminent physicists elect to disbelieve it. But his 'relativity' is valid – everything that happens is influenced by the characteristics of the observer. A physicist travelling close to the speed of light will see things and age differently from her companion who is not. Relativity in an analogous sense is common knowledge among therapists, who see mental disorders in radically different ways depending on their own personal standpoint.

Worse for the Reductionist or Absolutist is the finding that the heart of the atom does not ring true. The uncertainty principle is quite as unsettling as it sounds – you can either tell where something is, or which way it is travelling, but never both. The very building blocks of the universe are just perversely unknowable. It's like knowing where you left the dog, but not where it went since. Or knowing its speed, but not where it started from. What could be better calculated to confuse, to infuriate or to unsettle the ideal view that there really is a Newtonian universe out there just waiting to be discovered. Obviously with such a savage undermining of our cherished hopes and expectations, it is not to be wondered at that many will react in precisely the same way as traumatized children – they will deny that the problem ever occurred in the first place. Even eminent physicists who should assuredly know a great deal better, give credence to the notion that those who are sceptical because of quantum mechanics really don't understand – the truth is the other way around.

Enough of deconstructive scepticism. My year at Cambridge was spent half in Professor Zangwill's bereft bailiwick, and half in a dozen other faculties where the word 'philosophy' appeared in the title of the lectures – a truly universal education, setting my intellectual and spiritual journey on to pathways which I could never otherwise have discovered, and which though consistently contrary to the conventional wisdom, have led to a clear and fruitful outcome fulfilling my wildest expectations. Who would have guessed that the resolution of all these severe philosophical doubts and problems was being solved, almost as it were inadvertently, by the profession whose ranks I was set to join – clinical medicine.

A 'clinician' is one who works at the bedside, from the Greek *klinik* meaning a bed. So he or she cannot know everything that is going on, but must take the most important data, prioritize it, and act within a short enough time frame before the patient dies waiting for the 'results' to come back from the laboratory. Thus clinicians have been dealing with the concept of 'pain' for millennia, despite there being no objective definition or measure for this entity. Pain must be subjectively evaluated, since it can never be quantified or measured; it must be taken fully into account, even though it can be simulated and will forever remain 100 per cent subjective. Were clinicians to take the Logical Positivist's approach to pain, and exclude it permanently from their deliberations because its meaning could not be verified, they would *ipso facto* reduce themselves and their patients to the level of vets and their animals. And what applies to pain, applies in full measure to any emotion you care to name.

I well remember one of my philosophy professors, John Wisdom, who helped me with my Kantian studies, but not with my difficulties with the existence of other minds. He would place the back of his hands against his temples and wiggle his fingers, wrinkle his nose, and purport to be imitating an animal the very existence of whose mind was in question. He concluded firmly from this exercise that though the motions we observed might indicate something else going on within the creature's skull, we had absolutely no positive objective grounds for assuming that that beast had a mind. Now this reductionist position is still the established conventional wisdom. Though the great Objective Reductionist Scientific Belief System has sprung more leaks than a colander, research-giving bodies and award-making institutions are still manned by those who either believe in it as a matter of course, or religiously follow the advice of those who do.

It was no coincidence that Professor Zangwill abjured emotions, nor that his course was infinitely impoverished as a result – he was following the conventional wisdom of his day, however destructive that proved to be. Yet since emotions alone provide our mental furniture with its motion – there is no other way our mental bits and pieces can be moved – they are indispensable for any approach to mental events, or in particular to mental disease. Now whatever else they are, things of the mind are by common consent intangible and subjective – they can never be weighed, measured, bottled or counted. So if therapists elect to be purists and follow Zangwill and his ilk, they must consign themselves to the blankest (and boringest) therapeutic impotence. Only by launching into the unfashionable world of subjectivities, with due regard to the long-established clinical approach, can workaday therapists begin to ameliorate the palpable mental agonies which come their way week in week out. So here too therapists' witness and values can prove invaluable to wider social and 'scientific' issues.

And of course, once we notice that emotions move mental items around, then the next question is, can we control them? Are we living in a clockwork universe with not the slightest chink for individuality or variation from a pattern set many aeons ago, somewhere around the time of the Big Bang? Or can we run our own lives largely as we wish? I believe you would be surprised how many eminent theoreticians would flatly maintain that we unquestionably inhabit the former. The universe in the conventional view is Fully Determined, cause unquestionably follows effect (poor Hume has been excommunicated), and there is no question of any of us ever dreaming of having so diffuse and awkward a notion as Free Will, let alone Will Power.

And this is really rather odd, as the Red Queen might have said, because without deploying Will Power we can never hope to be sane. At one simple level, we need the determination to spring-clean all the obsolete garbage out of our heads – if we cannot decide to do this, then who is going to sort the wheat from that chaff in our inner mental worlds? More, what I am finding increasingly obvious is that consent forms the foundation stone for peace of mind, and peace of society. How can this possibly be meaningful if we have no freedom to put it into effect? Well, my view is now perfectly clear – let's get to work before the innumerable 'laboratories' send back their sterile objectivity protestations, or else the patient, not to mention our global society, might well not be here in the morning.

'Truth, trust and consent'

Practical therapists take what they see in front of them and try to ameliorate it. They pay less attention to the amenities of the room or other setting where the therapy is taking place, apart from ensuring as much physical comfort as possible; they pay more to encouraging their clients to expose their several mental discomforts. In the process there are wider issues which perhaps are introduced automatically, but which represent a different approach to human problems than is the conventional norm. Quite how different has recently been brought home to me in a particularly unpleasant and savage way.

Since the Special Unit in Parkhurst Prison, where I worked for five fascinating years, was prematurely closed because it conflicted with the Conservative Home Secretary Michael Howard's ideology, I have had time to reflect on the wider implications of my work there. In particular, it has become overwhelmingly obvious to me that the concept of 'consent' plays a positive and indeed active therapeutic role. The notions of truth and trust are prerequisites before consent can sensibly be invited, and I shall consider them briefly below. But consent itself is as powerful as it is indispensable.

At medical school it was constantly drilled into us that before any surgical procedure was embarked upon, of whatever nature, the patient must have completed a consent form. Various medico-legal complications were much bruited about – so we all well knew that only the foolish would be caught having operated without written permission. This was in striking contrast to the general (if unspoken) rule that what the patient actually said rated low and what they might agree to mattered little, which, with only a few outstanding exceptions, was regrettably the clinical norm in those days.

As the range of medical interventions moved steadily ever further from the obvious concrete surgical operations, the notion of obtaining consent from patients before treatment became ever easier to ignore. Pills and potions were prescribed on the often tacit understanding that patients consented to receive them. Advice and counselling was generally considered so far from what medicine was really all about, that the notion of specifically seeking consent before dispensing it was rarely explicitly stated or enacted. Starting therefore from somewhat lowly origins, the concept of consent has, in my estimation, travelled a long way – now it takes pride of place in my armamentarium, and carries the profoundest implications for society as a whole. Twenty years in general practice served to establish the notion of consent as entirely fundamental to any therapeutic intervention. Indeed I would go out of my way to discuss the pros and cons of various medicaments with the patient, and encourage them to choose which of the lesser evils they preferred. Their consent was quite essential to our compact – I would intervene medically only after they had agreed that I should. Fully informed consent became a way of life, as indeed it should.

Fortunately this earlier training stood me in good stead on my arrival in Parkhurst Prison Special Unit in 1991. These Special Units had been set up five years before for especially violent, unstable lifers who had been trouble makers in the system. On average they had spent two years in solitary confinement by way of punishment for ill-discipline. Quite a remarkable development in a generally punitive prison system, and one too fragile to survive Michael Howard's tenure as Home Secretary. It went without saying that if an individual prisoner or any other sort of patient did not consent, then treatment of any and all prescriptions was simply not proceeded with. The fact that those I was now treating were compulsorily detained, generally without their consent, weighed very much more heavily with other prison staff than it did with myself. The whole question of how much benefit is derived by deliberately disregarding the prisoners' consent in this matter of incarceration did not concern me so much at the time, though it has done since. However, prison staff in general, especially those at the 'sharp end', took grave exception at my stand on refusing absolutely to endorse involuntary treatments.

During the early months of my work on the Special Unit, there were three separate and highly dedicated attempts to remove me from my job. Mercifully, it so happened that the forces which were pushing one way on the first occasion, found themselves facing the other, subsequently. Had these happy conjunctions been slightly mistimed, or out of joint, then my stay at the Special Unit would assuredly have been short-lived. For the motivation behind these moves to expel me was fear – the master emotion. The prison officers believed that if the wing doctor refused to prescribe tranquillizing injections on demand, then not only would their work become parlous, but their very lives would be at risk. I had many hurdles to overcome and many challenges to vanquish during those early days, so converting coercion-prone prison staff to the virtues of a consensual approach was rather too high a mountain for me to climb initially. Nowadays, with the confidence my experiences there have given me, I would spend a great deal more time and energy setting out my decided opinions, as I am doing in this chapter.

This was quite a bruising time for me – I was uncertain how successful my model of the long-term effects of child abuse would be with violent and dangerous prisoners, unsure that the strenuous efforts I was making to persuade these damaged individuals to confront their most painful fears would really be to their long-term benefit – on top of this, I was faced not so much with the hostility of the prison staff, more with their complete disregard for my opinion. They knew how dangerous these men could be, they knew that heavy sedation reduced the risks – I was a mere neophyte, whose weeding out was an entirely trivial matter and something they knew exactly how to execute. They had rid themselves of troublesome doctors before and would readily do so again should the need arise.

In this atmosphere you can imagine my delight at the few crumbs of comfort which dropped in my path from time to time. Such a one was when a highly experienced officer went out of his way, in a discreet manner, to acknowledge that I was entitled to hold the views that I did. During one memorable conversation with this officer, I pressed him very hard on the point under consideration here. I asked him how he would tackle, say, a serious hostage-taker or other violent situation. Having worked in prisons for 20 or more years, he was well used to such eventualities, and I respected his judgement in dealing with them.

The 'macho' line, of course, would be to assemble sufficient force and overpower the culprit. I begged to differ from this, and set out to extract an agreement that, in the ultimate analysis, the wrongdoer would need to give consent to any final denouement. That without this consent, then there could really be no satisfactory outcome. Greatly to my delight this experienced man conceded that, yes, it really was quite essential to gain the wrongdoer's consent. He did not say so loudly, indeed the culture we were working in was very much against it – but nevertheless, this is actually a key component of prisons. Contrary to every item of Right-wing prison policy, prison riots occur or do not occur solely on the say so or the consent of the prisoners.

What completely astonished me was the latent power in this notion of consent, which heretofore had appeared commonplace, if not trivial. What I found was that it provides the pivot upon which mental health turns. And since we are considering here how the insights of workers in mental health can better inform the wider public, then this too is a crucial contribution we can make. For in order to give consent, not only must we have a mind with which to consider the point before consenting, but we must also have confidence in our own judgement and value our own position, in order to assert something of our own in giving, or of course withholding, consent.

Sadly those of a reductionist frame of thought, who actively doubt the existence of minds, cannot fully appreciate the wider implications of consent. It was not merely a matter of insisting that no treatment was ever given without consent, so too no consultation even, ever proceeded in its absence. I used to find myself in bizarre situations, bargaining with inmates as to whether or not they could find the time to come and see me, say at 10.30 or 11.00. We would haggle over which days of the week they might be 'available' and which not. And then the whole thing would dissolve into laughter, since they admitted that in a locked prison wing there was simply no place else they were likely to be.

I embarked on these escapades initially as a follow-over from general practice. I had got into the way of asking consent then and continued in the same fashion, despite the fact that I was now working in a maximum security prison. And yet, all the time, I was conveying a different message too. I was saying by this simple action that I needed something from them, that I valued their decision in this matter, and more, that I would not proceed against their wishes. No wonder the Conservative Home Secretary could not stand such a Unit existing in his prisons. Even in the depth of one of the most coercive contexts in a generally coercive culture, I was insisting, with absolute 100 per cent consistency, on securing consent before proceeding even to discuss matters with the prisoner.

At first, of course, my clients thought it was just a game. How could I, a major authority figure playing an important authoritarian role in a quasi-military setting, how could I possibly be entertaining the notion that an inmate might, on a whim, reject my invitation? And they would play along to find out what I really meant, what I was made of underneath, and how far they could push it in directing their decisions contrary to what they assumed I wished them to be. Happily my level of confidence was high enough to withstand the more serious buffeting, and happily too, enough inmates did not need to play this particular sort of game, so that when it occurred I had plenty else to keep me occupied.

What they were finding out was how important I regarded their views to be, and behind that, how I saw them. If I was merely play-acting, then I would just wait a while and then simply assert my power, and they would be compelled to do what I said. This is the model of the coercive society which is generally accepted as the only way to proceed. In fact it represents a cul-de-sac, which can only aggravate insanity. It is also the model in most families of how to deal with children, which again, once you can step outside the culture, you see is entirely counter-productive.

It is no exaggeration to say that consent distinguishes the men from the boys, or more generally the adults from the infants, the mature from the emotionally dependent. It became quite clear to me that the major root of Personality Disorder, which every prisoner I ever met suffered from, was delayed emotional maturation – in other words, inside their heads they were still infants. By taking them seriously; by behaving towards them, with 100 per cent consistency, as if they were responsible civilized adults who should have been quite capable of taking a decision on their own responsibilities; by simply acting in this way on the matter of consent, I was reinforcing such mature behaviour in them. As my confidence grew, I simply never allowed any other notion to enter my head – and this consistency began to tell on the inmates, who noticed that I was telling the truth. And after trying me out for a while, they began to believe me when I spoke. From this belief arose trust, the remaining pillar of mental stability and indeed of global stability. Once this process took hold, of course, my early hassles evaporated, and my work became delightful as true humanity blossomed even in this deepest of dungeons.

Truth, trust and consent are now the three points that I make to describe what I do. What delights me more than somewhat is that these are precisely the same values that attend any stable mental structure. Peace of mind is utterly dependent on this trio, as is peace within a family or across a globe. Here are values that every human can subscribe to, without needing any of the bizarre initiation rites or quasi-magical beliefs which too often surround today's religions.

Truth, in a pragmatic definition, is the degree to which you ensure that the mental model you have in your head corresponds as faithfully as possible with what is actually happening out there. In verbal terms, this means deploying deceit as little as possible, and working hard to convey what you understand to be going on, rather than deceiving first yourself and then your neighbour. Truth is actually the corrective for the Logical Positivist – we none of us can define what we say with 100 per cent accuracy, so we must build up a reputation for keeping our accuracy and our truth as close as we can make it to this unattainable ideal. There is all the difference in the world between trying to be honest and trying to acquire gains through deceit. Perfect accuracy may be as illusory as finding an exact numerical equivalent for π, but just as no engineer could get anywhere without as close an approximation as possible for this 'irrational number', so too no human being can begin to approach peace of mind without relying on truth.

Trust follows when you begin to believe the truth of what you are being told. Again this might sound simple, even simplistic. But what I found so clearly from my Parkhurst work, is that these three pillars must be learned.

Just as it takes many years to become fluent in a natural language, so too it takes a long time to learn quite how these three components of mental stability operate.

The notion of trust is commonplace. We all of us trust the floorboards we walk on not to collapse and drop us on to the floor below. When that trust is shown to be misplaced, then we scour the ground for rotten boards before putting another foot forward – and exactly the same happens in our human relations. The reason so many prisoners were where they were was because they had never had any experience of trustworthy human relations. A large element of my therapy with them was offering them a reliable, predictable and trustworthy relationship. Even so, it took months, even years for them to venture out and risk any of their 'weight' upon it.

Once truth and trust are in place, then, and only then, have you a stable platform from which to begin to exercise your new facility for consent. In order to give meaningful consent, you first have to have control of your own mind, faith in your own value and self-image, and confidence that those relating to you will respect your consent, will seek it as an asset and deliver upon it with care and fruitfulness.

Again, though these three items may seem eccentric and out of the ordinary they are in truth common enough already in human society. If instead of verbal currency we examined our fiscal coinage, clearly we need true and honest dealings if we are to come to trust the value of the money which is now indispensable to our survival as a civilized society. 'Confidence in sterling' is now so widely spoken of that we give it little thought. Too much embezzlement, too many occasions where an honest day's pay is not given for an honest day's work, or where the value of currency is stretched by all the means the economists list – in these cases the coins are known to be devalued, and they are either used much less freely, or when they are, are surcharged. Exactly analogous effects are seen with verbal currency. When Margaret Thatcher told the British electorate in 1979 that she would not raise VAT, while at the same time discussing doubling it with treasury officials, the reliability and therefore the value of her verbal currency fell. Kenneth Clarke, the Conservative Chancellor, had then less weight behind his assurances that VAT would not be extended to food in 1997.

I am in the process of devising a score or quotient to cover these three points, which I am terming the Quaker Quotient, in view of its provenance from the religious tenets of that sect (see Figure 9.1). The quotient is still in its infancy, but it can apply to partners, governments, self, work or community, that is, to any human relationship, since the latter provide the only possible basis for peace of mind, sanity or indeed for civilization. By scoring it as indicated, the total can be expressed as a fraction of ten, which is the maximum. Further details will be available from the James Nayler Foundation; the address is given below.*

---

* James Nayler Foundation, PO Box 1, Ventnor, Isle of Wight, PO38 2YX.

0 for NO
1 for maybe, iffy
2 for YES

1	TRUTH	Is he/she truthful?	
2	TRUST	Is he/she trustworthy?	
3	CONSENT	Does he/she seek your consent?	
4	PRESENT	Are you happy with the way things are between you?	
5	FUTURE	Are you happy with the way things are going between you?	

TOTAL = _____

FIGURE 9.1   *The Quaker Quotient – a score for sanity or peace of mind*

Psychopaths

Diseases in the New Testament were viewed as almost exactly the reverse of what they are today. Epileptics, in those days, were thought to be evil, the work of devils which could sometimes be 'cast out'. Those addicted to violence, on the other hand, were treated with compassion, with the advice to 'turn the other cheek'. Nowadays, of course, we treat our epileptics with a great deal of sympathy and perhaps too much heavy medication – but we reserve the 'evil' tag for our violent wrongdoers upon whom we dispense ever further physical degradation, heaped remorselessly upon their heads. Unsurprisingly, the former do quite well, and the latter appallingly.

This notion that violent criminals are 'born evil' has taken a firm hold. It was commonplace among the prison officers, one of whom stated quite baldly, and without even very much emotion: 'I have known Tommy for 20 years, and you'll never change him. He was born evil. You are wasting your time and taxpayers' money talking to him – but that's up to you.' This comment was made in an off-hand manner, it was not even intended to be offensive – it was a statement of fact which this particular officer knew beyond doubt, and he felt he was stating the obvious rather than a variant opinion. It just showed him how out of touch these so-called professionals could be, not that it was any of his concern, just that since he had been asked, he might as well say what everyone else already knew but had not cared to mention.

This viewpoint is not an isolated one. Michael Howard, perhaps not the most constructive Home Secretary this country has had in recent years, capitalized on just such a body of opinion. The 'tougher' he could be on crime, the more votes he expected to garner, whether in the general election (which followed shortly after the time of writing), or in the leadership election for the Conservative Party which, as widely expected, followed it.

But like most political prejudices, this one does not bear close dispassionate examination. And if I have learned nothing else since working in Parkhurst, it is that treating dangerous criminals demands a whole network of social support.

Howard is on record as excoriating 'do-gooders' – since I earn my living by seeking to do good wherever I can in the mental health field, it could be said there was an element of incompatibility between us. Unfortunately for me, we live in a feudal society, and once Howard knew of my work it was only a matter of time before he closed it – there being a desperate dearth of democratic countermeasures available to wronged citizens, be they inmates or prison doctors. Here is another reason why writing this chapter is so important for me. Our prisons are currently perpetrating appalling degradation of our fellow citizens – this makes them more dangerous, whatever Howard may suggest to the contrary, and we need a radical reappraisal of them, throughout society. Here too is a vital contribution that mental health therapists can make.

Listening to Howard explain how he wants longer and longer sentences for second and third offenders, one is tempted to ask, if incarceration is such a wonderful remedy for crime, why does not one dose suffice? His claim to be protecting the general public is shown to be eyewash, when the 'treatment' he advocates at such expense is well known to make violence worse. But in his own way, he is demonstrating another human truth. He is responding to the notion of retribution or punishment with more than mere political alacrity. Quite clearly his parents punished him, as many parents do, and thereby taught him that punishment is a 'good' in itself – sadly for many, he still believes them.

But punishment never improves human relations, it never improves peace of mind, nor the ability to learn. And when it is dispensed on a wide, even national, scale as in the Criminal Justice System, then it is building up for society's future a time bomb of seismic proportions. For just as the supposed desirability of punishment is learned in childhood, so too is that of violence. For there is no doubt in my mind that violence is a disease, and it is a learned disease. As such it can be unlearned. Far from violence and other wrongdoing being genetically determined, every human being is born sociable, lovable and non-violent. I certainly did not believe this when I started work at Parkhurst in 1991, it is one of the deeper insights I gained from working there. But I now hold it to be true beyond doubt.

Accordingly, if I come across, as I frequently do in my medico-legal work, a man who has exploded with rage, violence or terror, I immediately set about disclosing where the normal emotional development went wrong, and how deeply the sociable, non-violent and lovable parts of his personality have been buried. Provided I have time enough, and can build up sufficient stocks of truth, trust and consent between us, then we invariably uncover overwhelming evidence to support this counter-cultural view. Doing good in this context is not only beneficial to the individuals concerned, but also to the wider society to which we both belong.

Labelling something or someone 'evil' merely indicates just how great is our fear and ignorance of them. Epileptics in biblical times behaved in quite incomprehensible ways, and could give no rational account of why they did so. The consequences of their disease were not so socially destructive as say, those of a serial killer, but in superstitious times they could have been terrifying. Now, of course, we are in the grip of a Hollywood culture which feels entirely at liberty to erode in turn each of the three pillars mentioned. Thus we have too many films extolling coercion over consent, celebrating terror over trust, and condoning deceit over truth. Small wonder the death penalty is sweeping across each of the United States of America – within a decade, so strong has been the pro-violent media propaganda, there will be few if any States without it.

'Psychopath' when I was a medical student was a label given by doctors to those patients they could not treat – it was a fig-leaf to cover medical ignorance and incompetence. Since then, 'Severe Personality Disorders' have displaced the label, but not generally the therapeutic impotence. I had no particular interest in psychopaths or indeed similar disorders when I started work at Parkhurst – what I did have was a model of the adult consequences of childhood trauma, and it is that which provides the clue. Just to reassure the more sceptical reader, I should point out that the method deployed, together with the social support the staff gave, in this Extra Special Prison Unit reduced the incidence of violent assaults by over 90 per cent, from 42 in the first seven years, to one in the last two; the annual consumption of major tranquillizers from 150g per inmate to 10g; and from an annual average of 20 alarm bells, none at all were rung either by staff or inmate for the two years up to October 1994. So however incomprehensible the following description may appear, bear in mind that in practice it produced results in a maximum security prison wing that were unique throughout the world. Sad to think that Howard crushed it on an ideological whim.

Many a benevolent therapist will have become 'burnt out' by the recalcitrance of, and the deliberate, persistent and totally opaque anti-social abilities of, the psychopath. It is crystal clear to me that any approach other than the truth, trust and consent already mentioned carries its own failure, as perhaps it should. But in addition, the Severe Personality Disordered patient suffers from a peculiar mental lesion, which unless it is addressed proactively and directly will flummox all therapeutic approaches however benign or well meaning their intention.

The lesion for all mental disorders, in my view, comes from a frozen terror from childhood. The growing infant is exploring the world when something catastrophic happens, and the child decides that if that is what reality is really like, then they do not wish to know about it ever again. Worse, they believe, and it was my explicit task to disabuse them of this, that even merely *thinking* about that event would render them instantly liable to destruction by it. Only by firmly keeping their heads below the sand can they hope to survive. Rather similar to the theoreticians earlier –

they understand the world they know, and they are not prepared to risk exchanging it for any other. Certainly if they doubt the truth and the trust of what is offered, they will never consent to it. Thus there are many pitfalls into which the unwary may all too easily slip.

So here we have a different approach to 'talk therapy' than is the norm. In a nutshell, to break the above impasse it is my task to persuade the person in front of me to think the last thing they want to think, always with their consent. This is just as much a mouthful to do, as it is to say. But that is the size of it. The more powerful the mental furniture, the denser and more effective is likely to be the blockage behind which an infantile terror still lurks. The tragedy is that too few therapists have the confidence and persistence to prevail upon these destructive individuals to revisit the most terrifying incident they have ever experienced, and persuade them that the abuse has now stopped and will never recur. First, the therapist must him or herself be aware that this is the case, must know of his or her own terrors and have dealt with them, and must be prepared to deal with all the wriggling and squirming which anyone would put forward if they thought that the alternative meant their certain death – which is precisely what abuse victims fear would follow confronting their abuser. Quite a pickle.

I suppose it is a bit like being born into a concentration camp and learning from day one that everyone with any power is determined to exterminate you. It would take exceptional circumstances to alter this belief system, especially when punitive prison policies reinforce it at every available opportunity. What I had not accounted for was that as soon as we got the system working, and the inmates stopped chopping each other up, that the Home Secretary's change of prison policy, would bring about the Unit's premature demise.

Let me give a flavour of the type of transformation that is required, and the nature of the lesion as I see it today. As an example, I am taking not a prisoner but a seven-and-a-half-year-old, Sam, whose mother I had treated for regular bouts of self-harm – she would bite her hand or bang her head against the wall whenever she had a tantrum. When Sam sat down he was a typical giggly seven-year-old, with matchstick legs, alternately chatting away and stuffing his hand in his mouth to hide his shyness. When he had settled, I said to him 'When your mother bit herself, you were frightened' – an unexceptional comment in any circumstances. Sam agreed, and showed his agreement by vigorously nodding his head, while giving me powerful non-verbals that that was sufficient answer and that he now wished to move on to other topics which might be of interest.

Since I was not conducting a conventional conversation, but embarking on emotional education, I simply asked him, as I would any adult in the circumstances, to repeat the words I had said. I proactively overrode his unwillingness to press the matter forward. I needed his consent to do this, and his trust. The effect was dramatic. His jaw dropped open. His chattering ceased. He looked stunned. When pressed, as I did very gently, he said 'I forgot what you said', which was an inaccurate description of what had happened. He had not so much 'forgotten' the most important emotional event in his short life – he had blocked it. His thinking apparatus had frozen – he could not repeat the simple words that I had said, and which he had non-verbally signalled were perfectly true.

Here we have a young *Homo sapiens* not being able to think. And that, for any of us, is a most serious condition. This I believe is the true root of all irrationality, whether of Home Secretaries or otherwise – they are too terrified to think through the problem before them, and they confabulate irrational or obsolete thought patterns in lieu. With Sam, I gently repeated what I had said and encouraged him to do the same. When eventually he did so, his face cleared, and he suddenly realized that speaking these dreaded words did not bring the roof down about his head, nor cause his mother, his supposed protector, to destroy him entirely. I am convinced that he had in this way driven a highway through the mental garbage in his mind – without proactive and expert direction, he might never have done so throughout his entire life, any more than Freud did in his, but that is another story.

There are many other avenues, just beginning to open up, which it would be entertaining to explore in considering how therapists' experience can witness to a wider social awareness. There are moves towards a Neo-Enlightenment, which explores the wonder of other human values, and suggests how we can continually expand our mental capacity, learning more all the time, and advancing social cohesions. But most urgently we must find out, and then spread more widely, just what our minds are for. Publish more widely abroad how in the 'real' world, where blood circulates, social support does much the same, and is quite as essential to keeping us all sane. For if we fail in this, then judging by the century just gone, the coming millennium will assuredly be our last.

10

Therapy as a spiritual process

William West

> Our experiences in therapy and in groups, it is clear, involve the transcendent, the indescribable, the spiritual. I am compelled to believe that I, like many others, have under-estimated the importance of this mystical, spiritual dimension.
>
> Carl Rogers (1980)

> My own belief at present is that anyone who wants to be a good psychotherapist has to have their own spiritual discipline which they follow.
>
> John Rowan (1993)

Reflecting on my own therapy and self-development, work with individual clients and groups, and contact with colleagues, and my research activities, I am moved to put forward the notion that therapy is essentially a spiritual process. This will probably strike many people as absurd or even irrelevant. However, I intend to present here some evidence and opinion supporting this view. Perhaps the best point of departure would be to define the word 'spiritual'.

Spirituality

The world 'spiritual' is given a whole range of meanings which can vary from all forms of self-awareness (Farrow, 1984) to all states of awareness which possess 'values higher than average' (Assagioli, 1986). This linking of the spiritual to higher ethical values is common despite the appalling historical, and in some cases current, record of organized religion. What is clear is many people in the UK are pursuing spirituality outside of conventional religions. In this context then it is necessary to separate spirituality and what that means for the individual from the practice of organized religion.

In the mid-1980s at Pepperdine University a team of researchers under the guidance of Professor Elkins (Elkins et al., 1988) decided to explore spirituality from a humanistic and phenomenological perspective. They investigated what people mean by the word 'spiritual' and produced the following definition:

> Spirituality which comes from the Latin *spiritus*, meaning 'breath of life', is a way of being and experiencing that comes through awareness of a transcendent dimension and that is characterized by certain identifiable values in regard to self, others, nature, life, and whatever one considers to be the Ultimate. (1988: 10)

Their mention of 'a way of being and experiencing' is crucial. We find that public opinion surveys in the USA and in the UK (Hay, 1982; Hay and Morisy, 1978) show that up to a third of the adult population have had religious or spiritual experiences at some point in their lives, even in the UK where traditional church attendance is at a low ebb. So such experiences do not correlate with church attendance and appear to be cross-cultural (Hay, 1982).

In addition, there is also growing evidence of the benefit to health of spiritual experiences and spiritual development. Correlations have been demonstrated between: having spiritual experiences and well-being (Hay, 1982; Hay and Morisy, 1978), personal flexibility and spiritual experiences (Thomas and Cooper, 1980), self-esteem and religious faith (Forst and Healy, 1990), and having divine relations (that is, claims of contact with God) and well-being (Pollner, 1989). Religious experiences can also be interpreted as a self-healing mechanism (Valla and Prince, 1989).

Halmos (1981) was one of the first to point out the decline in the number of clergy and a rise of medical and psychological solutions to people's problems, with a corresponding huge increase in the number of people offering counselling. Nelson and Torey (1973) point to a similar phenomenon in the USA and maintain that many people who would have belonged to church groups are now in therapy groups instead, although some 'progressive' churches now offer counselling.

Spirituality and therapy

It is apparent then from the above brief survey that spirituality is an important part of many people's lives and that it can make a significant contribution to personal health and well-being. As a result it might be expected to be part, perhaps an important part, of counselling and psychotherapy.

Indeed, counselling and psychotherapy have spiritual origins to be found in the practices of witches, priests and shamen (Benner, 1988; Ellenberger, 1970; Healey, 1993; McLeod, 1993; Pietroni, 1993). The word 'psychotherapist' is derived from the Greek words *psyche* meaning soul or breath of life, and *therapeia* denoting attendant or servant. Psychotherapist therefore means servant or attender of the soul (Tick, 1992).

Despite these spiritual antecedents, counselling and psychotherapy have an uneasy relationship with spirituality. Many modern-day, largely secular therapists tend to ignore spirituality, or see it in terms of regression, as something for the client to grow out of. In this respect many therapists are following the lead of Freud (1963), who linked humankind's need for religion with early childhood experience: 'The derivation of religious needs from the infant's helplessness and the longing for the father aroused by it seems to me incontrovertible' (1963: 9).

Freud saw religion as providing people with an explanation for the uncertainties of life; it also gave them a benevolent God, a father figure who could be appealed to in prayer. Religion could, at best in Freud's view provide a 'crooked cure' (quoted in Hay, 1982) to life's problems. However: 'The whole thing is potentially infantile, so foreign to reality . . . It is painful to think that the great majority of mortals will never be able to rise above this view of life' (Freud, 1963: 11).

With regard to people's claims to have had spiritual experiences, Freud was initially neutral and stated: 'I cannot discover this *oceanic* feeling in myself' (1963: 2). This did not lead him to deny such feelings in other people, but he did not see them as the primary root of religious needs. He regarded these oceanic feelings as 'strange' and commented that they, 'fit in so badly with the fabric of our psychology' (1963: 2). He suggested that such feelings could be traced back to infancy, where the child did not see itself as separate from the world. To Freud, the only non-pathological adult experience of such a loss of boundary occurs when two adults first fall in love.

However, although Freud's view of religion and spirituality dominated the world of psychoanalysis, even in the early days there was a counter-viewpoint expressed by Carl Jung. Jung viewed religion not in terms of creeds but in terms of experience: 'The term "religion" designates the attitude peculiar to a consciousness which has been changed by experience of the numinosum' (1958: 8). 'Numinosum' was a term Jung took from Otto, which he defined as: 'a dynamic agency or effect not caused by an arbitrary act of will' (1958: 7). Jung regarded organized religion as being founded on such numinous or spiritual experiences, but he questioned whether such experiences were now available to church-goers.

So Jung saw the practice of being religious as intended to produce changes through numinous experiences, and according to Levy: 'Both Jungians and transpersonal psychologists view the experience of the numinous as intrinsically therapeutic' (1983: 47). (The transpersonal approach to therapy will be explored below.)

Jung recognized the psychic reality of the spiritual or religious need in all of humankind and stated: 'A psychoneurosis must be understood ultimately as the suffering of a soul which has not discovered its meaning' (1958:

330–1). Jung was convinced that our neuroses had present as well as past causes, otherwise, he insisted, they would cease to be active. Consequently he regarded: 'the religious problem which the patient puts before me as authentic and as possible causes of the neurosis' (1958: 333).

Thus, in contrast to Freud, Jung saw spirituality and spiritual experiences as a potentially healthy aspect of our being. He is often quoted as saying: 'Among my patients in the second half of life – that is over 35 years of age – there has not been a single one whose problem has not been in the last resort that of finding a religious outlook on life' (Jung, 1933: 164).

The world of therapy today can be divided into four different broad waves beginning with Freud and psychoanalysis around 1900, followed around 1920 by behavioural and latterly cognitive-behavioural, humanistic approaches around 1940, and finally transpersonal around 1960. Since then it could be argued that a fifth wave exists around systemic approaches (Cumming, personal communication, 1994) or is about cross-fertilization of existing schools resulting in eclectic and integrative approaches (Norcross and Dryden, 1990), or that multi-cultural therapy forms the next wave (Ponterotto et al., 1995).

It could be said that cognitive-behavioural approaches to therapy have little to say on the topic of spirituality (Rowan, 1993). However, some recent developments have occurred in which the use of cognitive-behavioural treatments with religious content have met with some success with religiously orientated clients (Payne et al., 1992). This has not depended on the spiritual viewpoint of the therapist, indeed therapists without a religious viewpoint have produced better outcomes in their clients than those religiously inclined! Marsha Linehan (Linehan and Schmidt, 1995) has integrated the use of Zen Buddhism and behavioural therapy in the treatment of clients with borderline personality disorders.

Within the humanistic tradition the issue of spirituality and how it is worked with therapeutically varies between therapists and between schools. One of the key founders of humanistic therapy was Carl Rogers. Towards the end of his life Rogers identified a new spiritual dimension in his work, and added to his long-established trio of core conditions for effective counselling (unconditional positive regard, congruence and empathy) a further quality which he had observed in himself and other experienced counsellors (Kirschenbaum and Henderson, 1990). He called this 'presence':

> I find that when I am closer to my inner, intuitive self, when I am somehow in touch with the unknown in me, when perhaps I am in a slightly altered state of consciousness in the relationship, then whatever I do seems to be full of healing. Then simply my *presence* is releasing and helpful . . . I may behave in strange and impulsive ways in the relationship, ways which I cannot justify rationally, which have nothing to do with my thought processes . . . At these moments it seems that my inner spirit has reached out and touched the inner spirit of the other . . . Profound growth and healing energies are present. (Rogers in Kirschenbaum and Henderson, 1990: 137)

Rogers is describing the conditions that he feels make 'presence' possible. However 'presence' is still a source of controversy in the person-centred world (McLeod, 1993; Van Belle, 1990). Mearns (1994) suggests that 'presence' can be referred to without using mystical language and can be understood within existing concepts like blending of the core conditions together with a counsellor's ability to be truly still within him or herself. However, removing the mysticism from Rogers' discussion of 'presence' helps to keep counselling separate from spirituality.

Other counsellors and psychotherapists have noticed similar developments, for instance, Thorne describes a quality of 'tenderness' which is akin to Rogers' 'presence' (Thorne, 1985, 1991; Mearns and Thorne, 1988). He states that he no longer has to 'leave my eternal soul outside the door' of the counselling room, and that he can now 'capitalize on many hours spent in prayer and worship' (Mearns and Thorne, 1988: 37). Thorne is bold enough to state that: 'The future of the person-centred approach may well depend on its capacity to embrace the world of spiritual reality' (1991: 127).

A similar viewpoint is to be found in the philosophical writings of Buber (1970), which have had considerable impact on Gestalt psychotherapy in Britain, and also in the work of Maurice Friedman (1992) and others with dialogical therapy in the USA. Buber says that there are two types of relationship: the 'I–It' relationship in which one treats the other as different from oneself, as something of an object, and the 'I–Thou' relationship in which the other is treated as kin. Within an 'I–Thou' relationship an energetic merger between the two people becomes possible. In such a meeting, according to Buber, God is to be found.

Transpersonal psychology, which is often seen as an offshoot of humanistic psychology, deserves to be seen as a unique psychology in its own right:

> Transpersonal approaches draw upon the first three forces [that is, psychoanalysis, behaviourism, and humanistic therapy] while going beyond to see humans as intuitive, mystical, psychic, and spiritual. Above all humans are viewed as unifiable, having the potential for harmonious and holistic development of all their potentials. (Hendricks and Weinhold, 1982: 8)

Transpersonal psychology is a blanket term that embraces a number of approaches (Boucouvalas, 1980; Guest, 1989) that are able and indeed encourage clients to contact their 'higher selves' (Assagioli's term for the soul). Transpersonal psychology draws on elements from psychosynthesis, Jung's analytic psychology, and, according to Boorstein (1986), ideas and techniques from meditation, chakras, dreamwork, imagery, healing, Sufism, Buddhism, astrology and after-death experiences.

There are relatively few transpersonal therapists in the UK, and it is still regarded very much as an innovative therapy (Jones, 1994). However, transpersonal approaches have spread by diffusion and are to be found in complementary medicine and in New Age spirituality. Some transpersonal approaches like guided fantasy and creative visualization have been widely adopted.

Spiritual experiences in therapy

As we have seen in the above survey, the attitude of the therapist towards spirituality and spiritual issues will vary with the school the therapist belongs to and in some cases the individual therapist. Indeed, Allman et al. (1992) found in a survey of US psychotherapists that spiritual experiences were being misdiagnosed and mistreated. Responses varied between humanistic therapists who were least likely to view such experiences as pathological (in some instances even when psychotic elements were present) and those therapists who regarded all mystical experiences as pathological.

It is apparent that not all spiritual experiences are healthy or wholly healthy. Ken Wilber (1983), a leading transpersonal theoretician, insists that we distinguish between 'authentic spiritual experience' and abnormal or pathological states, a point also made by Grof and Grof (1986, 1989), Assagioli (1986), Vaughan (1989) and Lukoff (1985). Lukoff goes further and argues for a new diagnostic category of mystical experience with psychotic features. He provides a clear basis for making such a judgement as well as suggestions for a treatment programme. Grof and Grof (1986, 1989) write about when spiritual emergence turns into a spiritual emergency and of the kind of support necessary during such spiritual crises.

Assagioli (1986) suggests that there are four critical stages in a person's spiritual development or awakening:

1 crises which precede the spiritual awakening;
2 crises caused by the spiritual awakening;
3 reactions following the spiritual awakening; and
4 phases of what Assagioli (1986) calls the 'process of transmutation' of the personality, in which higher or more spiritual levels of self-realization can be achieved.

Both Assagioli (1986) and Grof and Grof (1989) insist that more and more people are now experiencing spiritual awakening, though only anecdotal evidence is put forward to back up this claim.

Models of spiritual development

Implicit in these ideas of spiritual awakening or emergence is a model of spiritual development. Various models have been put forward ranging from Assagioli's (1986) famous 'egg diagram' (see Figure 10.1) which includes his

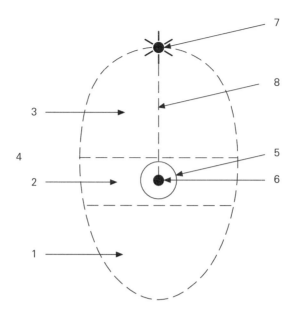

1 Lower unconscious
2 Middle unconscious
3 Higher unconscious
4 Collective unconscious
5 Field of consciousness
6 'I' – the conscious self
7 The higher self (soul)
8 The will – libido – link between 'Self' and 'I'

FIGURE 10.1   A *map of the person*: Assagioli's *'egg diagram'* (Jones, 1994)

concept of the higher self, to that of Wilber's (1979) ten-stage developmental view of consciousness. We will consider Wilber's model in more
detail here since Wilber has become probably the key theoretician for
transpersonal psychology and his model is a very inclusive one.

Two aspects are crucial to Wilber's view: first that each stage of development includes the previous stage, and second that the whole model is a
spiritual one even though the early stages of development, which more or
less match those of western psychology, would and could be seen as secular.
Wilber's model, in effect, unites western therapy with eastern ideas of self-
development (Wilber, 1980). Indeed Wilber recommends that if we want to
develop spiritually we first need to do some western therapy and then follow
this up with some eastern forms of spiritual development.

Wilber's model has been criticized for being too linear and too hierarchical – Rowan (1993) provides a concise summary of Wilber's model
and explores some of the criticism of it – but it does provide a framework

for understanding where spiritual experiences, spiritual awakening or emergence fit in, and how we can understand them within a therapeutic perspective. John Rowan's adaptation of Wilber's model, which reduces Wilber's complex ten stages to four (see Table 10.1), clearly brings out Wilber's notion that the forms of therapy or spiritual support offered need to match the spiritual development of the client.

Rowan's table provides us with an answer to the charge often levelled against therapists working with an openness to their clients' spirituality: how does this relate to short-term therapy, to real-life practical problems around poverty and so on? Later on I discuss work I did with two clients that had a spiritual element to it; neither client had more than six sessions. So a spiritual element in the therapy work does not necessarily mean long-term working. Some clients do present problems of a very practical nature which need appropriate help (though the solution to mass unemployment is not merely a series of individual changes), such as those mentioned under method in Rowan's column 1. However, as all therapists soon realize, the presenting problem may be the tip of a bigger iceberg. A spiritually aware therapist aims to be open to whatever level a client needs to work at, and of course open to the client choosing not to work at the spiritual or any other level.

Therapists' spiritual development

Of course the notion of spiritual development can be applied to therapists. Indeed we find that therapist training courses, with the possible exception of those on behavioural and cognitive approaches, usually involve some personal development work on the part of the trainee. Trainees often greatly value such work. In contrast, models of therapist development tend to de-emphasize or even ignore the role of personal change, focusing primarily on the therapist's development as a practitioner. However, the therapist is not a fixed, unchanging person who simply acquires therapy skills and then becomes increasingly effective in the practice of therapy. The process of personal change continues well beyond the end of initial training. Many therapists comment on the impact of their work on their own development. This personal development of the therapist can include the spiritual, which therefore needs to be considered as an aspect of therapist development.

A number of writers and researchers (for instance Hawkins and Shohet, 1989; Skovholt and Ronnestad, 1992; Stoltenberg and Delworth, 1988) have explored and presented models of therapist development, although these do not include the spiritual.

Therapy theories often include models of human development. Indeed, the practice of therapy can be seen to be about helping people to mature, whether this is understood in terms of Freud's (1933) stages of ego development, Erikson's (1977) eight stages of man, or Jung's concept of

TABLE 10.1 *A comparison of the four positions in personal development*

	1	2	3	4
Wilber level Rowan position	*Persona/shadow* *Mental ego*	*Centaur* *Real self*	*Subtle self* *Soul*	*Causal self* *Spirit*
Self	I am defined by others	I define who I am	I am defined by the Other(s)	I am not defined
Motivation	Need	Choice	Allowing	Surrender
Personal goal	Adjustment	Self-actualization	Contacting	Union
Social goal	Socialization	Liberation	Extending	Salvation
Process	Healing – ego-building	Development – ego-enhancement	Opening – ego-reduction	Enlightenment – questioned ego
Traditional role of helper	Physician Analyst	Growth facilitator	Advanced guide	Priest(ess) Sage
Representative method	Hospital treatment Chemotherapy Psychoanalysis Directive Behaviour modification Cognitive-behavioural Some transactional analysis Crisis work Rational-emotive therapy	T-Group method Gestalt therapy Open encounter Psychodrama Horney etc. Bodywork therapies Regression Person-centred Co-counselling	Psychosynthesis approach Some Jungians Some pagans Transpersonal Voice Dialogue Wicca or magic Kabbalah Some astrology Some tantra	Zen methods Raja yoga Taoism Monasticism Da Free John Christian mysticism Sufi Goddess mystics Some Judaism

Focus	Individual and group	Group and individual	Supportive community	Ideal community
Statement	I am not my body I am not my emotions I am not my desires I am my intellect To say anything more would be presumptuous	I am my body I am my emotions I am my desires I am my intellect I am all these things and more	I am not my body I am not my emotions I am not my desires I am not my intellect I am a centre of pure consciousness and will	Not this, not that
Questions	Dare you face the challenge of the unconscious?	Dare you face the challenge of freedom?	Dare you face the loss of your boundaries?	Dare you face the loss of all your symbols?
Key issues	Acceptability Respect	Autonomy Authenticity	Openness Vision	Devotion Commitment

Source: Rowan (1993).

individuation. However, such theories, with the exception of Jung's and those of the transpersonal, tend to ignore spiritual development.

On the other hand, Wilber (1979) with his spectrum of consciousness (explored above), Heron (1992) with his unique view of the transpersonal self (in contrast to Wilber, Heron maintains that our progress is not linear through the stages of development and also that the highest stage of development does not involve loss of individual identity), and Fowler (1981) who puts forward a model of stages of faith, all see human development in terms that include the spiritual. Finally, Benner (1988) offers us a useful model that has two dimensions – a structural or psychological one, and a directional or spiritual one – while insisting on what he calls 'our psychospiritual unity'. Benner insists that we cannot separate out the psychological from the spiritual.

If Wilber and Heron are broadly correct – that is, that our mature development as human beings includes the spiritual realms – then it is to be expected that some clients in therapy will tend to move towards these realms, if not inhibited by their therapists. Heron maintains that people who have done a lot of therapeutic work on their 'wounded child . . . tend to open up to transpersonal development' (1992: 83). Therapists open to their own development will tend to do likewise as a result of their own unfolding and also possibly triggered by their clients' explorations of these areas. Therapists often comment that their clients frequently work on issues that are alive in themselves.

It can also be argued that the practice of being a therapist, in which one pays attention to one's own inner processes while being simultaneously aware of one's client, is in itself a spiritual practice akin to meditation (Tart and Deikman, 1991). Doing this week in week out with clients over a period of years will inevitably lead to spiritual development in the therapist.

It is striking how a number of well-known therapists, curiously all male (Heron, 1992; Jung, 1983; Reich, 1969; Rogers, 1980; Rowan, 1993), began to take a deep interest in spirituality and the part it played in their work as they grew older. Of course such a phenomenon is not confined to therapists or only to men. Maybe it represents a more striking change, a break with what western men are raised to think and believe.

For instance, Jocelyn Chaplin talking of her early life speaks of her rebellion against her family's Christianity:

> Yet I had some kind of inner strength, a faith in that harmony I had dreamt of as a child . . . I still had a sense of not being alone in a spiritual sense. It almost felt as though I had some kind of 'inner' guide. (1989: 172)

Looking back she feels that she would have liked someone who could 'connect with the spiritual as well as the emotional and sexual side of my life'. Years later she realizes that she wanted to be that therapist she never had.

Spirituality within the therapy room

Recently I have been conducting research into therapy, healing and spirituality from the perspective of the therapist (West, 1995a, 1996, 1997). One therapist, a Gestalt psychotherapist, described an experience that occurred during the course of one of his regular client's therapy which he saw as representing a 'quantum leap' in that client's therapeutic process. Usually the therapeutic work with this client was fairly mundane. This time things were different from before the client even arrived. The therapist commented:

> I don't think I've ever experienced anything quite like it; it was just a totally different level of functioning of consciousness for us . . . It started before he arrived. I started to become aware of a sort of great calmness and a sort of contentment and peacefulness. He arrived, and we went into the therapy room and very quickly the room was filled with an incredible sort of soothing energy, totally undemanding energy.

This was experienced as healing by both client and therapist, and perhaps more importantly the client went on to make 'momentous decisions' about his life during that same therapy session.

Twenty-seven of the thirty people interviewed for this research filled in a follow-up questionnaire. Twenty-one reported feeling part of something bigger than themselves and their clients from time to time in their therapy work:

> I'm very aware that when I'm with clients, there's a third party present, if you like. It's very difficult to explain, but I'm just aware of an other that makes sense of and helps what's going on.

> There was a sense of being with another person within a context which was now somehow very much greater.

This last respondent was convinced that this new development in his work was at least in part due to:

> A very much greater deepening of my relationship with the essential core of my own being, or putting it theologically to encounter God within.

Another respondent understood this sense of being part of something bigger than himself and his client in terms of resonance of the aura or energy field of himself and his client:

> When a certain level of resonance is achieved something comes in. It's a little bit like if you wanted to describe the mechanics or the dynamics behind the phrase

'when two or more are gathered together in my name'. If you take that phrase and the implication of that – when two people are in resonance, when there is a common purpose and there is something of a common field, and there is harmony there – I do think that there is often at that moment something else, something of the 'other' comes in at that point. That is my experience, that suddenly there is more than just two people in the room.

This has echoes of Buber's I/Thou relationship in which God can be found (discussed above). However, just as it is possible to view Rogers' concept of 'presence' in non-mystical terms (see above), it is possible to view such therapeutic mergers with one's client in non-spiritual terms. This view has been put forward by Alvin Mahrer (1978, 1993) with his concept of transformational psychology during which the therapist and client merge and share their experiencing. In this process: 'To some extent, the therapist's identity (personhood, self) becomes coterminal with that of the patient' (Mahrer, 1978: 387). Carl Rogers advocated empathy as a core condition that therapists need to embody in their work and for their clients to be aware of their therapists' empathy. Rogers always added a rider or limit to such empathy: 'To sense the client's private world as if it were your own, but without ever losing the *as if* quality' (Kirschenbaum and Henderson, 1990: 226). Mahrer insists that his transformational psychology goes beyond empathy, and indeed seems to lose this 'as if' boundary: 'Instead of being empathic with the person, you are fully being the person. Instead of knowing the person's world, you are living it' (Mahrer, 1993: 34).

To most people who experience such mergers with their clients it is a relatively rare experience that comes about apparently fortuitously. Mahrer in contrast has devised a method of bringing about such mergers with his clients (1993).

The spiritual space

Part of the research mentioned above involved a small group of the respondents meeting together as a human inquiry group (further details in West, 1996) over four weekends to research the group members' experience of therapy and healing.

One of the key outcomes of this group was the concept that the therapeutic space can be seen as a spiritual space; that the therapists can hold in their mind that the therapy space is spiritual, and that this will allow the client to explore their spirituality and spiritual issues if they so wish. As one group member put it:

> Space is where the spirit is. Space is where we get out of the way and allow whatever we may call it, God's spirit, whatever, to be. That's like a healing because we are not interfering, allowing whatever it is to happen.

Another member was moved to add:

> Unless you keep some spiritual dimension in your mind as you're dealing with the
> client, the client is not going to transcend his or her normal self.

David Hay (1982), in his work on spiritual experiences referred to above,
talks of the taboo that exists for people in talking about such experiences
and the difficulties people have in finding appropriate language to discuss
them. As a result, it is important that therapists communicate a clear
acceptance of spirituality and spiritual experience for this can help to
overcome this taboo. This challenges the largely secular world of therapy. It
is also apparent from my research that therapists themselves experience the
taboo, for a number of them felt either unable to discuss spirituality with
their therapy supervisors (West, 1995b) or experienced some difficulty in
this area. As one respondent said rather wistfully, 'I'm careful who I talk to
about spirituality, even my supervisor.'

My own experiences

In order to present some of my own experiences here it seems helpful to do
so in the context of the evolution of my work as a therapist. I began working
as a therapist in 1979 within the Reichian tradition of bodywork
psychotherapy (West, 1984, 1988). Reichian therapy, which is a bodymind
therapy, focuses very much on the body, on how our problems are expressed
in muscular tensions, bad posture and poor breathing. However, underlying
the theory of Reichian therapy is a concept of life energy and how it pulsates
and flows in our bodies, in all living things and in the universe at large.

In the spring of 1982 my relatively secure world was disrupted by some
psychic experiences. These were not especially powerful experiences but
were deeply disturbing for me. I had vivid dreams before and after the death
of my aunt, I saw colours around people, sometimes I saw faces near
people, I became aware of ghosts and heard some imaginary voices. I
recognized that these were classic schizoid symbols and I felt scared for my
mental health, but fortunately was directed to seek help from some
experienced healers.

I was helped to come to terms with what was happening to me, with
advice to meditate and to accept these experiences, and in time to make use
of the talents involved. A period of real therapeutic work followed as I came
to terms with this new aspect of myself. This involved facing a lot of fear and
a lot of grief, as I seemed to both become more compassionate and to wrestle
with being less emotionally involved with other people's problems.
Gradually there was also a spiritual shift, a deepening of my awareness of
my place in the order of things, a spiritual quest that led me to continue my
exploration of heretical Christianity and eastern ideas of karma, reincarna-
tion and meditation. This led me, after some training, to become a spiritual

healer in 1984. Interestingly, there was no doubt in my mind that my healing, or rather my channelling of healing energies, was intrinsically spiritual.

For a while I saw clients separately as a therapist and as a spiritual healer. Inevitably some of my therapy clients heard about my healing work and asked for healing. I was then faced with the dilemma of whether to offer this or not. This decision needed to be taken in the light of the client's therapeutic progress, whether a healing would help their development or not. There were other consequent changes in my work at that time. I later wrote:

> I now do less physical or any other sort of interventions in my Reichian therapy practice. The energy field, the atmosphere I bring, or which appears around me, seems to have a bigger part to play. People speak of how good it feels. (West, 1984: 36)

I remember around 1984 a woman coming to consult me for the first time for healing, although it could have equally well been for therapy. She came in and sat down and there was a moment of silence which I was about to break when she suddenly started sobbing. She had actually come for a healing of a neck injury, but she said the atmosphere in the room had brought her tears on.

There were other ways in which my new skills could be put to use. Being able on occasion to see colours around people could give a clue to what was troubling them. A strong red might point to an anger that they had yet to talk about and an orange might hint at relationship difficulties. I had to use such information with discretion and timing, and I had to become clear as to what the colours actually meant.

I also picked up symbols. On two occasions during therapy groups I got the symbol of a cross. In one case it was a very faint cross and the woman involved was married to a church warden but was losing her faith and wondering how on earth to talk to her husband about it. For the other woman I saw a small but very clearly defined cross. She was at the point of returning to her childhood religion and seeing what meaning it might now have for her.

For both clients, my picking up of the cross symbol was important to them and facilitated them talking about the issues involved. In effect, it gave them permission. Of course, sharing such information with clients can increase the strength of the therapeutic bond with them, can cause them to see one in a very special and misleading light, and so it needed and needs to be carefully handled. However, it can speed up the therapeutic process in a very useful way.

It is not only religious symbols that I can pick up from clients. With one counselling client I had an image of him as a beaten dog. When I chose to share this image with him a story poured out of him about having a mother who would beat him without any warning and on at least one occasion he was locked under the stairs.

It is possible to regard such symbols not in spiritual terms. They do seem to be about being tuned in to the life world of the client involved and can be discussed in terms of countertransference – that is, reactions in the therapist to the client that the therapist can monitor and use to guide their therapeutic work with the client. It is possible to argue that the mechanism for such countertransference is the mingling of the energy fields or auras of the therapist and client (see Mollon, 1991). Again, we can view this phenomenon in spiritual or non-spiritual terms.

The calmness and the patience involved with spiritual healing had an increasing impact on my therapeutic work. Gradually my Reichian work, hitherto very cathartic, became less so. I became less interested in making things happen, indeed less interested in offering spiritual healing, and more in leaving a space within which the client could unfold in his or her own way.

Looking for a new way forward, in 1990 I decided to do a combined Diploma/MA in Counselling Studies at Keele University. To my delight I discovered Rogers' concept of 'presence', which seemed to match so much my development at that time, as did the patience shown by Rogers and his trust in allowing the therapeutic process to unfold for the client (Rogers, 1980).

At the same time I 'accidentally' found myself at a Quaker meeting and realized that after 25 years of wandering in the spiritual wilderness that I had found my spiritual home. To my delight I found that the Quaker silence was full of colour and energy for me – much like the phenomena that occur with spiritual healing – and that it was also a place of rest and healing. I felt too that there was a strong link between Rogers' acceptance of his clients and the Quaker acceptance of people, and that Rogers' description of 'presence' matched my experience of the Quaker meeting (West, 1995c). However, it took me some time to break the taboo I felt about talking about my spiritual experiences even to my new Quaker friends, who showed every sign of being accepting.

Inevitably, within the academic climate I was drawn first of all to raise questions about spirituality via a student seminar group we established for this purpose. It also gradually became clear to me that I needed to do a Ph.D. focused on the relationship between therapy and healing, and in particular how the practitioner handles the issues involved. Some of the findings of my doctorate are referred to above.

Meeting with many fine people who were wrestling with the issues involved in combining therapy and healing inevitably had a great impact on me, as did the academic discipline I needed to adopt in order to do my Ph.D. I discovered that other therapists and healers were moving away from dramatic forms of working, away from doing and towards being, focusing on the client unfolding and an increasing awareness that this unfolding needed to be seen as spiritual.

There seems to me in all of this a great sense of trust, in Julian of Norwich's words 'All will be well' (Jantzen, 1987), perhaps a hard philosophy to adopt in a world full of so much pain and suffering. However, this being with our clients did seem to make sense, did seem to deliver results. Paradoxically, allowing things to unfold takes great skill. It is a lot easier to choose some technique to make things happen and indeed many clients may need just that. It also demands a high quality of supervision, by a supervisor not put off by spirituality.

The value of allowing the client to unfold their process in what is felt to be a spiritual context and trusting the unfolding is illustrated by a client who came to me in the early 1990s. He was in his mid-20s and had taken time off work as he was clearly in a crisis. He was staying with a close friend of his who lived in the same city as me. There were several themes he explored during a four-week period of seeing me twice a week. One was a maturing of his sexual desires away from teenage boys and towards adult men; another was a shift away from comparative success in the world of business and towards wanting to do caring work with people. Underlying this change of his was a deep, though mostly implicit, feeling of a spiritual shift. There were intense times of grief and self-questioning for him. My part as his counsellor was to be present for him, to be a witness and a sounding-board. He did the work, much of it outside of the counselling sessions. I was his anchor and lifeline.

Recently I was presented with a different challenge from a counselling client. She was an ex-member of a Buddhist group which appeared to act as some kind of sect or cult in a way that I found was contrary to my understanding of Buddhism. However, I had to put my prejudices aside and listen to her ambivalence about leaving the group, about what had been good and creative and indeed spiritual for her within that group, and what had been painful and unhelpful. She was also faced with a lack of a spiritual home and whether in leaving the group she was someone condemned to a Buddhist equivalent of hell.

My approach to working with her was to give her the opportunity to explore her experiences within the sect and her thoughts and feelings about her life with the group (it was a residential community), and her reactions on leaving and now being in the outside world. I also sought to be accepting of her spiritual side (even though I only have limited knowledge of Buddhism and its tenets) and how she would engage with her spirituality in her world outside of the community. It was a painful, questioning time for her as she adjusted to her new life outside the Buddhist community.

I hope in this brief description of the unfolding of myself and my work I have shown something of what it has been like to allow the spiritual to be present in me and in my work with clients over the last ten years or so.

Implications

One of the implications of this is plain: whatever our own view of spirituality it is an important and often health-giving aspect of many people's lives. It seems to me too facile to have a knee-jerk reaction like Freud's that religion and spiritual experiences are infantile and neurotic. It also strikes me as absurd if therapists were to decide that as soon as a client utters the word religion or spirituality they must be immediately referred on to a priest or other spiritual professional. (Of course there are cases where such referral is necessary.) My contention here is a broader one, that as therapy can be viewed as a spiritual process then therapists in training need to familiarize themselves with spirituality.

A few suggestions follow as to what preparation therapists in training and afterwards could usefully consider:

1 Their own prejudices and biases around spirituality and religion, both positive and negative.
2 Familiarizing themselves with some of the literature around spiritual experiences (for example, Hay, 1982; James, 1901) and pastoral therapy (Lyall, 1995).
3 Exploring a religion from a different culture than their own including attending a religious service (see Lee and Amstrong, 1995).
4 Addressing the assessment issues involved, including when a spiritual experience might have psychotic elements to it, when a client needs a spiritual referral and who to refer the client on to, and the part played by spiritual emergence and spiritual emergency in some people's spiritual development (Lukoff, 1985; Grof and Grof, 1989).
5 Getting a sense of some of the main maps and theories of spiritual development, Wilber in particular.

Even though spirituality is a very alive issue to many clients and not just the third of the population who have had spiritual experiences, it is not expected that therapists will all be willing to see themselves as having a spiritual nature and even more to actively engage in their own spiritual development. However, I believe it would be unethical for therapists not to be aware of the role spirituality plays in many of their clients' lives, and at least to suspend a rush to judgement on the neurosis or otherwise of such beliefs and experience their spiritually orientated clients have. Spirituality for many people is an ordinary part of their lives, but it is often something they will quickly shut up about if they sense a lack of receptivity in their listener. The challenge to us therapists is clear: 'Can I be present for my client's spirituality?'

Conclusions

I hope then that I have put forward evidence and opinions in support of my notion that therapy is a spiritual process. My current working position as a therapist is to take a phenomenological person-centred viewpoint: how is it for you, what meanings do you attach to spirituality should you choose to raise it? I hold the notion that therapy is always implicitly spiritual and that the therapy space is a spiritual space which I hope will allow my clients to be spiritually present. I am aware of research into spiritual experiences, have some knowledge of differing religions, and I have some maps of spiritual development. Finally, I have explored and continue to explore my own spirituality, and I follow Rowan's (1993) dictum quoted at the start of this chapter that all therapists should be pursuing their own spiritual development.

Acknowledgements

The ideas expressed here have been drawn together from a number of sources over the years but I especially want to mention those who took part in my research, especially the members of the PsychoSpiritual Initiative. My PhD. supervisor Professor John McLeod was a sounding-board for many of these ideas as have been my students and colleagues. Useful feedback on an early draft of this chapter was provided by Colin Feltham, Mary Berry, Henry Hollanders and Jane Orchard. As ever, the support and interest of my wife Gay was crucial.

References

Allman, L.S., de la Rocha, O., Elkins, D.N. and Weathers, R.S. (1992) 'Psychotherapists attitudes towards clients reporting mystical experiences', *Psychotherapy*, 29 (4): 654–569.

Assagioli, R. (1986) 'Self-realisation and psychological disturbance', *Revision*, 8 (2): 121–31.

Benner, D.G. (1988) *Psychotherapy and the Spiritual Quest*. London: Hodder & Stoughton.

Boorstein, S. (ed.) (1986) *Transpersonal Psychotherapy*. Palo Alto, CA: Science and Behavior Books.

Boucouvalas, M. (1980) 'Transpersonal psychology: a working outline of the field', *Journal of Transpersonal Psychology*, 12 (1): 37–46.

Buber, M. (1970) *I and Thou*. Edinburgh: Clark.

Chaplin, J. (1989) 'Rhythm and blues', in W. Dryden and L. Spurling (eds), *On Becoming a Psychotherapist*. London: Tavistock/Routledge.

Elkins, D.N., Hedstorm, L.J., Hughes, L.L., Leaf, J.A. and Saunders, C. (1988) 'Towards a humanistic-phenomenological spirituality', *Journal of Humanistic Psychology*, 28 (4): 5–18.

Ellenberger, H.F. (1970) *The Discovery of the Unconscious: The History and Evolution of Dynamic Psychiatry*. London: Allen Lane.

Erikson, E. (1977) *Childhood and Society*. London: Paladin.

Farrow, J. (1984) 'Spirituality and self-awareness', *Friends Quarterly*, 19 (2): 213–323.

Forst, E. and Healy, R.M. (1990) 'Relationship between self-esteem and religious faith', *Psychological Reports*, 67: 378.

Fowler, J.W. (1981) *Stages of Faith*. San Francisco: Harper & Row.

Freud, S. (1933) *New Introductory Lectures of Psychoanalysis*. London: Hogarth Press.

Freud, S. (1963) *Civilization and its Discontents*. London: Hogarth Press.

Friedman, M. (1992) *Religion and Psychology: A Dialogical Approach*. New York: Paragon House.

Grof, C. and Grof, S. (1986) 'Spiritual emergency: the understanding and treatment of transpersonal crisis', *Revision*, 8 (2): 7–20.

Grof, S. and Grof, C. (1989) *Spiritual Emergency*. Los Angeles: Tarcher.

Guest, H. (1989) 'The origins of transpersonal psychology', *British Journal of Psychology*, 6 (1): 62–9.

Halmos, P. (1981) *The Faith of the Counsellors*. Milton Keynes: Open University Press.

Hawkins, P. and Shohet, R. (1989) *Supervision in the Helping Professions*. Milton Keynes: Open University Press.

Hay, D. (1982) *Exploring Inner Space: Scientists and Religious Experience*. Harmondsworth: Penguin.

Hay, D. and Morisy, A. (1978) 'Reports of ecstatic, paranormal, or religious experiences in Great Britain and the United States – a comparison of trends', *Journal for the Scientific Study of Religion*, 17 (3): 255–68.

Healey, B.J. (1993) 'Psychotherapy and religious experience: integrating psycho-analytic psychotherapy with Christian religious experience', in G. Stricker and J.R. Gold (eds), *Comprehensive Handbook of Psychotherapy Integration*. New York: Plenum.

Hendricks, G. and Weinhold, B. (1982) *Transpersonal Approaches to Counseling and Psychotherapy*. Denver, CO: Love Publishing.

Heron, J. (1992) *Feeling and Personhood*. London: Sage.

James, W. (1901) *The Varieties of Religious Experience*. London: Collins.

Jantzen, G. (1987) *Julian of Norwich*. London: SPCK.

Jones, D. (ed.) (1994) *Innovative Therapy: A Handbook*. Buckingham: Open University Press.

Jung, C.G. (1933) *Modern Man in Search of a Soul*. London: Routledge and Kegan Paul.

Jung, C.G. (1958) *Psychology and Religion*. London: Routledge and Kegan Paul.

Jung, C.G. (1983) *Memories, Dreams, Reflections*. London: Fontana.

Kirschenbaum, H. and Henderson, V. (eds) (1990) *The Carl Rogers Reader*. London: Constable.

Lee, C.C. and Armstrong, K.L. (1995) 'Indigenous models of mental health interventions: lessons from traditional healers', in J.G. Ponterotto, J.M. Cases, L.A. Suzuki and C.M. Alexander (eds), *Handbook of Multi Cultural Counseling*. Thousand Oaks, CA: Sage.

Levy, J. (1983) 'Transpersonal and Jungian psychology', *Journal of Humanistic Psychology*, 23 (2): 42–51.

Linehan, M. and Schmidt, H. (1995) 'The dialectics of effective treatment of borderline personality disorder', in W.T. O'Donohue and L. Krasner (eds), *Theories of Behavior Therapy: Exploring Behavior Change*. Washington, DC: American Psychological Association.

Lukoff, D. (1985) 'The diagnosis of mystical experiences with psychotic features', *Journal of Transpersonal Psychology*, 17 (2): 155–81.

Lyall, D. (1995) *Counselling in the Pastoral and Spiritual Context*. Buckingham: Open University Press.

Mahrer, A.R. (1978) 'The therapist–patient relationship', *Psychotherapy, Theory, Research and Practice*, 15 (3): 201–15.

Mahrer, A.R. (1993) 'Transformative psychotherapy sessions', *Journal of Humanistic Psychology*, 33 (2): 30–7.

McLeod, J. (1993) *An Introduction to Counselling*. Buckingham: Open University Press.

Mearns, D. (1994) *Developing Person-Centred Counselling*. London: Sage.

Mearns, D. and Thorne, B. (1988) *Person-Centred Counselling in Action*. London: Sage.

Mollon, P. (1991) 'Psychotherapists' healing attitude', paper to symposium The Crucial Factor in Psychotherapy and Psychoanalysis, Dept. of Psychotherapy, Manchester Royal Infirmary, 9th November.

Nelson, S.H. and Torey, E.F. (1973) 'The religious function of psychiatry', *American Journal of Orthopsychiatry*, 43: 362–7.

Norcross, J.C. and Dryden, W. (1990) *Eclecticism and Integration in Counselling and Psychotherapy*. London: Gale.

Payne, I.R., Bergin, A.E. and Loftus, P.E. (1992) 'A review of attempts to integrate spiritual and standard psychotherapy techniques', *Journal of Psychotherapy Integration*, 2 (3): 171–92.

Pietroni, P. (1993) 'The return of the spirit', in A. Beattie, M. Gott, L. Jones and M. Sidell (eds), *Health and Wellbeing: A Reader*. Milton Keynes: Open University Press.

Pollner, M. (1989) 'Divine relations, social relations, and well-being', *Journal of Health and Social Behavior*, 30: 92–104.

Ponterotto, J.G., Casa, J.M., Suzuki, L.A. and Alexander C.M. (1995) *Handbook of Multi Cultural Counseling*. Thousand Oaks, CA: Sage.

Reich, I.O. (1969) *Wilhelm Reich: A Personal Biography*. New York: St Martin's Press.

Rogers, C.R. (1980) *A Way of Being*. Boston, MA: Houghton-Mifflin.

Rowan, J. (1989) 'A late developer', in W. Dryden and L. Spurling (eds), *On Becoming a Psychotherapist*. London: Tavistock/Routledge.

Rowan, J. (1993) *The Transpersonal, Psychotherapy and Counselling*. London: Routledge.

Skovholt, T.M. and Ronnestad, M.H. (1992) *The Evolving Professional Self: Stages and Themes in Therapist and Counselor Development*. Chichester: John Wiley & Sons.

Stoltenberg, C.D. and Delworth, U. (1988) *Supervising Counselors and Therapists*. London: Jossey-Bass.

Tart, C.T. and Deikman, A.J. (1991) 'Mindfulness, spiritual seeking and psychotherapy', *Journal of Transpersonal Psychology*, 32 (1): 29–52.

Thomas, L.E. and Cooper, P.E. (1980) 'Incidence and psychological correlates of intense spiritual experiences', *Journal of Transpersonal Psychology*, 12 (1): 75–85.

Thorne, B. (1985) *The Quality of Tenderness*. Norwich: Norwich Centre Publications.

Thorne, B. (1991) *Person-Centred Counselling: Therapeutic and Spiritual Dimensions*. London: Whurr Publishers.

Tick, E. (1992) 'Attending the soul', *Voices*, 28 (2): 7–8.

Valla, J.-P. and Prince, R.H. (1989) 'Religious experiences as self-healing mechanisms', in C.A. Ward (ed.), *Altered States of Consciousness and Mental Health, a Cross-Cultural Perspective*. Thousand Oaks, CA: Sage.

Van Belle, H.A. (1990) 'Rogers' later move towards mysticism: implications for client-centred therapy', in G. Lietaer, J. Rombauts and R. Van Belle (eds), *Client-Centred and Experiential Psychotherapy in the Nineties*. Leuven, Netherlands: University of Leuven.

Vaughan, F. (1989) 'True and false mystical experiences', *Revision*, 12 (1): 4–10.

West, W.S. (1984) *Loving Contact*. Self-published monograph, Leeds.

West, W.S. (1988) *Melting Armour*. Self-published monograph, Leeds.

West, W.S. (1993) 'Spiritual experiences in therapy', *Self & Society*, 21 (5): 29–31.

West, W.S. (1995a) 'Integrating psychotherapy and healing: an inquiry into the experiences of counsellors and psychotherapists whose work includes healing', Ph.D. thesis, University of Keele.

West, W.S. (1995b) 'Supervision difficulties for psychotherapists and counsellors whose work includes healing', paper presented at First Annual Research Conference of the British Association for Counselling, Birmingham University, 25th February.

West, W.S. (1995c) 'The relevance of Quakerism for counsellors', *Friends Quarterly*, 28 (5): 222–6.

West, W.S. (1996) 'Using human inquiry groups in counselling research', *British Journal of Guidance and Counselling*, 24 (3): 347–55.

West, W.S. (1997) 'Integrating psychotherapy and healing', *British Journal of Guidance and Counselling*, 25 (3): 291–312.

Wilber, K. (1979) 'A developmental view of consciousness', *Journal of Transpersonal Psychology*, 11 (1): 1–21.

Wilber, K. (1980) *The Atman Project*. Wheatstoner, IL: Quest.

Wilber, K. (1983) *A Sociable God: Towards a New Understanding of Religion*. Boston, MA: Shambhala.

Index